Books by Emmet John Hughes

The Ordeal of Power

A POLITICAL MEMOIR
OF THE
EISENHOWER YEARS

EMMET JOHN HUGHES

The Ordeal of Power

A POLITICAL MEMOIR
OF THE
EISENHOWER YEARS

NEW YORK ATHENEUM *1975*

*Ex Umbris Et Imaginibus
in Veritatem*

Contents

vii

Contents

The Ordeal of Power

A POLITICAL MEMOIR
OF THE
EISENHOWER YEARS

A Recollection of some men and events of the 1950s, personally and anxiously witnessed, mingling appreciation and dismay, along with a few judgments—aided immeasurably by the marvelous faculty of hindsight—bearing not only upon the recent past but also upon such present and abiding matters as: the role of President in the American nation, the uses of power in a democracy, and the arduous art of free government . . . upon all of which things may depend the fate of many men, and the nature of many events in the 1960s.

EMMET JOHN HUGHES

CHAPTER ONE

A Word of Introduction

To begin at the end . . .

The end came in Washington, D.C., in the numbing cold of late morning, on Inauguration Day, Friday, January 20, 1961. Just before eleven-thirty, President Dwight David Eisenhower and President-elect John Fitzgerald Kennedy strode down the broad front steps of the White House, climbed into the black limousine awaiting them, and began their ceremonial journey together along Pennsylvania Avenue to Capitol Hill. Vice Presidents, wives, and Secret Service followed in solemn, poised attendance. Tens of thousands along the route shivered in the icy wind, but they warmly waved and breathed great gray puffs of cheer into the frosty air. And yet, as the two men sat back and stretched their legs—the older man seated on the honored right for the last time—they both were, seriously and inescapably, quite alone in the world. Probably, each was alone with his own sober thoughts and tense emotions. Certainly, both were alone in their silently shared knowledge of the awesome power and the poignant isolation—the matchless hopes and hazards—of the office that would pass in a few moments from the one to the other.

The scene and the encounter were arresting. Beside the President who, at the age of seventy, had become the oldest Chief Executive in American history, there sat the man who, at forty-

5

three, was the youngest ever elected to the office. He was the first, too, born of his particular religious faith, as well as the first born in this particularly tempestuous century. The lives of both were renowned—their words and acts, their countenances and gestures, already long familiar to millions. In the sight and thought of the nation, therefore, they were logically, almost intimately linked. Yet they were not at all known to each other. Until a few weeks before, they had barely met or spoken.

Behind this meeting, of course, lay an encounter of quite a different kind: the conflict of ideas and of parties that had been the 1960 National Election. The younger man had accused the older one, by sharp word or broad insinuation, of many lacks and failures—above all, of letting the political conscience of his country slumber, leaving the people to blink and gape at the surge of crisis in all the world of free men. The older man, drawn into a fray he would have shunned, had turned scorn on the young critic, chastising him for a poverty of experience and a wealth of misinformation. For all its stridence, the clatter of words occasionally had given true sign of their serious clash of views upon the standing of the nation and the state of the world, the role of government and the duty of a President, the strength of American arms and the force of American convictions. And back of *this* conflict lay the eight years of the older man's regime, with all those years' historic events and symbols: Camp David and Little Rock, riots in Berlin in 1953 and riots in Tokyo in 1960, summits and Sputniks, Korea and Lebanon, Cuba and the Congo, "open skies" and offshore islands, hope at Geneva in 1955 and humiliation at Paris in 1960, spectacular presidential missions to distant lands and faltering missile-flights to outer space, the cheering millions of the Far East, the sneering mobs of Latin America, the whine of British bombers over Egypt, the crash of an American plane on a mission of espionage deep within Soviet frontiers.

Did the two men speak of such things this day, as they rode slowly toward the Capitol? No. It was a more quiet, resigned time. Bracing for the cold, they had just sipped coffee together

6

at the White House. The President had decided to honor the occasion by the precedent of donning a top hat, and the young President-elect had laughed appreciatively when Mrs. Eisenhower had said gaily to her husband: "Till seeing you in *that*, I never noticed how much an Irishman *you* look!" Now—alone —they chatted easily, and the older man set the subject. He groped back beyond memories of the days when he twice had taken his own oath of office, back to the past beyond all his life in the presidency. He returned, in thought and speech, to the time of World War II, when he had been Commander of all Allied armies in Europe, while his youthful companion had been a courageous but obscure PT-boat officer in the distant arena of the Pacific waters. Their political views of the world of today seemed almost as remote from each other as then were their military assignments. And as their limousine rolled on, the President murmured his reminiscences of the Allied invasion of Normandy in 1944. The historic amphibious operation across the English Channel, he recalled, had been greatly aided by an element of surprise that had turned on so seemingly minor a matter as accuracy of weather forecast: the Allied prognosticator had caught glimpse of a little spell of calm weather, benignly moving in from the Atlantic, that had wholly eluded the German watcher of the winds . . .

A rapt eavesdropper might well have wondered: was it suggestive or significant that the man should fill these particular moments, near the instant of surrendering the presidency, with remembrances of so distant and so different a scene? Were these memories more consoling or more assuring than those of years more recent? Perhaps all the talk meant no more than an agreeable wish to find bland conversational matter to fill the void of this ceremonial hour. Or—could it have been prompted by some vague but troubling awareness that the tricks of human fortune, ruling lives and decreeing history, had lately been much less kind than the Atlantic winds and the Channel water of that unforgotten late spring day? . . .

Only a few moments later, President Kennedy, his oath of office taken, delivered a stirring Inaugural Address. All the while, ex-President Eisenhower watched and listened. He seemed grave, attentive, and approving. Quite clearly, he liked the words: "Let every nation know, whether it wishes us well or ill, that we shall pay any price, bear any burden, meet any hardship, support any friend, oppose any foe to assure the survival and success of liberty." He may have noted, even pondering somewhat the worth of words, that he himself had said much the same thing on precisely the same occasion in 1956—and earlier too, in 1952, a full eight years past. But now, with this Inauguration: "Let the word go forth from this time and place, to friend and foe alike, that the torch has been passed to a new generation of Americans."

But the young man, through the august ceremonies, had been watching the older man, too. For he found something at which to marvel a little. He explained the matter, late that night, when all the rituals of Inauguration were done, and he found himself sitting quietly with a few friends, recalling what had so forcibly struck him. "The vitality of the man!" he exclaimed. "It stood out so strongly, there at the Inauguration. There was Chris Herter, looking old and ashen. There was Allen Dulles, gray and tired. There was Bob Anderson, with his collar seeming two sizes too large on a shrunken neck. And there was the oldest of them all, Ike—as healthy and ruddy and as vital as ever. Fantastic! . . ."

The young President voiced his wonder, at day's end, in the living room of a gracious house in Georgetown. The hour had been past 2 A.M. when he had startled his friends by knocking on the door and entering, as naturally as a neighbor, to find relaxation in some amiable, aimless conversation to close his unforgettable day. Trim and buoyant and festive in his tuxedo, still a little excited in voice, he sat slowly sipping a glass of champagne, his left ankle casually thrown over his right knee but moving restlessly and rhythmically—the only physical sign of the inner tension he hoped to ease a bit, far from official throng and duty, before retiring for his first night of sleep in the White House. But *his* reminiscences did not go back beyond the recent political campaign. All the stir of Inauguration itself had done nothing to upset the cool detachment of his view of that contest —or of his own political self. Candidly, he assessed his election as "a miracle." Professionally, he marveled at the seeming folly of his Republican antagonists. With uncompromising realism, the man who had become President of the United States less than fifteen hours earlier calmly insisted that he could have been routed by a stronger opponent.

He had more to say of Eisenhower, however, ai.d the subject plainly fascinated him. He acknowledged having been impressed by the older man, more than he had expected, in their few talks between Election and Inauguration: "He was better than I had been prepared for. . . . Takes a simplified view of most things, but . . . better than I had thought." Yet what deeply excited his attention was the personal drama of his predecessor's so sudden departure, now, to private life. "What a transformation, what an adjustment it must be! Just to go off like that by himself . . . President this morning—and now . . ." Thrice he came back to this reflection, as if it nagged and troubled him. And suddenly one sensed the obvious: the young President was thinking less of Eisenhower on this day than of himself, on the same day four years or eight years hence, facing the extraordinary experience of becoming a *former* President—at the age of forty-seven or fifty-one.

The older man, by this hour of this night, was far from the official scene. The Inaugural formalities completed, he had attended the modest retirement ceremony of a luncheon with his Vice President and some of their close colleagues and wives. Then he had left Washington by car. There had been no grand official cavalcade. He had been escorted only by his family and a token Secret Service detail, soon to leave him altogether and abruptly to his privacy. And in the frosty, fading sunlight of this late January afternoon, he had reached his farm at Gettysburg.

There, for as long as he lived, he would be listening with interest—with a sharply questioning glint in the bright blue eyes, a serious set to the strong mouth, a deep grimace or a swift smile

9

—as various voices swelled the slow-rising chorus that, some day, would speak the judgment of history upon what he had done and what he had left undone.

2

I did not see him this day, nor had I seen him for many, many months before it. Strangely, it was his young successor who, in our chance meeting as this day ended, told me something of his mood and words. And yet I had shared with him quite a few passages through the years that had led, slowly or swiftly, toward this day.

We met first in September of 1952, six weeks before he would be elected President. I worked on his staff, shaping ideas and words toward speeches and pronouncements, through the climax of that National Election. When he assumed office two months later, I took reluctant leave of my journalistic profession to serve him in the White House, assured by the understanding that I would not be pressed to stay beyond a few months, as Sherman Adams urged, "just to help us get things started." The contract of impermanence was respected, though the months became the greater part of 1953. Nor could the time and the experience ever be regretted, for this first of the Eisenhower Years—now it seems so clear—set the mold for most national policies and political practices for the rest of the decade. After 1953, we corresponded through the years. I returned to join him for the two months of his second campaign in 1956, and this brought renewal of the peculiarly intense comradeship that marks any such political engagement. During his second term, our irregular correspondence continued. I returned to Washington to see him a number of times—to give help in the bipartisan battle for foreign aid, the outstanding cause that bound us, or to murmur uninvited comment in spheres where our convictions were not so congenial. But our ways and our views steadily grew more gravely apart. I spoke aloud my doubt and fear over the drift of the nation's foreign policy, with a book published in 1959. The rest, between us, was silence.

Such is the spare graph of my acquaintance with the man who was President for most of a troubled decade. It made of me a witness.

Yet the kind of witness I would be had been largely determined before we ever met. It stood essentially beyond his or my powers to amend or to temper or to improve. For it had been decreed by all things first bringing me to this political scene— all the untidy but sovereign miscellany of one's own convictions and commitments, granite beliefs and fragile fancies, clean perceptions and gray illusions.

I must briefly state the sum of these. For, with a witness in politics, they are as basic and material as name and address with a witness in court.

I was—and am—of the Generation of the New Deal. Both principles and passions in politics were profoundly affected by all the churning issues of the 1930s, by the contrast then starkly set between the nation's two great political parties, and by the lasting force of the memory of Franklin Roosevelt. While accident of age and wartime duty and foreign assignment kept me from voting in any national election until 1952, I would have voted without exception, until that date, for all Democratic candidates for the presidency. I felt, as I professed and lived, independent of any formal partisan affiliation. I cared far too much about such issues as civil rights or foreign aid to pause and frown over the question of whose partisan banners might flutter in triumph as particular battles were fought, each new citadel taken, in the long course of crucial and continuing struggles. In terms of political philosophy, after almost a full decade of life in Europe, I broadly shared the views and spirit of the Christian Democratic Left in Western Europe. In terms of American politics, I most commonly found myself a comrade, in purpose and temper, of the Democrats—and not the more conservative ones. I still do.

Only some singularly sharp and explicit appraisals could have cast such a citizen, in 1952, in the anomalous role of fervent labor on behalf of a Republican candidate for the presidency. In immediate political terms, the emergence of Adlai Stevenson on the Democratic scene somehow had excited my attention less than the massive struggle on the Republican scene between the forces of Robert Taft and the forces of Dwight Eisenhower. I believed—with considerable inexactness, as the years have proved —that this struggle would determine, perhaps for long to come, the character of the Republican party, its role in the nation, and hence, in serious measure, the nation's role in the world. And this unusual preoccupation with the destiny of the Republican party sprang from anxious scrutiny of both the domestic scene and the world scene.

As for the national scene: I believed the essential vigor of the nation's two-party system to stand in clear and present danger. This concern had quickened with the years I had spent in Europe, there witnessing the political price paid by those nations whose political parties had become enfeebled or fragmented. In 1952, for the life of the two-party system, it was "time for a change." But I thought this change essential—paradoxically—less by reason of the political faults so loudly imputed to Democrats, too long in power, than by reason of the political follies so willfully practiced by Republicans, too long in exile. After twenty years of Executive power, it was true, the Democratic Administration, all too often, looked flabby and sounded stale. Yet graver still, I thought, was the fact that the Republican opposition throughout two decades, with only so rare an exception as an Arthur Vandenberg, appeared even more slack and less inspiring. Its voices seemed stammering, its organization lax, its aspirations timid, and its premises obsolete. If the democracy of the American two-party system were to endure, all *this* had to change. And there could be no more effective cure, so it seemed, than the summoning of Republican leadership to learn again, and to suffer, the cleansing anguish of responsibility and decision.

As for the world scene: this seemed to proclaim a need even more imperative. On the Republican side, although there was little in the party's recent record eloquently suggestive of either bravery or creativity in foreign policy, the Eisenhower candidacy clearly appeared to offer a critical chance for the party to establish at least a speaking acquaintance with twentieth-century responsibility in world affairs. Conversely, a defeat of Eisenhower could condemn the party to the indefinite dominance of the xenophobes. On the Democratic side, while there was much to respect in a leadership with the courage and imagination to develop a Marshall Plan to save Europe—and to fight a war to save Korea—the ruthless facts of American political life seemed to have driven Democratic foreign policy into a dangerous dead end. Whether or not the causes were rational or just, the leadership of the Democrats, in world affairs, was failing to win the confidence of either the Congress or the people. As a result, the architects of national policy were threatening to sound and to act like prisoners of their critics. And if one believed, as I did, that American diplomacy urgently needed freshness of thought and boldness of deed, one had to conclude that Democratic leadership, whatever its inner will, was almost powerless to generate such energies. Any initiative would be pitilessly choked off by domestic political opposition. Any diplomatic ventures—daring or conciliatory—seemed doomed to fall, instantly upon conception, before the furious rifle-fire of charges of "appeasement" or "recklessness." And indeed a great part of all the people's discussion of foreign policy seemed to have become either rigid or irrelevant. In lieu of grave debate, the land seemed to hear little more than sulphurous invective or saccharine clichés. The fumes of McCarthyism filled the air. Words like "negotiation" were spat out like obscenities. And such a situation could be purged of its absurdities and its perils, I believed, only by a profound change in the whole political climate. And so one truth seemed to emerge: only a Republican administration would have the *freedom*—the *chance*—to think anew and to act anew. And if such an administration confidently seized this chance, it could surely do much.

Such were the mingled hopes and fears and convictions that

would so seriously affect my own vision as a witness to the Eisenhower Years.

Any citizen holding such beliefs—sophisticated or simplified, reasoned or biased—found himself embarked, from the year 1952 onward, upon a most uncertain, occasionally heartening, often troubling journey.

3

An intimate witness can be an incompetent judge. If he be fair, he admits that he has never, at any moment, seen more than fractions of a dark sum. His very closeness to men or events may have clouded, rather than cleared, his vision. And he knows that no document is to be scanned with more skepticism, or cited with more caution, than the memoir that pretends to be definitive.

I sense these cautions. I shall do my best to respect them.

And yet . . . there are still more cautions—to be shared with others. For each and every written thing *belongs*, in the truest sense, not only to its author but equally to its reader. The intent of one, without the understanding of the other, means little and achieves nothing: it can only be a marriage of minds—unconsummated. And the unfearful seeking of some truth—which alone makes the act of writing or the act of reading worth the doing— requires an honest union of two.

In this spirit, then, I invoke a literary tradition of centuries past, thereby to address to you—*Gentle Reader*—a brief word. . . .

Let us both know well what are—and what are not—*the reasons for this testimony.*

Do not seek here the stunning revelation of political secrets . . . or the solacing confirmation, by shrewdly contrived argument, of your prejudices or mine . . . or the final thunderous proclamation of indictment or eulogy.

For if these things be your quest, you will be wasting our *time. And we will, at the end, part company disappointed.*

Let me give yet another warning.

Do not be too startled—in pleasure or in dismay—to hear a man who was President speak many thoughts in his own words, more fully and precisely, perhaps, than you have heard his voice in the memoirs of others.

If the prospect excites, I must caution: you will hear him speak only of matters and of men wholly in the domain of public concern.

If the prospect distresses, I must caution: you will find no opinion recorded, no attitude revealed, whose essence is not already known to the individuals concerned and to all notable leaders of both our political parties.

Within these fixed limits, then, this President often will speak plainly for himself . . . for no true history can be written in deference or surrender to the privileges of a small and fortunate elite of the informed.

Let it—lastly—be understood why these pages are written now: *not years earlier, nor years later.*

They might *have been written much earlier, indeed.* Five *years ago, the reporting of some of these events would have served to sharpen my own public criticism of the nation's foreign policy.* Three *years ago, too, this might have lent force to my concern— again plainly stated—over a Republican leadership urging the nation in 1960 to carry on serenely as before, at home and in the world.*

I felt constrained—on both past occasions—to do no such thing. For all the men critically involved still held the highest offices—and, as individuals, still struggled for the highest stakes— in the political life of our nation. To have cited personal experience for polemical advantage, at such a time, would have been to turn words into weapons and facts into bludgeons.

The electoral verdict at the end of the Eisenhower Years now has long since been recorded—as well as a midterm electoral judg-

ment upon a wholly new Administration. The personal political fortune of no man who significantly figures in these pages can, any longer, be either enlarged or diminished by whatever here is written.

And I do not believe it an act of either courtesy or courage to hoard all testimony about the leaders of a nation until all of them are dead—and voiceless. Some men most important to these late years have died; others still live; and to segregate them thus would defy sense and history, for their story is one story. To stifle speech until a man's death is to be spared the fear of all complaint. This may be more safe. I doubt that it is more just.

And perhaps important above all else: there is the abiding responsibility of a free people to know itself.

The problem of knowledge in a free society is twofold. One part requires, of course, that we, the citizenry, conscientiously seek to learn whatever we do not know. But the other part requires that we share—and wisely use—all that we do *know.*

Our need for such knowledge grows with each passing year. The gravest facts of modern life—the mysteries of science and the refinements of weaponry, the intricacies of politics and the delicacies of diplomacy—all conspire relentlessly to reduce the sum of vital knowledge securely possessed by a free people, the number of supreme decisions truly shared by them. Thus may the essential sovereignty of a people threaten to become more remote and more vicarious. And thus must we all try to open every room that must not be sealed, to admit the fresh air and the free mind.

To this end, then, this testimony is given.

If it be fairly stated and honestly read, it may enable us, as we look candidly backward, to see more clearly ahead. It may strengthen us, a little, in shunning the rule of myth or fetish or slogan. And this can fortify our reason and our discernment—as we seek, in all our nation's life and governing, the tangled truths and their slow unsnarling.

And so—to begin at the beginning. . . .

CHAPTER TWO

The First Campaign: 1952

The world and we have passed the mid-way point of a century of continuing challenge.

These were the first official words, following a brief prayer for divine guidance, spoken by President Dwight David Eisenhower after taking his oath of office on January 20, 1953. All through the preceding weeks, almost every sentence of this first Inaugural Address had undergone numberless versions, as the restless and fretful discontent of the President-elect had seemed to quicken with each passing day. Words, phrases, paragraphs—spirited exhortations and sweeping affirmations—had been shuttled in and out of the speech so often, so excitedly, and so confusedly that, quite often, the derided deletion of yesterday ended as the prized text of tomorrow. And so, although he did finally utter these opening words of his Inaugural Address, only a few days earlier the President-elect had scrawled in pen beside them his angry marginal comment: "I hate this sentence. *Who* challenges *whom? What about?*"

The comment—I well knew at the time—was wholly characteristic of the man. He rebelled against rhetoric. He distrusted abstractions. He shied from generalizations. And all such aver-

17

sions reflected not merely his semantic taste but his historical sense. For he had found through the years—as he once told me —only one particular pleasure in history: the mental exercise of memorizing majestic dates, so that a glance at the page of a calendar on his desk might prompt him to note the anniversary of a historic battle, as promptly as if it were the birthday of a cherished friend. But the more cryptic and elusive uses of history—the grave deduction or the bold appraisal—provoked but a doubt and a frown. As the word should be plain, the concept should be concrete.

The comment, I thought recently, upon rereading it, now almost seemed suggestive of something more. The phrases of dismay were written after a hotly fought national campaign, vivid with passions and promises, as always. Great hopes and gleaming assertions had shimmered brightly in the political air. A campaign had been called a Crusade. With the triumphant end of the struggle, all the rewards and responsibilities of victory were ready for the taking. And the questions so pithily stated at such a moment—*Who challenges whom? What about?*—carry to the ear, years later, with an oddly disconcerting ring. For they stir one to a different kind of wondering: how truly and clearly were the challenges of that day sensed and known? Were the victorious leaders really ready to meet the nation's tomorrow—and give it meaning? How firm and defined was their purpose? *What* was all the political stir *about?*

The campaign of 1952 itself had given some clues to these questions and their future answering.

There were things of high and honorable purpose to be read in its story.

And there were, too, things of a different kind—or, at least, their warning portents.

2

A historic figure may have enormous force and impact *physically*. The biographers of the great are wont to weigh the strength of a man in more lofty terms—the range of his wisdom or the fiber of his courage, the elegance of his words or the richness of his talents. Yet it would seem unwise to ignore the most obvious: the simple *presence*. The stride and the stance of a man, the timbre of his voice, the command of his eyes, the vigor of his gestures, the authority of his movements—these can affect profoundly the whole world he inhabits. They can endow and empower him. And they did so with Eisenhower.

Upon first encounter, the man instantly conveyed one quality —strength. Our first meeting took place September 13, 1952, in the private suite of his political headquarters in New York, Room 615 of the Hotel Commodore. He had come into the room with that loose, rolling, yet somehow assertive stride that provoked, I remember, the odd first thought: this general walks like an admiral. On being introduced to those present, he smiled and spoke that pleasant but vague, "Hello—welcome—glad to see you," which is the half-brave, half-faltering attempt at graciousness by a man already weary of strange faces. But there was a feature of his face impossible to ignore or to forget—the blue eyes of a force and intensity singularly deep, almost disturbing, above all commanding. They were, I would quickly learn, eyes astonishingly expressive, almost *articulate*. In the months and years to come, I would watch them moving quickly and inquisitively from face to face around the Cabinet table, staring solemnly over a hushed audience, darting impatiently from paper to paper on the immense desk in the oval office in the White House—and drooping heavily with fatigue. Always they would speak of the moment and the mood: icy with anger, warm with satisfaction, sharp with concern, glazed with boredom. And

19

always somehow—was it their eloquent explicitness of feeling? —they conveyed an image and a sense of strength.

The physical fact symbolized a political fact. The man, throughout the campaign of 1952, seemed in firm and sure command of himself and of all around him. Nor—standing close to him—did one feel this command compromised or shaken on the few occasions when his own instinct did bow to another's urging. For when he deferred to a contrary judgment, the act seemed never to issue from weakness or meekness. It rather seemed a gladly given sign of healthy self-confidence in a man who felt no need to prove the steel of his will by mere stubbornness of opinion. This easy air of personal authority seemed, of all hopeful facts of 1952, the most promising for the future. For years thereafter, the force of this image would persist, profoundly affecting all who stood near him, defying all suggestions of vacillation or laxness, so ominous to viewers more remote and detached. And indeed some residue of this quality, some still-kindled spark of it, flared in the sheer *vitality* so appreciatively witnessed by his young successor eight years, two terms—and one dream—later . . .

Between the mid-September of that first meeting and the exhilarating climax of Election Day, I learned the spectacular disorder and the savage stress—the noise and the waste and the frenzy—that a watching nation generally imagines to be a presidential campaign ruled by deliberate strategy and cunning design. The east corridor of the ninth floor of the Hotel Commodore housed the populace of draftsmen, researchers, stenographers, mimeographers, teletypists, who would help piece together all of the candidate's appeal to his listening electorate. The throng was swelled, as it always is, by a long and unmajestic procession of visiting counselors—senators and congressmen, volunteers and organizers and enthusiasts of all kinds—each of whom came to tell, with implacable insistence, of the discovery, by singular revelation, of the one *"idea,"* the one speech, the one act certain to assure electoral triumph. (Double old-age pensions? Slash taxes?

Declare war on Mao? Leave the United Nations? A gold laurel for the noble brow of General Douglas MacArthur?)

Yet the real tyrant of such a period was simply the timetable —the pitiless schedule of the campaign train. The clatter of its wheels across distant states of the Union ruled the rhythm of my typewriter, chattering frantically to keep pace. Words, words, words—faster, faster, faster—write, edit, stencil, telegraph: there was no place, here, for the verb, "to think." Coin that epigram, edit that peroration, sharpen that retort, catch that headline: these were, and remain, the crude imperatives. Policy meant one thing: produce speeches in number to match scheduled engagements. Strategy gave its crisp corollary: do it faster. There was one solace. There remained no leisure time for reflecting, sagely or sadly, whether this was a responsible way for a great democracy to make its great decisions. And there was some further solace in the giddy humor spurred by the near-hysteria. For the favored way to take a phone call from a particularly persistent member of the Congress soon came to be the greeting: "Good morning, this is Clichés Incorporated."

Some faint, blurred lines of a pattern of work did emerge. Gathered figuratively around my typewriter, in relaxed but fairly continuous discourse, were three men: Attorney General-to-be Herbert Brownell, Jr.; Harold E. Stasson, the undeterrable candidate; and C. D. Jackson, a volunteer from Time, Inc., like myself, and a man whose quickness of mind and patience of temper specially endowed him to cope kindly with all gratuitous notions for "strategy" and their zealous authors. The four of us found ourselves—in rarely troubled harmony—acting as a loose kind of council at campaign headquarters, exchanging thoughts and criticisms on most of the words rushing from the garrulous typewriter; and these discussions contrived such modest "strategy" as ever existed. The agreed point of departure for any speech was never more explicit than "a foreign policy speech" or "a good place to talk about inflation" or "another high-level

21

statement of moral purpose." With that, I would write. Often but not always, the four of us would jointly review the text a day—sometimes barely an hour—before its dispatch to the ever restless campaign train. And on the most feverish days, this train loomed before me like an absurd apparition, a gluttonous steel monster that had to be fed paper and words, quite as much as electricity or coal, if it were to stay alive.

The train had to pause now and then, however, and so did the candidate. Upon such returns to New York, Eisenhower would meet with us in conferences of three and four hours, to weigh the endless questions—which states to visit, which candidates to help or to ignore, which audience to pick for a chosen subject, whether a motorcade was imperative or an airport appearance might suffice—and whether we were winning or losing ground. From each foray across the country, the candidate would return weary. He would be weary of the travel and the din, the sound of his own hoarse voice, the tedium of the phrases worn thin by repetition, the forced smiles and the lavish handshaking as the hordes of local politicians descended upon the visiting train.

But the resilience of the man was stunning. After such a journey, of an evening, the lines in his face would look deep, the muscles tight, the lips sealed in strain, the eyes dulled with fatigue. Told of the scheduling of yet another speech or, worse still, another motorcade, he would grate his teeth in wrath and grind out the cry: "Those fools on the National Committee! Are they trying to perform the feat of electing a dead man?" But the next morning, a fresh reminder of his latest burden would evoke only a brisk assent, snapped out: "Okay. Fire away. Whatever they want, I'll do." And the full color in the face—above all, the renewed glint in the eyes—would signal, once again, the physical miracle that is a soldier's night's sleep.

Over our meetings, the ex-soldier would truly preside. When he spoke, he was heeded in respectful silence. When he argued, many a head punctuated each sentence with rhythmic nods of agreement. When he decided, any dissent, with rare exception, went unspoken.

He was aided, in this quiet exercise of confident command, by the fact that most men present accorded him the deference of distance: not many had even known him personally a few months earlier, and none enjoyed the kind of intimacy that encourages brusque speech or blunt challenge. The central group—Brownell and Stassen and Jackson and I—would occasionally and somewhat capriciously be joined by others. Two of these did know Eisenhower better than the rest. They were Major General Wilton B. ("Jerry") Persons, who would later direct White House liaison with the Congress, and the Boston banker, Robert Cutler, who would deal with National Security Council matters in the coming Administration. Others only lately acquainted with the candidate included Gabriel Hauge, the articulate young companion of the candidate on the campaign train, who would be chief economic adviser on the White House staff; and Arthur E. Summerfield from the Republican party's National Headquarters in Washington, who appeared in the campaign's latter weeks to try to bridge the chasm in communications between personal and party headquarters. Also in occasional attendance was the candidate's brother, Dr. Milton S. Eisenhower—a genial and thoughtful man often a little embarrassed when his brother introduced him to a newcomer as "the only really *bright* one in the family." Of these various voices, the most effective and persuasive, those most attentively heard by the candidate, usually were those of Brownell and Milton Eisenhower. This fact was somewhat indicative, and not wholly reassuring, for both men were given to the softly modulated speaking of common sense. This seemed good, so far as it went, but . . . Zeal never stirred these councils. Debate was never profound. Panic was unknown. Passion would have seemed strange.

And throughout these meetings—especially as they grew in size and shifted from the hotel room on Forty-second Street to the spacious living room of the candidate's residence at Columbia University—the most striking things to be observed and remembered were simply the personal marks and manners of the man. And we all came to know these well: the deep-furrowed frown, almost a scowl, signifying utter attention . . . the burst of appreciative laughter, a prolonged gruff guffaw, saluting some sudden jest . . . the quick, sharp twist of the jaw as angry words came through clenched teeth . . . the soft and sunny delight erasing lines from the face as grandchildren scurried past . . . the conventional and affectionate husband's tone, at once self-commiserating and a little self-mocking, when his wife, on rare occasion, intruded with a banal domestic problem . . . the slow, rhythmic beat of the pencil tapping his crossed knees, as he listened to the reading of a speech draft . . . the hand roughly pulling the muscles of his face, and the wide and unblinking eyes, in the long moment of silence just before stating a terse opinion or a final decision . . .

His scrutiny of a specific speech draft took place either in these larger meetings or in quieter sessions alone with me. In both cases, a rather regular procedure soon evolved. I would read aloud the text that I had prepared, and he would listen to its entirety without comment. His attention would never wander—and this brought my first awareness that, for him, the ear was keener than the eye, the spoken word more persuasive than the written. The reading finished, he would never—utterly without exception—make a general comment or judgment of any kind. (Was this yet another sign of the distrust of *all* generalizations?) Rather did he invariably go to a specific matter or phrase, precisely noted, and observe: "Right. Now at one point, along about the second page, you say . . . This doesn't seem right to me because . . ." And such criticism would range from details of substance to points of style, structure of sentence, questions of grammar. The man whose own sense of syntax, as displayed over years of presidential press conferences, would invite smiles and jokes, possessed, nonetheless, a remarkably quick and exacting faculty for editing.*

Through these encounters—the dialogues either between us or in larger groups—there came rare chance, as words and ideas were weighed and refined, to learn the man's intellectual tastes and distastes. And his greatest aversion was the calculatedly rhetorical device. This meant more than a healthy scorn for the contrived and effortful. It extended to a distrust of eloquence, of resonance, sometimes even of simple effectiveness of expression. All oratorical flourishes made the man uneasy, as if he feared the chance that some hearer might catch him *trying* to be persuasive. Simple repetition, the rephrasing of some central thought more than once in a long address, aroused like suspicion. With the austere logic of a mind practiced in swift scrutiny of factual military memoranda, he would rebel with the complaint: "This *sounds* very good, but isn't the idea pretty much the same as what we say way back at the beginning?"

Equally rigid and equally revealing was his distaste for direct personal critique—or, worse still, counterattack—in the political arena. In a long discussion we once had on the question, pro-

* The relationship between a President (or a presidential candidate) and an aide helping to prepare his public statements is intricate enough for a lengthy essay, but it here requires only a footnote. Its most striking quality is the fullness and intimacy of intellectual contact that it affords. Any official preparing drafts of presidential pronouncements may well know the mind of the Chief Executive better than any member of his Cabinet, for the dialogue between the two is boundless. But the weight of the aide's role is easily exaggerated. With the rarest exceptions, no presidential utterance is the creation of one mind: authorship is almost always shared or diffused. Moreover, the *only* politically meaningful fact is not what the aide writes but what the President says. The former may give important inflections to the latter. But the only *decision* of political moment belongs, wholly and unqualifiedly, to the President. Whatever he publicly declares is profoundly *his*.

In the pages of this memoir, I shall be quoting, of necessity, from presidential statements that I sometimes helped to form and write, and I shall occasionally report their apparent impact. The necessity is inescapable, but I am spared self-consciousness for the reasons given. All that Dwight Eisenhower chose to "wear" in public belonged wholly to him, not to any valet or tailor of his language. And in this spirit, I shall so report it.

25

voked by my proposing some retort to a charge by the opposition, he expanded: "I simply do not believe it does a damn bit of good wasting time answering the other fellow. All you do is to double the audience he had the first time when he proclaimed whatever it is you are trying to answer." As the campaign moved toward its climactic weeks, with President Harry Truman sharpening his attacks, the private retort of Eisenhower was: "I'm sure they would like me to get down to *their* level. Well, that's *one* satisfaction they will *never* have." And this hot feeling of personal pride ruled his whole personal attitude toward the campaign—the sense of personal integrity so keen that it could, at times, impute *lack* of integrity to anyone guilty of failing to recognize and respect his.

One October day, he gave me an incisive little speech on the matter. "All I can hope to do in this or any other campaign," he affirmed, "is to say what *I* believe. And this does *not* mean always getting into wrangles and scuffles with the other fellow, to the point where the people can't any longer figure out just what we're fighting about. The people who listen to me want to know what *I* think—not what I think about what someone *else* thinks. This is all I have to offer. If the people believe in what I say and do, nothing else matters—and they will vote for me. If they don't, there's nothing I can do about it." And then came a note struck often, not only in these months but also in years to come. "If they don't want me, that doesn't matter very much to *me*. I've got a hell of a lot of fishing I'll be happy to do."

All these conversations gave early testimony to marks of character and habits of thought that would stamp themselves on so much the man would do, and refuse to do, in the years ahead. There was the stubborn search for the simple—the striving, only partly conscious and deliberate, to reduce all issues to some bare essence, starkly seen and graphically stated. From this, however, a paradox would follow. The man who so shunned all hint of the personal in political life would, by this coveting of simplification, often apply an intensely personal definition to the most historic world matters—as when, as President, he would impose the test of "sincerity" upon the conduct of the Soviet Union.

There was visible here, too, the slightly disdainful aloofness from aggressive politics; and it was hard, for example, to imagine such a man wielding the sharp-edged weapons of patronage for coldly planned effect. And there was, clear above all else, the aversion to rough political combat, especially the hurtful political thrust, that would temper so drastically his conduct toward Republican enemies as well as Democratic opponents.

Dominant in all he said—in every response and in every urging—was an almost fiercely stubborn resolve to respect the truth as he saw it. There were times, before the campaign ended, when advisers could persuade him either to do something personally distasteful or to stifle what he most wished to say. There were times, too, when he would blurt out thoughtless phrases, unreflected and imprecise, sometimes even harsh. But it was unthinkable—and everyone near him knew it was unthinkable—that he would willfully twist a fact, distort an issue, or delude with an empty pledge.

Accordingly, again and again, whenever confronted with any suggestion of a politically expedient posture or phrase, he would sharply caution against any falsifying note. The blunders in foreign policy? He would emphasize: "Sure, I'll talk about the mistakes of others—when they've got it coming to them. But I want to be sure, now and in everything we say in this campaign, that I don't sound like just another politician with the wisdom of hindsight." Taxes? He would snap: "I'll talk about the burden of taxes and their danger to a people's initiative, but let me tell you—I'll be darned if anyone is going to talk me into making any idiotic promises or hints about elect-me-and-I-will-cut-your-taxes-by-such-and-such-a-date. If it takes that kind of foolishness to get elected, let them find someone else for the job."

On another rather notable occasion, his fervor edged on anger. The provocation rose from a review of the whole matter of national defense and its fiscal burden. Oddly, his own defense policies in years ahead would seem to mute, if not refute, the sentiments voiced at this time. But the words, now, were: "Look. Let me tell you something. I know better than any of you fellows about waste in the Pentagon and about how much fat there is to be cut—because I've *seen* those boys operate for a *long* time. But let me tell you something else. I am not going to go around this country making any stupid promises about slashing our defense costs. Anything I say on this subject is going to make perfecly clear that nothing—and I mean *nothing*—is going to come ahead of assuring the safety of the United States."

The sturdy intent, of the words and of the man, was as plain as his integrity. Toward such a man, all kinds of dissent or doubt on particular issues could conceivably be directed—except personal disrespect. This would be, in fact, the unchanging thing, among so many things that would seem to change.

3

The immediate matter, in those nerve-fraying weeks of September and October 1952, was not the analysis of a man. It was the winning of a campaign.

The issue should not have been in much doubt. Sometimes it is the man, sometimes it is the circumstance, that contrives to give one party great advantage in any presidential election. In this instance, the man was a national hero, and the plainest political circumstance appeared to be the people's fatigue with Democratic leadership. Both personally and politically therefore, Adlai Stevenson seemed most poorly armed for a national duel with Dwight Eisenhower.

Yet one could never serenely *feel* that the outcome was splendidly predestined, and a nagging doubt would linger until a fortnight before the election: by then, I felt certain of both victory and its size. Until then, there were a number of facts to temper one's confidence. Perhaps above all, I always believed that a national campaign—far from being a kind of superfluous carnival to

celebrate a secretly accomplished fact—reached the stage of decision only in its last three to four weeks. To that point, the time
was essentially spent in two exercises: the slow striving to catch
the ear of the people, and the gradual staking of claim to positions and policies on which to speak loudly, once the people's
attention was truly engaged. After that point, almost anything
could happen. No initial advantage could ever be so huge as to
be wholly safe from slow squandering or sudden shattering. At
the heart of the matter, then, there was a critical paradox. Almost certainly, it was never possible for Adlai Stevenson, out
of his own political resources, to win the 1952 campaign. Most
certainly, however, it was possible for Dwight Eisenhower to
lose it.

There were more specific causes for some concern, at the
mid-September moment when I joined his campaign staff. These
reasons were summed up in the editorial lament of one newspaper
chain, wholly sympathetic to the Republican cause, mourning
that the general was running "like a dry creek." Rhetorically, he
had made his wildest swing at the Democratic Administration
with a profession of scorn for men in high office "too big for
their britches and too small for their jobs." Such stridence, aside
from being singularly out of character for the man, could suffice,
at best, for a frantic skirmish, but it was hardly the stuff that
effective campaigns are made of. Substantively, he had not done
much better. His one attempt at serious discussion of foreign
policy, early in September in Philadelphia, had failed, in fact, to
be serious. Its firmest assertions had not risen above the level
of indisputable platitudes. And its harshest charges against the
Administration—for having "abandoned China" and "bungled
us perilously close to World War III"—had come unpleasantly
close to the ambiguous, bellicose, and misleading rhetoric all too
familiar at recent Republican National Conventions.* The unwanted effect of all this had been heightened, of course, by the
contrasting skill and clarity of most of Adlai Stevenson's
speeches.

* New York *Times*, September 5, 1952.

29

Scanning and appraising this situation, I fairly soon discovered that, in politics and in government, there can exist one peculiar recompense for general confusion: the freedom that such confusion leaves for individual initiative. For I found myself enjoying rather blithe and unquestioned liberty in making a number of elemental decisions hopefully designed to lend greater force and precision to the candidate's public policy. These simple decisions went unchallenged—essentially, I was sure, because they went unnoticed. They affected style and substance, nonetheless, in both domestic and foreign affairs. For one matter, I struck from the current vocabulary any use of the words "Crusade" on the national scene, and "liberation" on the world scene. Their presumption seemed to me offensive, and they nowhere appeared in any passage of any speech that I prepared for the rest of the campaign. In similar spirit, I shunned the hitherto favored rhetoric about "the mess in Washington." The description seemed to me petty, self-righteous, and extravagant.

Most importantly, there were lines of argument that had to be drawn clearly if discussion of foreign affairs was to be rational and responsible. In particular, it seemed essential to avoid three types of argument most common in Republican oratory. The first of these argued—in bellowed indictment or whispered innuendo—that Democratic leadership was chronically addicted to stumbling into war, rather the way delinquent adolescents stumble into trouble, whereas a mature and sagacious Republican leadership would never have become entangled in the Korean War. The second line of equally meretricious argument—quite inconsistent with the first, but this fact never seemed to perplex its political merchants—charged this same Democratic leadership with weakness, timidity, or something vaguely more sinister, in *evading* direct retort to Communist challenges around the world. And these blurred insinuations encouraged yet a third argument, the cry that had been dramatically raised by General Douglas MacArthur: the war in Korea had to be pressed massively toward full victory over North Korea and Communist China. All these arguments mixed those strains of isolationism and chauvinism most truculent and least attractive in conservative Republican oratory about world affairs. Even in diluted form, they could have crudely corrupted the positions taken in the 1952 campaign. My disrespect for them was total. What was vastly more important, Eisenhower disdained and ignored them.

There had to be woven, then, a pattern of argument that took critical account of the seeming drift in foreign policy. The courage and rightness of the 1950 decision to enter the Korean War obviously could not be brought into doubt. All that could reasonably be questioned were a seeming slackness in the diplomacy that had preceded the conflict and, eventually, the air of indecision that had seemed to settle like a cloud upon its military conduct. Here, as in all discussion of foreign policy, the essential imperatives were to avoid either brash charge or bloated promise. And from these convictions were shaped the two speeches that, in utterly different ways, were probably the most important of the 1952 campaign: the address on October 16 to the Alfred E. Smith Memorial Foundation dinner in New York, and the speech on the Korean War in Detroit on October 24.

The New York address was an adequate example—to be repeated, curiously, in the 1956 campaign—of the importance of a speech that, by the yardstick of political sensation, looks not important at all. This particular text was a long and rather somber document, delivered at a late hour to an after-dinner audience, a large portion of whom were left bored and yawning. Yet it held a signal place in the campaign, by reason of what had preceded it. The candidate had just completed a long midwestern tour that, on many occasions, had dismayed a host of his eastern friends. His back-platform remarks from hasty notes—or "ad-libs"—had not read well in the press. The allusions to world affairs had sounded superficial and uninspired. All too typical had been an ambiguous suggestion that any Far Eastern conflict would best be fought by "Asians against Asians"—a phrase of such obscure meaning as to invite the inference that an excellent idea might be to leave Koreans on their own to fight Koreans. In New York headquarters, an increasingly anxious staff fell to asking one another: "When is he getting back and out of that damn jungle in the West?" To the impact of all of this, an antidote was urgently needed—an appearance and an address of mature tone and serious substance.

In these same days in Moscow, Stalin and the Nineteenth Party Congress had just reviewed, for the world's hearing, the doctrines and the threats of Soviet Communism. This provided the material for our text—an analysis of the scope of the Communist challenge, a warning of its complexity, and a statement of the demands and sacrifices it would impose on the American people. I spent far longer working on this speech than on any other of the campaign. The candidate returned to New York from the West only the day before its scheduled delivery, and the time for editing left to us was less than an hour—in a car rushing him through Manhattan streets to join a motorcade in northern New Jersey. Late that night, the listening audience nodded rather indifferently through the long text. The following morning, however, the *reading* audience of the world-oriented community of New York greeted the candidate's review of the international scene with sighs of relief and approval. And a New York *Times* that had been wavering nervously toward an endorsement of Adlai Stevenson promptly hailed the speech "skillful and penetrating" and shortly declared for Eisenhower. For a candidate who had theretofore evoked little support in the nation's intellectual community, this was a pertinent victory.

There was nothing so obscure about the import of the other major speech of these weeks. This contained the candidate's pledge that, if elected, he would go to Korea. Psychologically, this declaration probably marked the end of the campaign. Politically, it was later credited—by vast exaggeration, I believe—with turning millions of votes, sealing the election itself. Whatever its exact effect, its genesis and its aftermath reveal, rather strikingly, how very different can be the perspectives, on such an event, of a participant and an observer.

The origin of the speech was simple and inexorable in political logic. It rose from the need to say something affirmative on the sharpest issue of the day—*without* engaging in frivolous assurances and *without* binding a future administration to policies or actions fashioned in mid-campaign by any distorting temptations of domestic politics. I have been unable, to this date, even to conceive what Eisenhower could have said, to meet these basic requirements, other than what he did say. Confronting a military issue that was both the most distracting and the most dramatic of the day, the candidate, who happened to be the nation's most renowned military figure, pledged himself to look at the arena personally. The statement, it seemed to me, was, for him, natural and appropriate, almost to the point of being banal.

The steps in the preparation of this declaration varied not at all from the familiar procedure. In late September, during one of the many diffuse discussions of scheduled speeches, it had been agreed that at some unspecified date, before some unspecified audience, a foreign policy speech of unspecified content should deal with Korea in an unspecified way. All such discussions, even with Eisenhower present, largely exhausted themselves in review of technical details and arrangements. As in this instance, substance was almost never debated, at least not until a text was ready for immediate review. The notion of the candidate promising to visit Korea, however, had formed in my own thoughts weeks before the scheduled speech, and—in the fashion of the day—I never raised the matter for debate but decided to test the proposition in the prepared text. It was easy to conclude, also, that the most apt timing for such a proposal would be some ten days before election—a date late enough in the campaign to assure a high level of popular attention, yet not so late as to invite criticism as a last-minute device, slyly delayed to escape rebuttal. The timing seemed to me as obvious and unremarkable as the proposal itself.

33

Accordingly, and with a belatedness also typical of the pace of the days, I prepared "the Korea speech" two days before its scheduled delivery in Detroit. Herbert Brownell came by my home, at my request, to look over the draft before its dispatch to the campaign train the following morning. When he asked if I had discussed the proposal to visit Korea with the general, I replied: "No, there hasn't been time, and it just makes sense, so why not try it on him?" Brownell was more excited than I in anticipating its political effectiveness—indeed, I had been more concerned about its prudent avoidance of commitment on future Asian policy—but, by the following morning, we had agreed the matter important enough to warrant sending Harold Stassen to the campaign train, then en route to Detroit, to lend any necessary advocacy to the proposal when Eisenhower read it. The effort was superfluous. The candidate approved the speech immediately, only slightly modifying its phrasing to make the proposal stand out even more emphatically. And the next night, the pledge was given: "I shall go to Korea."

The reactions—on both political sides—wrote a few amusing footnotes to the whole electoral battle. Adlai Stevenson and one of his closest advisers, George W. Ball (who would be Under Secretary of State in the Kennedy administration), had received and read an advance text of the proposal—as Ball smilingly later told me—with no great concern at first. While others on Stevenson's staff reacted with quicker dismay and anxiety, only a day later did Stevenson begin to appraise the issue as gravely damaging to himself. An explanation for this relative unconcern lay in a curious fact. Months earlier, Stevenson and his advisers had weighed his making precisely the same pledge. They had concluded, most reasonably, that the promise of a visit to the Korean battlefront by an Illinois governor was hardly a dramatic thrust, if even a sensible notion. Suddenly confronting the appropriate enough promise by the nation's military hero, however, the Stevenson staff now groped urgently for a retort. The most bizarre and ill-advised response, which almost came to be delivered, was a speech drafted to explain the simple truth of Stevenson's earlier pondering of such a post-election journey and, in effect, echoing: "I, too, shall go to Korea." Wiser counsel prevailed, to veto so limp a retort. Instead, the decision was made to assail the very idea with furious indignation as a "slick" and theatrical campaign device, crassly exploiting a foreign crisis. The indictment proved unwounding.

The response of Eisenhower, in the days following his pledge, reflected still more of the temper of the man. While his staff exulted over the political reaction, he betrayed no special interest and, in our conversations, never even alluded to the Detroit speech. When he finally did mention it, more than a week later, the matter came up strangely. Sitting in his living room one morning, he told me of receiving a letter from Bernard Baruch that seriously troubled him. The letter, he explained, deplored the thought of any post-election trip to the Korean front as a reckless act on the part of any President-elect. Eisenhower frowned with concern, as he told me this, and added glumly: "I just don't know about that speech, now. We may have won —or we may have *lost*—the whole election right there." And he never brought up the subject again.

Politics in a democracy is a playground for paradox, and all of the campaign of 1952 gave fresh proof of the fact, in matters both major and minute. Thus, the most dramatic political speech of the campaign left the candidate who delivered it in a state of doubt almost as pained as the distress of his opponents who sufferingly heard it. Another of his most important pronouncements was as beneficial to his fortunes as it was boring to his audience. And in all the campaign's great glut of words, there probably were none uttered quite so important as the phrases— in promises or in polemics—that he scrupulously, steadfastly refused to speak.

4

The act of omission can play as critical a role in political life as in all human affairs. A man or a policy can be most forcefully dramatized by the thing quite deliberately not done. A leader can make his political profile sharp, and his identity unmistakable, by the company he refuses to keep, as well as the enemies he is willing to make. The worth and wisdom of a major pronouncement, partisan or national, may rest quite as much upon what is suppressed as upon what is spoken. And the councils of a leader are truly distinguished, not only by the qualities of the men present but also by the number—and the nature—of those absent.

One of the striking marks of the group around Dwight Eisenhower in the 1952 campaign was the absence of several who might have been expected to be present. Among those most conspicuously not present, in fact or in spirit, was General of the Army Douglas A. MacArthur. He was the military hero, if not the national hero, of Republican conservatives. Some decades before, Dwight Eisenhower had been a junior officer on his staff in the Philippines. Only weeks earlier, MacArthur had been the keynote speaker before the Republican Convention that finally had nominated Eisenhower. For millions of orthodox Republicans, MacArthur was both the supreme symbol of, and the supreme authority on, the most sensitive issue of the political hour—the Korean War. Despite all this, his counsel was never invited, his association never encouraged, his name never invoked, and his judgments never embraced.

The absences of others were equally interesting, for other reasons. Collectively, the Republican National Committee in Washington was quite absent from any decisions on the strategy, substance, or style of what the candidate had to say. While Arthur Summerfield late in the campaign came to New York to attend occasional meetings on such matters, his presence essentially was treated by the candidate merely as a convenient way to let the National Committee know his decisions—never to seek its counsel. And equally striking was the absence of Sherman Adams from all such strategy sessions. So burdened was Adams, as the candidate's personal campaign manager, with the mountainous labor of schedules and arrangements that he never attended a single discussion of the substance of what the candidate would endorse or decry. Like much else of these campaign weeks, this, too, foreshadowed the future—in this instance, the role, so largely administrative and operational, that Adams would fill in the Eisenhower administration.

Yet not at all indicative of things to come was the total absence from the scene of the figure soon to become so familiar to the nation and the world: the tall figure, hunched shoulders, and mournful countenance of John Foster Dulles. That Dulles was missing, even as an advisor at the far end of the long-distance telephone, was remarkable. At the time, he was widely presumed to be the most probable Secretary of State in any Republican Administration, and the electoral battle was being waged heavily in the terrain of foreign policy. Most key speeches that I prepared dealt with world crisis and foreign policy. Yet only once during the whole campaign—in the case of a statement of October 4 rebutting Democratic assertions on Asian policy—did Eisenhower even suggest that I consult Dulles on substance or language. This evident unconcern with the judgment of the Republican party's venerable authority on foreign affairs came to seem more remarkable, speech after speech, week after week. I could only infer, without necessarily lamenting, a significant lack of rapport between the two men. And I accordingly came to hold some doubt, shared by many others, that Dulles would ever be named Secretary of State.

Of all those absent from the intimate circle of advisers, however, none were more conspicuous—or more remote—than two men who would do much to shape, or to twist, the history of

37

the Republican party in this decade. The two were vice-presidential candidate Richard M. Nixon and Wisconsin's Senator Joseph R. McCarthy. And these two, so distant from the intense and intimate frenzy of Eisenhower's personal headquarters, were to cause the two most painful moments in his progress toward the White House.

I became acquainted with the details of the incident of "the Nixon fund," and its impact upon Eisenhower, only indirectly. I had, at the time, no personal acquaintance at all with Nixon. Neither lack of knowledge was a source of serious regret.

The story of the rather unorthodox personal political fund, by which Nixon had been defraying his California political expenses, broke into the campaign at a time when the Eisenhower train was proceeding upon its appointed rounds in the Middle West. Not once thereafter did I hear Eisenhower refer to the crisis that so suddenly erupted. But all those close to him on the train testified with sorrow and emphasis, upon their return, that the event had staggered and shaken the presidential candidate.

It could hardly have been otherwise. The episode meant more than a soldier's rough introduction to the unpoetic side of politics. It threatened to demolish, with eloquent mockery, the more righteous pretensions of a campaign that had christened itself, without excessive modesty, a "Crusade." It invited the Democratic candidate, with his proven gift for satire, to caricature the massive display of Republican righteousness as a shabby kind of political revival meeting. And, for the startled general, the immediate circumstances could scarcely have been more confusing and confounding. For he and his advisers aboard the campaign train found themselves, at the moment of crisis, almost prisoners of a curious kind of isolation, imposed by the ruthless rule of their itinerary. Without breaking their scheduled commitments, they lacked means or time to assess realistically either the political facts or the public reaction. Their only sources of information were frantic phone calls to New York and California, or the bundles of newspapers avidly seized and scanned, at each station-stop.

There was no panic at New York headquarters, but a mixture of other emotions, ranging from a cool and somber concern to an instant and heated exasperation with the man causing all the trouble. A disjointed but far from dispassionate kind of debate ensued, as Herbert Brownell undertook an informal poll on the blunt question: should the vice-presidential candidate be dropped from the national ticket? Bizarre and drastic as this action would have been—and strenuously opposed as it was by the Republican party headquarters in Washington—the notion won wide support. It came to be approved, even urged, by a considerable majority of the volunteers and independents, including myself, who felt vastly more concern with the political fate of Eisenhower than with the political embarrassment of the party. We were joined, moreover, by two others whose opinions could have much greater weight in such a situation: New York's Governor Thomas E. Dewey and General Lucius D. Clay, one of Eisenhower's oldest friends and supporters. In these days, I had a long discussion of the matter with Clay and found him to be angry and vehement, for he felt particular responsibility—and disenchantment—as one who had urged upon Eisenhower, at the Republican Convention, the choice of Nixon as his running mate. And all these largely hostile opinions were finally assessed and collected by Brownell, who decided to report them personally to Eisenhower on the campaign train.

But events—not for the last time—were to outrace an Eisenhower decision. Suddenly and dramatically, Nixon, from Los Angeles, was telecasting his apologia to the nation. The vice-presidential candidate made his dog, his wife, her clothes, his debts, and his mortgages famous in American campaign annals. A wave of popular sympathy surged in his support. And the President-to-be eyed its crest in some wonder and, in effect, shrugged and nodded.

The episode meant more, however, than tinsel melodrama.

39

It threw glancing light on some qualities of its central characters, and it would subtly affect their personal relations in the political future. For Richard Nixon, this had been a scarring ordeal, a time of desperate tension, a summoning and exhausting of all faculties to meet a mortal test. Within moments of concluding his televised self-defense, the tension broke—and he burst into tears. For he was sick with the certainty that he had failed persuasively to vindicate himself. As his car carried him away from the television studios, he slumped beside his wife and his close friend and adviser, William P. Rogers, and glumly stared out the window of his car—to discover a huge Irish setter bounding along senselessly beside them. Wanly, Nixon grimaced and said: "Well, we made a hit in the dog world, anyway."*

When Nixon shortly discovered the success he had scored in the political world, however, his elation turned to shock and rage—when Eisenhower failed to announce promptly and categorically his own satisfaction and his confidence. Instead, there came the general's summons to journey across the country, to receive at their personal meeting in Wheeling, West Virginia, what seemed to Nixon a needlessly belated benediction. From this— and from his awareness of the hostility, throughout the incident, at Eisenhower headquarters in New York—there came the first stirrings of emotions that would cloud much of Nixon's future relations with Eisenhower and the White House staff. As these sentiments persisted and evolved, they would inspire in Nixon much detachment, some disparagement, and a little distrust. And, in varying degrees at different times, the White House would reciprocate.

The conduct of Eisenhower, too, had illuminated something

* Years later, the published recollection by Nixon of this memorable moment in his life was markedly different. He recalled (*Six Crises*, pp. 117-18) the emotional tears as falling from the admiring eyes of the television camera crew, and he related that he immediately felt he had been successful, citing the incident of the dog as a happy jest expressing relief and assurance. Here I have noted the recollection of his friend, William P. Rogers, as he related it to me—a few months after the event.

of his character. He had been assailed by a clamor of conflicting counsels, immediately upon being thrust into the most unforeseen of crises. A certain steel of will was required to avoid all hasty action, even a hasty word, under such pressure. At the same time, Eisenhower, to the end, voiced no judgment that could be taken as a thoughtful appraisal of the merits of the matter. He had simply waited, albeit under conditions making this no easy exercise. And thereby he gave his first significant public display of the faculty for holding his peace—for "letting the dust settle." This particular description of a political posture had been made famous, of course, by Democratic Secretary of State Dean Acheson, and Republican campaigners never tired of caustically citing it as a confession of lethargic Democratic diplomacy in the Far East. Ironically, the years ahead would often suggest that no great political leader, in the nation or in the world, could surpass the Republican President-to-be in determined practice of this precept.

The major event of the 1952 campaign involving Senator Joseph McCarthy revealed still more of the man who was Eisenhower and the President he would be.

This incident began with a quiet discussion that the candidate had with me—late in September, in the living room of his home at Columbia University—as we noted that his schedule shortly called for his entering Wisconsin to deliver a major speech in Milwaukee. The mere prospect was distasteful to him: he had long resisted the Republican National Committee in planning even an appearance in the home state of Senator McCarthy. For he logically bracketed McCarthy with Indiana's Senator William E. Jenner as two reckless vilifiers of a man whom Eisenhower deeply admired, General of the Army George C. Marshall. (When Eisenhower appeared in Indianapolis, and Jenner exploited the public platform to clutch Eisenhower in a near-embrace, the candidate later told me: "I felt dirty from the touch of the man.") Suddenly, in our discussion of the Milwaukee speech, he leaned forward, bristling with excited indignation, and said: "Listen,

41

couldn't we make this an occasion for me to pay a personal tribute to Marshall—right in McCarthy's back yard?" I was more than mildly enthusiastic. And the text I accordingly prepared contained these affirmations:

Freedom is not only a precious but also a complex privilege. It is essentially the most generous way of life known to man. . . . It places its faith in the ultimate ability of the people to think clearly, to choose wisely, to act compassionately.

So full and generous a way of life must never be allowed to become narrow and stingy. The most awful poverty for people in this way of life would be a poverty of ideas. Their food for thought can never be rationed, nor their diet dictated by either an intellectual elite or self-appointed censors . . .

To defend freedom, in short, is—first of all—to *respect* freedom. This respect demands, in turn, respect for the integrity of fellow citizens who enjoy their right to disagree. The right to question a man's judgment carries with it no automatic right to question his honor.

Let me be quite specific. I know that charges of disloyalty have, in the past, been leveled against General George C. Marshall. I have been privileged for thirty-five years to know General Marshall personally. I know him, as a man and as a soldier, to be dedicated with singular selflessness and the profoundest patriotism to the service of America. And this episode is a sobering lesson in the way freedom must not defend itself.

These last words, supposed to be spoken on October 3 in Milwaukee, were stricken from the candidate's text, as his campaign train rolled across Wisconsin. At his dismayed New York headquarters, we quickly came to understand that Wisconsin's Republican leaders had convinced those closest to the candidate on the train—notably "Jerry" Persons—that the insult to McCarthy, in his home state, would sound excessively harsh and gratuitous. His counselors found Eisenhower at first almost snarling with impatience at their caution. But he finally assented. So late was the censorship performed that the press was fully aware of the fact, from its knowledge of the prepared text. The nation thus quickly became aware that Eisenhower, righteously stirred to defend his longtime friend against the vulgar assaults of Jenner and McCarthy, could be dissuaded from so serious a resolve by the exigencies and protocol of Wisconsin politics. Already, early in the campaign, he had been accused of "surrender" to Taft, when the two men had conferred in New York to heal some of their deep differences; and the Ohio senator had managed to convey the impression of having exacted the soldier-candidate's conformity to his own kind of conservatism. And now occurred this far more self-effacing performance, in the name of party unity.

The scent of irresolution in politics is never pleasant, and this time was no exception. Yet the most compassionate response to the dismal event came from one of those who, personally, was most dismayed. This was Harold Stassen, and I recall his tempered remarks. "It is easy to judge harshly," he cautioned, "sitting back here in New York and not knowing the pressures that go on inside that insane campaign train. You are trapped there. There are just a few people near you whom you trust. You don't have a chance to get out in the clean air and think things through. You have to decide fast. Time is always running out on you. And when all of them around you gang up, to insist you do this or that, it is just about impossible to fight back."

I could not help wondering at the time, however, if a problem might not lie at a deeper level. The sheer force of Eisenhower's authority and presence could not be leveled by mere number of dissenters—if he were firmly committed in his own mind. And this was an instance when he hardly could have been troubled by the faintest doubt of the rightness of his own position. It seemed, therefore, that the event gave warning that certain qualities of the man, even virtues in themselves, could be wrenched in the play of politics and made to seem misshapen. Clearly, there was in him a profound humility—a refusal to *use* the full force of his personal authority or political position against a critical consensus. He saw himself realistically as a man of military affairs, a stranger to political affairs, surrounded by

43

Republican leaders who—by their own testimony, at least—were political "experts." He would have abhorred any image of himself as the man-on-horseback, crudely importing military disciplines into a civil arena. Hence, even if the self-denying constraint drove him close to a teeth-grinding anger, he must shun the merest suggestion of martial arrogance. He must show and prove himself, in short, a modest enough member of "the team." He would use this particular phrase through the years, long after it grew stale, to describe or to commend all his political associates, be they his Cabinet or his White House staff, his Administration or his party. I am sure that the word "team" genuinely expressed for him a set of virtues transferred from the military life: coordination and cooperation, service and selflessness. Yet I often wondered if the simple, terse exhortation were not addressed, perhaps only half-consciously, as much to himself as to others.

The negative, then, held quite a notable place throughout this campaign of 1952.

There were the words left unspoken. There were the advisers not consulted. And there were the convictions not imposed.

All, for better or for worse, would prove relevant to the history ahead.

5

The headline on the front page of the New York *Times* of Monday, November 3, 1952, pronounced the circumspect conclusion: ELECTION OUTCOME HIGHLY UNCERTAIN, SURVEY INDICATES. This last of seven exhaustive surveys by the nation's leading newspaper, published on the eve of the election, judiciously reported: "Neither Gen. Dwight D. Eisenhower, Republican, nor Gov. Adlai E. Stevenson, Democrat, can be regarded as of now as certain of election." And the following morning, the nation's voters proceeded to give Eisenhower the greatest victory-by-landslide recorded by any Republican in the twentieth century.

To most of Eisenhower's staff, such an outcome had come to seem quite sure in the campaign's closing days. Some of this confidence was fired by the special impact of the Detroit speech on Korea, dominating the news and the mood of "the moment of truth" that is the final phase in any national campaign. My own expectation of a huge margin of victory rested, however, on a different proposition. The public opinion polls, unanimously and tenaciously, stressed the heavy percentage of "undecided" or "independent" voters. Here, with this group, there obviously rested the power of decision. But the polls seemed to draw the plausible, but quite unwarranted, inference that such a "floating" vote would tend to divide rather evenly, making the final verdict perilously narrow. The contrary seemed to me more true politically: so large a group of "independent" voters, cautious and uncommitted and reflective, possessed, by its very definition, a certain political coherence and unity. It would, therefore, be most unlikely to sunder, at the last instant, approximately into halves; instead, in whichever direction it moved, it would tend to move massively.

And so it did . . .

Election night—at campaign headquarters in New York's Hotel Commodore—crackled with the electric excitement of this unique political moment.

This is, inescapably, a time of drama, personal and political, raised to the highest power. The stakes could not be higher: the presidency of the most powerful nation on earth. As the minutes tick and the hours toll toward decision, the history of four years seems to stand—waiting, listening, poised—ready to be suddenly born and set upon its course. The mind feels a little dazed by the almost harsh finality of it all, as all complexities and subtleties of political life suddenly descend to the level of the crude, basic verdict of the spinning wheel or compass . . . Red or Black?

45

. . . North or South? . . . President—or one-time nominee? . . . A subject for biographies—or for textbook footnotes? . . .

The nerves of all political workers, attending the answer, dance a little crazily, in human frames physically and mentally exhausted from the tension of some hundred days or more. Any moment of any one of those days, from high noon to midnight, could have brought the event or the act, the speech or the phrase, secretly triggering—it will *now* appear—the chain of occurrences finally decreeing this victory or this rout. In these last hours, no man, however unfavored in forecast, is so icily realistic as not to feel the teasing quiver of hope. And no man, however assured by prophets, is so stoutly confident that he does not have to swallow, a few times, a swelling lump of doubt—a fear that he might, after all, have misread some false glitter in the golden omens.

Of this particular night of electoral victory, I recall but a few scenes of the festive post-midnight hours, as all the small and bleak hotel rooms seemed to grow large and stately and gay, swelled by the cheers and the laughter, the relief and the hopes, belonging to the exuberant instant . . . I remember the President-elect and his beaming wife, huddled in a tiny room, as he battled a tangled switchboard to make his first phone call after victory—to Herbert Hoover. The sentimental gesture was true to the man *trying* to identify himself with a tradition—a "team"— that was still essentially foreign to himself. . . . I remember him, again, grinning boyishly in the suite reserved for family and intimates—his strong face flushed red with excitement, his grin restlessly alive, and the thin hair throwing out lively wisps of gray. A cherub, one thought, had become President . . . Then, as the minutes wore on without a formal concession from his overwhelmed opponent, there came his flash of impatience: "What in God's name is the matter with that monkey?" For some reason, the expletive of "monkey" already had become his civilian substitute for the more muscular language of the barracks. . . . Then, not long past midnight, it was all over officially. The popular-vote plurality surged past six million. Of 531 electoral votes, Eisenhower captured 442—from 39 states. The sweep of the victory carried both "left" and "right": at one and the same time, he had captured the big urban vote of the North while scoring unprecedented advances into the conservative South.

For Eisenhower, it was a personal triumph of rare magnitude. Precisely because it was so personal and so sweeping, the event carried implications of both hope and caution for the political future. Professional Democratic politicians—like James Farley— might ascribe the size of the victory to the meeting of the issue of the Korean War. Professional Republican politicians—like any of a score or more state chairmen across the nation—might point to some local victories to suggest various pockets of party strength. Yet the thoughtful and the candid knew it to be a victory for the *man*—and the respect, the affection, and the hope that *he* summoned. Twenty years of Democratic leadership, highlighted by the popular triumphs of Franklin Roosevelt, had been brought to an end with a Republican victory almost comparable to the greatest wrought by Roosevelt. And the name of Eisenhower carried with a resonance—through the world as well as the nation—matched, in a whole generation, only by the name of Roosevelt.

Yet these same dramatic facts posed a peril and a question: might not its extraordinarily personal nature warn that this victory rested on too narrow a base of politics? For this electoral triumph of 1952 found neither reason nor reflection in the structure or the life of the Republican party itself. No aspect or resource of the party—neither its discernment of world affairs nor its political imagination on the national scene, neither its richness of talent nor its strength of organization—could be credited with a vital role in this victory. And the wary observer might draw from this a rather dark inference: if the years ahead saw any notable failure or slackness in *personal* leadership, there would be meager resources within the party to enlist for atoning or compensating.

Another shadow, slow to fall, could hardly be seen, though vaguely sensed. For the very sweep of the Eisenhower victory, through both Deep South and urban North, left the party still to debate, within itself, its very identity. Led to triumph by an Eisenhower, it did not have to make a choice. To the one side, "liberal" northern champions of civil rights, and to the other side, "conservative" southern devotees of states' rights: each could continue to lay loud claim to being the authentic voice of Republicanism and the hopeful herald of its future. The very greatness of the political victory thus exacted its price—by making easy the slurring of issues and the stifling of self-scrutiny. Basic decision could be deferred. Mere time could be bought. Thus early—instantly upon Eisenhower's first election—the politics of America began preparing a major bill for future reckoning. And the final payment would not be exacted until the 1960 National Elections, eight years distant.

At the exhilarating time, however, between Election Day in 1952 and Inauguration Day two months and two weeks later, there was little mood for such critical savoring of the taste of victory.

The labor of transition between administrations is always arduous, even for the veteran and expert in government. In this instance, a group of novices was taking over the government of the United States. None had known any experience in Executive decision or action at the national level. Behind them stood a Republican party whose twenty years of exile from the Executive Branch left it in a state of unreadiness, bordering on astonishment, before the prospect of working *with* the man in the White House.

Upon this near-empty stage, there came an onrush of new problems and new personalities. There were Herbert Brownell and Lucius Clay, commissioned by the President-elect to nominate men for the highest offices in the national government—with orders that little heed be paid to party counsel. There was Sherman Adams, taking charge of all the administrative machinery in New York, prior to overseeing its shipment to the White

House and assuming his own post as Assistant to the President. There were counselors on the fringes of the scene, like Thomas E. Dewey, mourning to Milton Eisenhower that his vast, if not triumphal, experience in national politics somehow did not seem to be viewed by the President-elect as indispensable. There were jobs to be found for men like Senator Henry Cabot Lodge—so prominent in sponsoring Eisenhower's appearance on the national political scene, but so conspicuous in defeat, in his own campaign for re-election, at the hands of young John Fitzgerald Kennedy. There was the work of the quickly appointed advisory committee on government organization, later given official status, consisting of Milton Eisenhower, Dr. Arthur S. Flemming, and Nelson A. Rockefeller. And in a different sphere, there was the slow labor of preparing an Inaugural Address and a State of the Union message.

Abruptly, in early December, there intervened the President-elect's journey to Korea—to be joined at Wake Island, on his return trip, by a group of some of us who would be working most closely with him. Following the rendezvous at Wake, on December 8, we passed three days on the cruiser U.S.S. *Helena*, en route to Hawaii, in round-table discussion of the most immediate matters before the incoming Administration. These included: a statement on the Korean War for release upon return to American soil, extended debate on the removal of price controls, summary review of a draft of the Inaugural Address and of the contents of the State of the Union message, and general discussion of Communist world strategy, especially in Asia.

Attentively attending almost all the discussions of those three days, I found in them a somewhat dismaying contrast between their actual substance and their public appearance. To the world's news agencies, flashing their crisp reports across the globe, these meetings constituted "the epic mid-Pacific conference." Naturally, Press Secretary James C. Hagerty did nothing to diminish this impression. Quite to the contrary, he gravely described the sense of urgency supposedly spurring the conference: "It is imperative to decide how best to combat Soviet-dominated Communism throughout the world." And in succeeding years, there were widespread rumors and reports of the portentous "strategic decisions" supposedly made aboard the *Helena.*

There were, in fact, no such decisions. Nor did anyone present delude himself on the matter. Thought and work were completed on only one immediate order of business—the President-elect's statement on the Korean War, broadly pressing the Communist leaders toward a settlement honorably acceptable to the West. Beyond this, there were not even any "strategic" military or political decisions concerning Korea alone. Nor was any major problem on the domestic scene—including price controls—debated to final resolution.

Yet there was value to these meetings. They provided time for the first serious communication, if not indeed their first introduction to one another, among some of the men who would most seriously shape the new Administration's personality and achievement. More important than the few of us who would serve on the White House staff were those who would be key members of the Cabinet-to-be. For the Department of the Treasury, there was George M. Humphrey: he conveyed instantly a personal charm and warmth matching Eisenhower's, a candor and simplicity of speech typifying the most generous traditions of the Middle West. Beside him, as Director of the Bureau of the Budget, stood Joseph M. Dodge: genial in manner, crisp in speech, logical in thought. For the Department of Defense, there was Charles E. Wilson: bluff and hearty, a passionate and uncompromising simplifier of issues, fresh from General Motors with abundant confidence that his corporate experience in Detroit's automobile industry would guide his path through all snares of politics, congressional or global. And at Wilson's side stood Admiral Arthur W. Radford, to be Chairman of the Joint Chiefs of Staff: a handsome, articulate, and assured man, with a deep concern for Asian affairs but with a disconcerting capacity for reporting such a fact as the presence of anti-colonial feelings among Asian peoples with the earnest and breathless excitement of one announcing a fresh and remarkable discovery. And—most important of all—there was John Foster Dulles.

Here on the *Helena* came the first occasion when I saw to-gether and in close contact these two men whose relationship would so critically affect the whole history of the Eisenhower Years. The impression they created was vividly memorable—and remarkably misleading. Through all the hours we spent sitting around the green-felt oval of the *Helena's* conference table, there were no moments more striking than those filled with the solemn monotone of the Secretary of State-designate. Whether expand-ing at philosophic length upon his estimate of the Communist challenge, or responding at legalistic length to a specific ques-tion of policy, Dulles apparently made one consistent impact upon Eisenhower: he bored him.

Time after time, as Dulles spoke, I watched the all-too-expres-sive face of the President-elect and the gestures of impatience made almost more plain by the half-successful efforts to suppress them. His reactions were always the same—the brisk nodding of the head, in a manner designed to nudge a slow voice faster on-ward toward some obvious conclusion . . . the restless rhythm of the pencil tapping his knee . . . the slow glaze across the blue eyes, signaling the end of all mental contact . . . finally, the patient fixing of the eyes on the most distant corner of the ceil-ing, there to rest till the end of the Dulles dissertation. When the end came, at last, Eisenhower was quite likely to rejoin the conversation with words sharply aimed away from all that had been said, without even acknowledging their utterance.

More than manner of speech or tedium of listening, how-ever, seemed to me to stand between these two men. Personally they had had remarkably little contact with each other before the November election. Nor had this distance been spanned by any assurance on Eisenhower's part that he would appoint Dulles as Secretary of State. After Election Day, a number of Republicans had counseled against the appointment—a sufficient number, causing enough delay in the President-elect's decision, to make Dulles fully aware that his selection had not been instantaneous. All this evidently troubled Dulles enough to make him appear awkwardly shy and diffident in Eisenhower's presence, as if almost pained by his unsureness of the other's confidence. And aside from such emotional matters, there loomed the contrast between the two in their very style of thinking. To a military man eager to discuss the tangible and the pragmatic, the lawyer offered a surfeit of abstractions and generalizations. Almost brusquely and sometimes insensitively, the President-elect seemed to spurn the offering as tasteless fare.

From the "epic" of these mid-Pacific meetings, I therefore returned with one impression that seemed, for the future, more important than all others. This was the serious expectation that, in the great labor of redirecting American foreign policy, the partnership of Eisenhower and Dulles would surely break, most probably within a year or two. It was a memorably erroneous conclusion.

Back in New York, in the less exotic surroundings of Eisenhower's headquarters, the days till Inauguration resounded with the commotion of any huge family struggling to assemble its wits and its belongings, pack its practical utensils and its lofty programs, and hastily move to a distant city and a strange home. The ceremonial highlight of the period was the novelty of two successive "Cabinet" meetings in New York, on January 12 and January 13, largely given to lengthy review of the Inaugural Address and to further discussion of economic controls. These meetings provoked a sudden flutter of hastily written papers from the prospective Cabinet members, directed by Eisenhower to send me their substantive contributions to the State of the Union message; but most of them responded with vague and hesitant generalities, as if they had been asked to weigh matters as esoteric as the formula for nuclear fission. And all the while there continued the flow of counsel from office-seekers, elated senators, or out-of-office congressmen—along with General Mac-Arthur and his crisp advice to end the Korean War by publicly threatening atomic attack. But all that later seemed worth recalling of the confused din was the occasional quiet moment, allowing another glimpse of the man to be President.

There was, each day, the quickening of his nervousness about his Inaugural Address, as the time for Inauguration neared. The text was spun, with increasing unreason, through circle after circle of verbal changes. The first "Cabinet" meeting had burst into spontaneous applause when the President-elect finished reading one draft to them; but five days later—and barely seventy-two hours before Inauguration—he seriously started laboring with an utterly new speech, only to discard quickly this impulsive notion. To the last hours—and his personal drafting of the prayer with which he preceded his speech—he felt a restless anxiety never displayed, before or later, about any speech. The problem, of course, was not merely semantic but deeply personal. The candidate, who had been able to talk almost cavalierly about "going fishing happily" if he were not elected, had now come face-to-face with the ceremony signaling the solemn consequence of victory. And the imminent encounter seemed clearly to leave him humbled, awed, a little troubled.

There recurred, too, throughout the hours upon hours of dialogue we shared in preparing his Inaugural Address, a constant, almost monotonous theme to which he kept reverting. He called it, quite simply, "the individual"; and he commonly linked it to the verb, "produce." And it would go thus: "All these generalizations about freedom and history do not mean too much. What matters to the average citizen is—what can *he* do? A carpenter or a farmer or a bricklayer or a mechanic—what is *his* role? The *individual*—that's what counts. It's not just a time of crisis for the statesmen and the diplomats. Every individual has got to understand and to *produce*. He's got to *work* harder than ever—and he's got to understand *why*." This was spoken with the same fervor, and asserted the same basic values, as a score of

53

kindred utterances on thrift, spending, and budget. For these values seemed to him priceless American precepts, immutable and indispensable, whose mere invocation could politically inspire the nation.

There were passing suggestions, too, through these days, of his sense of religious values—partly reverent, partly wry, intensely simple. With his first "Cabinet" meeting, he had set the precedent of asking Secretary of Agriculture Ezra Taft Benson, one of the Council of Twelve Apostles of the Mormon Church, to open the proceedings with prayer. Yet not many days later—impatient with Benson's slowness to define his farm program—Eisenhower could jest: "I really think Ezra is less concerned with his Department than with making sure I open every session with a prayer." At the same time, casual as had been his own traditional religious practice, he would exhort on few subjects so promptly and passionately as "spiritual" strength or "spiritual" precepts as the "real" sources of American power and greatness.

There occurred too, idle moments—over a quiet lunch or in early evening discourse—that conveyed insights more personal and explicit, including his plain-spoken views of some of his contemporaries. Thus a mere mention of Harry Truman's name brought fast flashes of antipathy—including wondering aloud "if I can *stand* sitting next to him" in the Inaugural procession. Stung by Truman's campaign rhetoric, Eisenhower bitterly recalled: "I remember his saying to me a while back, 'This politics is a dirty game, but nothing will affect us and our relationship.'" And he would reminisce, quite differently, of Winston Churchill—prompted by the current succession of transatlantic phone conversations with the British Prime Minister, as the crisis over Iranian oil had grown intense. "It's a lot easier talking to Winston by phone than in person, you know," he smilingly explained. "He's so darn deaf we can get a lot more business done at a distance." And many such casual remarks were passing reminders of his rare familiarity and ease with all the Western world's leaders—and the notable asset that this could prove to be in office.

A more personal and touching subject came up one day over luncheon in his office. This concerned his son, John, then a major on Korean duty. For John had cabled his hope—with "no offense intended"—that sudden orders reassigning him to Washington might be canceled. One could easily imagine him matching his father in disdain of unwarranted personal privilege. But his orders had been issued to guard against the possible danger of his capture by Communists on the battlefield. A little grimly, the President-elect explained: "I told him that, if he ever got surrounded, there'd be only one way out, because if he were captured—my God—I guess I'd just have to resign or something. How could I *then* deal with those boys?"

I have kept, from these days, a final memento. It is a small sheet of paper on which Eisenhower scrawled with hasty pen the essence of what he wanted to convey in his Inaugural Address. The words are few. A simple list of four qualities stands at the top of the page: *Understanding, Heart and determination, Productivity,* and *Readiness to sacrifice.* The list is bracketed, and beside it the collective comment reads: "These must be *universal.*" And directly below comes the particular: "*Leadership*—political, industrial, church, school, labor—must develop the above."

This well enough summed up the spirit and the perspective of the man, as he became the thirty-fourth President of the United States.

6

In Washington, on Inauguration Day, January 20, above the presidential platform on Capitol Hill, the sun suddenly struck through the low clouds of the chill morning. This was just minutes before Dwight David Eisenhower was to take his oath of office. A number of politicians, diplomats, and correspondents familiar with Eisenhower's career looked up at the sky's abrupt brightness. They smiled. They nodded knowingly to one another. And for some seconds they were murmuring to each other about the persistence of what they long had called "the Eisenhower luck."

Shortly, then, the soldier-President was speaking to his nation and to all nations. And among other things of like spirit, he assured them . . .

We are called as a people to give testimony, in the sight of the world, to our faith that the future shall belong to the free. . . .

The faith we hold belongs not to us alone but the free of all the world. This common bond joins the grower of rice in Burma and the planter of wheat in Iowa, the shepherd in southern Italy and the mountaineer in the Andes. It confers a common dignity upon the French soldier who dies in Indochina, the British soldier killed in Malaya, the American life given in Korea. . . .

We stand ready to engage with any and all others in joint effort to remove the causes of mutual fear and distrust among nations. . . . [Yet] we shall never try to placate an aggressor by the false and wicked bargain of trading honor for security. Americans, indeed all free men, remember that—in the final choice—a soldier's pack is not so heavy a burden as a prisoner's chains. . . .

We must be ready to dare all for our country. For history does not long entrust the care of freedom to the weak or the timid. . . .

No person, no home, no community can be beyond the reach of this call. . . . For . . . whatever America hopes to bring to pass in the world must first come to pass in the heart of America.

The peace we seek, then, is nothing less than the practice and fulfillment of our whole faith. . . . It signifies much more than the stilling of guns, easing the sorrow, of war.

More than an escape from death, it is a way of life.

More than a haven for the weary, it is a hope for the brave.

It seems not without meaning that—in 1953—the first Republican President in twenty years spoke so firm a commitment to America's role of service and of sacrifice, in the world of free nations.

It would seem, too, not without meaning that—in 1961—his young critic and successor would proclaim, in phrases more felicitous but in substance no different, his own and his nation's dedication to precisely the same purposes . . . still stubbornly standing, eight years later, just as far from fulfillment.

CHAPTER THREE

The Eisenhower Regime:
Its Roots and Its Men

The first of the Eisenhower Years foreshadowed all of them.

It was a time that inscribed, swiftly and deeply, the epigraph for a whole decade. The words and phrases now uttered—again and again—became facts and resolves forever after. For this was the time of seed: the elements of thought and the fragments of policy belonging to this initial year would seem to sprout and flourish in times and in crises twenty and forty and eighty months later. And this was the time of omen: the casual or sudden decision of this year would somehow live on, as sovereign precedent in the future, and the flaw first glimpsed now would slowly swell to the size of failure. And so most remembered moments of this year—notable or trivial, sad or comic—would find remembrance and response in the sighs, or the smiles, of the last of the Eisenhower Years.

Perhaps this manner of making history is not so remarkable in an Administration committed to conserving rather than creating, guarding rather than building. Perhaps, more likely, all this also reflects the relatively slow pace of change on the surface of modern American politics, despite all the pulse-quickening rhetoric: the slogans and the pledges may seem fresh as newly minted coins, but the currency of ideas—for a long time—has remained singularly stable. Or perhaps, more likely still, the revolutionary pace of events in the middle of the twentieth century so outraces a people's awareness and readiness that almost any leadership, even one passionately committed to "the new," soon finds that its practices and its postures fast tend to grow disconcertingly old.

And one pervasive fact of political life, in any modern democracy, would prove pertinent to all the Eisenhower Years: the sheer size and intricacy of government conspire to taunt and to thwart all brisk pretensions to set sensationally new directions. The vast machinery of national leadership—the tens of thousands of levers and switches and gears—simply do not respond to the impatient jab of a finger or the angry pounding of a fist. And thus it might even be recalled, for example, that, in the first hours of the Eisenhower administration, the White House frantically struggled with no great issue affecting the destiny of freedom or the welfare of the nation. The greater part of the memorable day was spent in trying to unscramble a White House office switchboard so snarled that husbands, assigned to this citadel of decision, had to cross Pennsylvania Avenue to a drugstore phone booth to advise their wives of the hour when they would be home for dinner.

2

The men who made up the leadership of the new Administration, for all their want of political experience, were—remarkably without exception—individuals of clean intent, sober commitment, and patriotic purpose. In a couple of them, vanity and ambition occasionally shivered near the surface, like uncontrollably twitching nerves. And they possessed, of course, quite varying tempers, attitudes, and perceptions. Even of those from the top ranks of the nation's business community, there was a sharp distinction between the political sophistication of a Joseph Dodge—who, under the Truman administration, had expertly directed currency reforms in postwar Austria, Germany, and Japan—and a George Humphrey, who deeply believed the destiny of all free peoples to depend almost wholly upon the stability of the American dollar. And the unselfish sense of service of a Sherman Adams offered a contrast, sharp as silent mockery, to the self-preoccupation of a John Foster Dulles.

All these men were bound and united, nonetheless, in a few elemental convictions. The relative simplicity of these did nothing to dull the edge of the fervor with which they were held. All of them believed the national government to be languishing in a state of decay or disorder, calling for swift remedy. They thought the world menace of Communism had been so idly abetted by American irresolution that some show of resolution—spiced with some specific, but not too costly, show of force—would change matters considerably. They largely conceived the solution of all political crises, nationwide or worldwide, to depend essentially on economic strength, and they gauged this strength, in turn, by the simple yardsticks of the "soundness" of the dollar and the "freedom" of the economy. They therefore felt a powerful sense of obligation to limit expenditures even for those government programs, including national defense, which they warmly endorsed in principle. And—even though *they* now *were* "the government" —they steadfastly believed that the less the government did, the more the people would progress and prosper.

The nation's new leaders seemed determined to apply this self-effacing theory immediately—in the practical labor of transition between old and new administrations. This awkward interval between regimes, never easy and usually untidy, always reveals something of each new regime's particular spirit and method of work. Thus, in 1960, the incoming Kennedy administration, in such key areas as the Departments of State, Defense, and Treasury, would go through elaborate and detailed self-education for the turnover of Executive power—with days of conferences, and weeks of contact, between incumbents and appointees on up to the Secretarial level. The approach was markedly different eight years earlier. In all the sphere of foreign affairs and defense policy, the sum of such educating contacts was two—one chilly twenty-minute exchange at the White House between Truman and Eisenhower, and one fifty-minute visit by Henry Cabot Lodge, officially designated as liaison officer for foreign policy, with the incumbent head of the State Department's Policy Planning Board. This was truly scanty preparation for a group of men already marked by their inexperience. And so casual a review of the great problems ahead seemed to make all the more incongruous a fastidious attention to inconsequential detail promptly displayed in the White House. Thus, presiding over the first meeting of the White House staff—which began and remained a daily 8:30 A.M. conclave—Sherman Adams devoted most of his time to cautioning against "eccentric habits" in "deportment," such as: secretarial office-gossip sessions, smoking in corridors, or disrespectful feet on executive desks. There was, indeed, a puritanical tinge to the new regime.

The travail of transition commonly entails no exercise quite so confused as the preparation of a new administration's first State of the Union message. The task is difficult enough in any normal year—as each head of department tries to shout over the clamor of all his Cabinet colleagues for presidential attention to his unique and urgent concerns. The portentous proceedings teeter toward chaos, however, when the department heads feverishly clamor for recognition of their future needs, even though they themselves have had no time to ascertain precisely what these needs may be. I still recall Eisenhower's cries of anguish upon seeing some of the incoherent suggestions and rambling phrases that many of his Cabinet members submitted as "programs"— including his unhappy awe at a contribution from the Department of the Interior distinguished for failure even to mention rural electrification. Wearily, through those days, from early

61

morning to late evening, he and I, often joined by his brother Milton, would labor over the bundles of drafts and re-drafts, suggestions and memoranda—during the day at his office desk, by late afternoon in his upstairs study, sometimes at night by his bedside. In such sessions, a few stubborn matters of substance defied mere verbal resolution. On the domestic scene, Ezra Benson conscientiously held out for views of farm-price parity that bluntly contradicted the party platform. In foreign affairs, John Foster Dulles insisted on a "repudiation" of any past dealings with foreign governments resulting in "secret agreements" —whose very existence stood in some doubt. And the Senate's most vociferous conservatives, led by Ohio's Robert A. Taft and Colorado's Eugene D. Millikin, missed no chance to deliver their admonitions against fiscal irresponsibility, unbalanced budgets, and lowered tariffs—seeming to appear almost daily to be sure that their protesting theses were nailed upon all White House doors.

Out of this political and verbal disorder, there finally emerged —as, miraculously, there always does—a document proclaiming the purposes of the most powerful government on earth. Down to its small details, Eisenhower contributed personally and knowledgeably—whether the matter concerned the disposition of the Seventh Fleet in the Pacific or the sundry reasons for the decline in the price of butter. With time to study the text of a paper, his editorial sense almost always stayed quick and precise. I recall, for example, in this first State of the Union message, his carefully changing the term "Stalinism" to "aggressive Communism" throughout the text. He offered me the matter-of-fact explanation: "'Stalinism' is too personal—it sounds the wrong note. For one thing, he's the most conservative of that gang in twenty-five years. And besides—it's always possible I'll be meeting and negotiating with him someday. So . . ."

As in the presidential editing of the Inaugural Address, so now I noted, in these days, his tendency to stress repetitively a single word and notion, more than a little revealing of the man.

This time the word was "instinct"—or "instinctive." Repeatedly he employed it in speech or on paper as synonymous with "conviction" or "principle." Always, it was used in a context signifying *good* "instinct." The fondness for simplification, so evident in the candidate of 1952, would be no less a mark of the President, for all his life in office.*

History in these months, however, was not presenting its problems in simple shapes or compact packages. The first year of the Eisenhower administration would witness, in Soviet Russia alone, the death of Stalin, the rise and fall of Malenkov and Beria, and the explosion of the first Soviet H-bomb. Elsewhere in the world, American policy would have to grapple with problems of armistice in Korea, crisis in Indochina, diplomacy toward Communist China, and differences with West European allies as measures for European unity faltered. And on the national scene, aside from the special stridence of McCarthyism, there was the noise of bitter debate among Republicans on world trade policies. Soon, on a score of issues, the Republican President would learn that his major domestic problem, too, was a question of "coexistence"—with the Republican party.

As the Eisenhower administration moved to meet this host of problems, it gradually displayed a particular *style* of politics. This was set not only by the character of Eisenhower but also by the talent and training of a few men around him. They—like his problems—largely stayed with him to the end.

Their images come vividly to mind—from diary notes of their words and responses, their myriad remembered acts and gestures . . .

---

* As it turned out, the State of the Union message was well enough received, including its promise of "a new, positive foreign policy." Typically, the Washington *Post* hailed "a clear statement of principle" that "had scope and grasp and even attained a certain grandeur of conception." It cheered, too, "the manner in which the President talked as an Atlas." No less appreciative was Walter Lippmann, as he saluted "the work of what is already, at this early date, an organized and remarkably coherent Administration." (Washington *Post*, February 3, 1953)

63

On the White House staff, from the first and through the years, the President's most important aides were three. They were: Assistant to the President Sherman Adams, Press Secretary James C. Hagerty, and Special Assistant Major General Wilton B. ("Jerry") Persons. And I doubt if any of these three could be surpassed, in the wishes of any President, for their professional dedication to their tasks and their personal devotion to "the boss."

The strength of Adams was the strength of candor and courage, uncomplicated by intellectual posturing or political ambition. At fifty-four years of age, he was physically lean and resilient, nervously tense and quick, mentally clear and pragmatic. He took in stride his twelve-hour days, sometimes filled with as many as two hundred phone calls, a score or more personal visitors, and monosyllabic decisions beyond count. Detractors found Adams curt and rude, especially if they were seeking favors, and if the monosyllable was "no." Undoubtedly, he alienated, at times needlessly, senators and congressmen who found him gruffly barring their entry to the presidential office. And garrulous argument or vacillating response sharpened his natural impatience to an edge of anger. Notwithstanding descriptions of him through the years as an enigmatic *éminence grise,* he scarcely ever sought to work as a policymaker. He interceded even in the planning of presidential speeches only occasionally and superficially. Sardonically, he described his role in the White House as "scrubbing the administrative and political backstairs." As an administrator, his sense of order was far from meticulous, and a rich variety of state papers and White House correspondence could disappear from sight on his cluttered desk. But the man hurled himself at his work with a kind of headlong force— a stoic disregard of self and a cold clarity of judgment—that seemed almost to beat matters into decent submission. On occasion, over the years, his partisan rhetoric would sound unpleasantly scathing or righteous. But his loyalty to the man who was President transcended mere partisanship, and he could retort to many insistent demands upon Eisenhower by party leaders with an acid dismissal: "Nuts! We're doing quite enough for the goddam Republican party." His sense of personal integrity was so fierce and final that he could not imagine anyone possibly questioning his actions or relationships or motives. The assurance, in truth, seemed amply justified, but it encouraged him in a tactical carelessness that would bring his term of service to a painful end.

One slight incident of a later date may suggest the man's freshness and vigor of judgment. In August of 1956, at the Republican Convention in San Francisco, I was scheduled to address the delegates specifically in the role of "an independent for Eisenhower." The idea for such an address had been the President's, but it had not been warmly welcomed by the party officials. It became positively distasteful when they found that my prepared text included some sharp remarks about those "within the Republican party" in whose minds "loyalty to America . . . was crudely confused with conformity"—while they "read the Constitution as if it were a partisan pamphlet." Buffeted by protests, Adams asked me, the night before the speech, to delete all such remarks, offering the plausible explanation: "It simply isn't courteous to be a guest of the Convention and rap one wing of the party." Briefly, I observed that this was precisely what any thoughtful independent would do: if he failed to do so, he would plainly be either not thoughtful—or not independent. Adams reflected for an instant, then briskly answered: "Right—let 'em have it." Thus it required perhaps less than one minute of conversation for him to decide to brush aside the complaints of most of his Convention colleagues. And this rare capacity for viewing any matter on its simple merits assured Adams remaining, throughout the years of his service to the Administration, a source of clean air, amid much that grew stale.

James Hagerty probably matched Adams in his rare fullness of commitment to his work and to his President. Like Adams, he neither possessed nor coveted any quality of the idealogue or the theoretician. Forty-three years old, quick and shrewd and indefatigable, he was a master technician of press relations. He entertained and expressed little concern with substance, except as he assayed its immediate editorial impact. Neither in national nor international affairs did he press his views of policy on others—though he, like Adams, came often to be imagined and reported in some such secret, powerful role. The terms in which he rejoiced or raged were elemental and immutable. What hurt the public image of the President was bad. What enhanced this image was good.

For General Persons, the ultimate criteria were identically the same. A mellow fifty-seven, warm in nature and rich in humor and steadfast in friendship, Persons minutely directed all White House relations with the Congress. By temperament and belief, he wished these relations, as constantly as possible, to be gently governed by cordiality and compromise. Over the years, he may have healed as many congressional wounds as Adams opened. Most important of all: from his experience as a Defense Department liaison officer on Capitol Hill, he inherited a respect, bordering on deference, for all congressional prerogatives and sensibilities. In practical terms, he frankly argued the rightness of this as a matter of mere arithmetic: "A vote by Jenner or McCarthy is worth just as much as any other senator's."

On one occasion in 1953, Persons told me an incident that revealed a good deal about both his and Eisenhower's attitudes toward this strategy of conciliation. The recital was provoked by one of many instances when I had frankly lamented his journeys to the Senate to assuage some distress of Senator McCarthy. And he candidly explained: "Just the other day, after I came back from seeing Joe, I went in to talk to the boss. *He* gave me hell, too. 'Jerry, I don't understand,' he said, 'how you feel you can come in this office altogether clean after shaking hands with that fellow.' And I told him: 'Maybe I'd feel that way, too, if I were up there trying to get something for myself. But if it's to get him to do something *you* want, I'll shake hands with him as often as I have to.'" Oddly but characteristically, the exchange between

the two men had ended on this tentative note—with issues un-
joined, principles unclarified.

Along with these three men, there come to mind the remembered faces grouped, week after week, around the long table of
the Cabinet room . . . seated in their high-backed black leather
chairs, gravely fingering the little white notebooks before them,
nodding solemnly whenever the President spoke, and murmuring comment or counsel on the bewildering array of matters—
from farm surpluses to departmental deficits, from ambassadorial
appointments to senatorial disappointments, from Democratic
strength in South Chicago to Communist armament in North
Korea—that makes up the agenda of American democracy at
work.

Among those in less sensitive offices, Interior's Douglas
McKay and Commerce's Sinclair Weeks sat, in rarely broken
silence, on the outermost edges of the conservative view of almost all matters. Men from opposite ends of the nation, McKay
from Oregon and Weeks from Massachusetts, they paired off
like parentheses—ready to close in upon words or views with
any too dangerously "liberal" ring, first to bracket, then to excise
them. Popping up between them, with impudent grace, would
often appear Oveta Culp Hobby, the first Secretary of Health,
Education and Welfare. While hardly a secret radical, she conscientiously argued on the problems charged to her and to her
deputy, Nelson Rockefeller, so that both of them might be
viewed by the suspicious as harboring egalitarian inclinations not
wholly appropriate to a Republican Cabinet. Nearby sat Herbert
Brownell, to speak and act, in effect, in a dual capacity. Probably
the most astute of Eisenhower's professional political advisers, he
also (along with Deputy Attorney General William P. Rogers)
presided over a highly competent administration of the Department of Justice, whose record of anti-trust action would surpass
that of most Democratic administrations. Genial and humorful,
unstirred by deep debate on world policy or political philosophy,

67

Brownell viewed political life with the partisan professionalism of a Farley and the personal detachment of a Falstaff.

Across from Brownell sat Arthur E. Summerfield, enjoying as Postmaster General the traditional reward of successful campaign management. A disciple of Senator Robert Taft, he punctuated Cabinet discussions rarely, then to recite in lugubrious tones the familiar details of Post Office deficit. A few chairs from Summerfield, toward the west end of the room, sat Ezra Benson, politically alone, more and more, as the years passed. He argued and acted like an implacably honest and politically intractable man. His views on farm parity were superlatively conservative, of course, from a Republican fiscal viewpoint. But even Summerfield and McKay and Weeks saw little virtue in taking conservative principles so literally as to assure, in any national election, the loss of fifty or sixty Midwestern electoral votes. Meanwhile, on the Labor front, James P. Mitchell—succeeding the politically short-lived Martin P. Durkin—brought a different accent. A veteran of eastern metropolitan labor affairs, untouched by the Taft tradition and ungiven to most conservative clichés, he could have sat perhaps as comfortably in a Democratic cabinet. And he represented about the full measure of whatever "liberal" tang there was to be found in this rather bland domestic wine.

On the side of foreign affairs, there was a different political flavor. Here stood the most candidly "liberal" or "modern" Republicans: United Nations Ambassador Henry Cabot Lodge, and Harold Stassen, Mutual Security Administrator and later Special Assistant to the President on Disarmament. Both had breadth of view on world affairs and sensitivity to the common problems of all free nations. Both had bruising and valuable experience in the political arena. Both were articulate and persuasive men. But both, oddly, suffered almost identical impediments. Many of their Cabinet colleagues were impressed, and not appreciatively, by the exceptionally high importance that each of these men seemed to attach to his own words—and his own ambitions. The imputation may have been unjust, and the basis for it was not easy to document. Yet each man contrived, in different ways, to provoke similar responses. Lodge succeeded through an unruffled composure and a fluency of speech somehow suggestive of complacency, evoking the kind of unease and distrust usually reserved by Midwestern Republicans for articulate Democratic professors on eastern college campuses. And Stassen achieved exactly the same effect by seeming to strive so studiously to avoid it. Not renowned for his enjoyment of a subordinate post in politics, nor for his acceptance of the rigidity of Dulles' posture toward the Soviets, Stassen disconcerted many a conference which he and the Secretary of State attended by his easy mastery of the vocabulary of self-effacement: "Whatever you think, Foster," and (as suffix to all suggestions) ". . . under your leadership, of course, Foster."

In this group of largely well-intentioned men, there did seem to remain some room for raw strength of personality and leadership. And strength, of one kind or another, came from the three most important officials in the Cabinet: Charles E. Wilson in Defense, George Humphrey in Treasury, and John Foster Dulles in State.

I had known Dulles before and outside the political scene of 1952. And I must acknowledge that his appointment had inspired a reaction no better than tentative and mixed.

The force of Dulles' personality, with its suggestion of vigor of spirit and toughness of intellect, was as indisputable as his experience and knowledgeability in foreign affairs. Probably no man in American history had prepared, for greater time or with greater desire, for the office of Secretary of State. Obviously, these were not trifling resources.

These assets, moreover, were sometimes lost to sight in the fury of controversy, as his tenure extended through the years. Almost always, there was a striking, even disconcerting, contrast between his intellectual postures in public and in private. Publicly, he often spoke in the harsh and doctrinaire theorems that

69

less suggested a sophisticated public servant than a politically naïve academician. Privately, however, he could restate the same issues lucidly and subtly, with fine regard for shades of meaning. Too frequently and unfairly, I thought, Dulles was appraised almost wholly and quite literally on the basis of his press conferences. Here he commonly displayed a rare talent for being arid and uneloquent. But too serious an emphasis on Dulles' deficiencies in the presence of journalists reminded me a little of a humorist's theory about ghosts—that scientists could not possibly prove their nonexistence, since the law of life for ghosts quite probably forbade them ever to divulge their presence to a scientist. A still more reasonable caution seemed to me the prudence of not judging a Secretary of State categorically in terms of his performance before the press. Within the public man there might live a ghost—of unseen skill and wit and courage.

Yet, although I tried to make such allowances, I did wonder from the first whether such secret gifts and faculties really existed. Early in 1952, as an editor of *Life* magazine, I had worked at considerable length with Dulles as he was preparing an article to set forth his basic views on foreign policy. It had seemed then extraordinarily difficult to persuade him to give clarity and substance either to his critiques of "containment" or to his exhortations on "liberation." Later, in the middle of the 1952 campaign, Eisenhower had felt compelled, on one occasion, to call Dulles to task for delivering speeches about "liberation" without even a qualifying phrase about "peaceful methods." For a man trained in law as deeply as in foreign affairs, such verbal lapses seemed a little curious and disquieting. Nor did the poise or subtlety or skill of a great diplomat seem suggested by his fondness for embellishing his political statements—usually rendered with the cold finality of judicial decisions—with moralistic flourishes more appropriate to church councils than to international conferences. Finally, to be reckoned with, there was not the mere fact, but the plain intensity, of his ambition to hold and to keep the office coveted for a lifetime. This could inspire in him the presumption, untempered by much modesty, which he confided to Eisenhower at the outset of their official partnership: "With my understanding of the intricate relationships between the peoples of the world and your sensitiveness to the political considerations involved, we will make the most successful team in history."*

The case of George Humphrey was profoundly different. In person and presence and temper, he resembled Eisenhower almost as strikingly as he contrasted with Dulles. Against Dulles' self-conscious stiffness, Humphrey offered effortless grace; to his cerebral coolness, a natural warmth; to his tension and sophistication, a modesty and simplicity, easily resting on quiet confidence. In personal life, even at the age of sixty-three, Humphrey's formulations of serious conclusions remained so bromidic ("In business, it is results that count.") that his wife collected them, in memory, as fondly as photographs for a family album. In political life, similarly, he arrived in Washington with an intellectual baggage uncluttered with complexities: a resolve to slice away billions of dollars of "waste," balance the budget, and quicken tax reductions to spur "individual initiative." Yet his preconceptions, so it seemed, were not forbidding barriers. Fresh facts kept breaking through, for he had a gift for listening. Never before close to public office or Washington life, he had presided for years over Cleveland's M. A. Hanna Co. and its labyrinthine empire of mills and banks and minerals. Politically discovered by General Lucius D. Clay, he had lived as far from public prominence—and with as little desire for it—as the reverse was true of Dulles.

As the relationship between Humphrey and Eisenhower grew and tightened over the years, it came to appear one of the major ironies on which the final story of the Administration would decisively turn. The two men had remained wholly unknown to one another throughout Eisenhower's campaigns for nomination and election, when the whole thrust of the President's political effort had been to summon the Republican party to power and

* Cited by Sherman Adams, *First-hand Report* (New York: Harper & Brothers, 1961), p. 89.

responsibility by leading it away from the neo-isolationism of Ohio's Senator Taft. Yet Humphrey—both in his passion for domestic economy and his dispassion toward foreign affairs —was an almost flawless political replica of his fellow Ohioan. By the start of the second Eisenhower administration in 1957, the stature and the assurance of this disciple of Taft were so impressive that he could publicly invite the Congress to cut back the national budget just submitted by his own President. Yet four years before this remarkable political spectacle, from the first weeks of Eisenhower's first term, the pattern of Humphrey's convictions was clear. Vigorously and bluntly, he enlivened almost every Cabinet session with little polemics on checking deficits, spoken as ardently as Dulles' exhortations on checking Communists. And Humphrey at times almost seemed to view the deficits as the more menacing of the two enemies. "To get real tax reduction," he warned one early Cabinet meeting, suddenly facing the prospect of a $5 billion deficit, "you *have* to get Korea *out of the way*. And after that you have to go on and do something more—figure out *a completely new military posture. . . .* We have to cut *one-third* out of the budget, and you can't do that just by eliminating waste. This means, wherever necessary, using a meat ax."*

As the months became years in the Eisenhower regime, the bold brandishing of such verbal weapons by Humphrey, seeming ever more to impress the President, more and more required counterthrusts from Dulles, who was not lacking in antagonists outside the Cabinet. This pattern, too, was set from the first Cabinet sessions. In one such typical dialogue, Humphrey made an impassioned plea for a cutback in expenditures to accompany the removal of controls: "If we end up by lifting controls and don't cut government expenditures, then, boys, we're in trouble. I really believe that in thirty days, or at the most sixty days, we *have* to make decisions that will be fundamental to the whole

* Cabinet meeting, EJH notes, May 1, 1953.

rest of this Administration." And Dulles, shoulders hunched and jaw drawn down—with the slightly heavy and weary tone of a man confronting one opponent too many—would drawl out his parrying remarks: "It's just not quite that easy . . . a lot of imponderables. . . . For one thing, we don't know yet what we're going to do in Korea—or in the whole Far East, for that matter. . . . And there's another thing you have to keep in mind. It's all very well for us to balance our budgets, but we have to remember that every other NATO country would like to do the same thing. If we tidy up our own shop nicely, they aren't going to take more kindly to our insistence on their defense buildups, leaving *them* stuck with unbalanced budgets."*

The long dialogue between these two men bespoke an anomaly strangely common in politics—the odd contrast, within each man, between the personal and the political temperaments. For it fell to the cool and withdrawn Secretary of State, a man of parochial spirit in many respects, to speak for a relatively more open, aware, and responsive view of the world at large. And the Secretary of the Treasury—a man of unusually warm and expansive personality—served as the uncompromising spokesman for a world view peculiarly grudging and parochial. So open and receptive a personality was Humphrey, so largely free of intellectual vanity or intolerance, that it seemed unlikely that much time could pass without his acquiring a wider vision of world politics. And the fact that no such change would occur probably offers as much commentary on the political environment in which he found himself, as upon the individual. The very vigor of his person and conviction and speech allowed him to tower over most of his political neighbors. He found himself surrounded by colleagues of whom rather few held profound convictions, while those who did possess them, perhaps more sensible and sensitive than his own, either fought for them only sporadically or lacked talents to make them persuasive. And so perhaps one of the most

* Cabinet meeting, March 20, 1953.

malleable of men in high office was allowed to stay and stand like stone.

In the third of the key Cabinet posts, the sixty-two-year-old Charles E. Wilson, fresh from General Motors, bore little resemblance to either Dulles or Humphrey. Within the Administration, he filled a role larger, in a sense, than Secretary of Defense. He was both a symbol and a test of one of the Administration's basic presumptions—the conviction that success in business was directly convertible into capacity in government. And Wilson's record left this presumption wounded by considerable doubt.

Eisenhower never lacked awareness of the obvious political risk of weighting his government with corporation executives. One of his most frequent cries against ultraconservatives on Capitol Hill was the exclamation: "Don't the darn fools realize that the public thinks the dollar sign is the only respected symbol in the Republican party?" But the President also felt deeply the exceptional respect that the career military often reserve for triumph in the business world: such triumph seemed the ultimate in civilian achievement, certainly surpassing the value of mere "political" distinction. His reliance on men successful in business, moreover, verged on an act of faith: they *stood for* the free economy that, for him, was both the base and the arsenal of American life. And out of this mixture of feelings Eisenhower would speak, to the business executives assembled in his Cabinet sessions, mingled words of confidence, compliment—and caution. Thus the President could warn, only a few weeks after taking office: "Now, we've all got to remember that we're called a *business* Administration. In fact, we invited that description, and it's fine— to a point. But the word *business*, in people's minds, is totally disassociated from the word *humanity*. So we have to be particularly careful to make clear that this Administration is truly interested in the *little* fellow—not just the banks and the corporations. In fact, we are interested in the little guys who *work for* the corporations. If we weren't, we'd have no business being here."*

* Cabinet meeting, March 20, 1953.

Such appeals were addressed, perhaps only in part consciously, to Wilson. For Wilson personified, occasionally almost to the point of caricature, a classic type of corporation executive: basically apolitical and certainly unphilosophic, aggressive in action and direct in speech—the undoubting and uncomplicated pragmatist who inhabits a world of sleek, shining certitudes. Like most of his colleagues, he felt utterly free of any selfish political ambitions, and he was given to saying: "I'm just in this damn town to get a job done." The job—as Eisenhower and he defined it—was to gear the defense establishment to a new way of life that would achieve drastic economy, reduce interservice rivalry, and impose greater unity under the strengthened civilian authority of the Secretary. The climactic fight for these issues—only partially successful—did not come until the President's Special Message on Defense Department Reorganization of April 3, 1958. But Wilson was charged from the outset with the running fight, within his own department, against what Eisenhower wryly referred to as "the supposed *requirements*" of the armed services. A man with thinner skin than Wilson's probably could not have fought off so resolutely the assaults of the several services, and even Wilson had to be stiffened at times by the tough, repeated injunction from Eisenhower: "You have got to be willing to be the most unpopular man in the government."

But the Secretary of Defense at times displayed an almost alarming willingness to earn precisely this reputation—from the broadest possible audience. His famous (and usually distorted) remark to a congressional committee about the identity of interest between the United States Government and General Motors was a clumsy but innocent enough attempt merely to suggest that he did not think the two institutions were working at cross-purposes. But his frankness of speech continued to be surpassed by his infelicity of phrase. Thus, in Detroit in 1954, arguing that workers in depressed areas should not wait for military contracts to spur local industries but should move elsewhere, he could explain: "I've always liked bird dogs better than kennel-fed dogs

75

myself—you know, one who will get out and hunt for food rather than sit on his fanny and yell."* The news of such Wilsonian indelicacies, carried to the President, would bring a response eloquent beyond words—the audible grinding of teeth, the strained tightening of the mouth, and the slow, pained rolling of the bright blue eyes heavenward.

Within the Cabinet, to the Congress, or before the world at large, Wilson was a man of almost imperturbable self-assurance. Swift to speak and vehement in argument, he listened grudgingly, as if the words of another were imposing rude delay upon his next remarks. At the first New York meeting of the Eisenhower Cabinet, for example, the President found occasion to dwell on a favored subject—the widening of trade and commerce throughout the world, including broader economic contact with Communist-controlled countries. He had barely finished a thoughtful exposition before Wilson snapped out his dissent: "Well, I'm a little old-fashioned—I don't like selling firearms to the Indians." And at the next Cabinet, he greeted a discussion of some probably unpopular economic decisions with the counsel: "Don't wait till April 30. There'll be spring in the air. The workers will feel it in their blood, and they'll go on strike just for the hell of it."† Even before he got to Washington officially —where his conflict-of-interest case, based on his General Motors holdings, would provoke the first public embarrassment of the Administration—the President, Adams, and Persons tried to prepare Wilson a little for harassments normally afflicted by congressional committees. Beyond dismay or caution, he replied on one such occasion: "I got a feeling that I'm going to be pretty pleased and surprised at how easily those boys can be handled." The surprise awaiting him, of course, was wholly different.

For world affairs, Wilson reserved that curiously and coldly apolitical attitude so common among business leaders and so baffling even to conservative politicians. On all domestic matters,

* New York *Times,* October 13, 1954.
† Cabinet meetings, January 12 and 13, 1953.

social or economic, the orthodoxy of his nineteenth-century views placed him well to the political right of Robert Taft and shoulder-to-shoulder with William Knowland. But the senator from California would have been aghast to hear Wilson, addressing himself to problems of a Korean truce, blurt out to the Cabinet one day: "Is there any possibility for a package deal? Maybe we could recognize Red China and get the Far East issues settled."*

Quite a few Cabinet meetings were jerked to quivering attention by such remarks. Their startling sound would fold the normally relaxed countenance of "Jerry" Persons into a grimace of pain. For it was Persons who, in effect, had to walk patiently in the path of Wilson through Senate and House on Capitol Hill, gathering up the scattered pieces of broken understandings or shattered congressional egos. And during one such session of the Cabinet, a Wilsonian succession of dogmatic irrelevancies moved the wincing Persons to scrawl an unhappy note and quietly pass it to me: "From now on, I'm buying nothing but Plymouths."

3

There were few things, in all the world of the 1950s, that most Republicans around Eisenhower viewed with such serenity and assurance as their ability to "clean up" a federal government whose practices and habits constituted so deplorable a "mess." In this faith, they were sustained—again—by a rare faculty for simplification. The dragons to be swiftly slain were: bureaucracy, bigness, waste, duplication, spending, incompetence, inefficiency, and plain laziness, not to forget disloyalty and homosexuality. Brightly shone the swords of virtue: common-sense, good-old-American, down-to-earth, shoulder-to-the-wheel, feet-

* Cited by Sherman Adams, *First-hand Report*, p. 99.

on-the-ground practices—all made efficacious by the supreme virtue of being business-like. A great part of the political education of these men, accordingly, required their collision with a sufficient number of realities to encourage the slow, sorrowful recognition that the arena and the processes of democracy resemble not at all the agenda and the deliberations of a corporation board meeting. And the awful truth about *business-like* methods came, at last, to be painfully suspected: politics might not be *like* business.

The tough tasks of government, of course, came close to teaching the reverse of what these men had confidently anticipated. Freed by popular mandate from Executive responsibility since 1933, the Republican party, with rare exceptions, had lost all collective memory of the problems of leadership or the pain of decision. Simple slogans, repeated like incantations, had become genuinely believable, precisely because so little else had been known firsthand. And twenty years is a long time during which to have no direct acquaintance with what one is talking about.

Once propelled into power, however, some Republican critics of the past began honestly to acknowledge to themselves a freshly inverted view of matters. As they came to know the labyrinthine ways of government—by simple virtue of getting lost in them so often—they sighed with relief, more often than not, that the public image of governmental process and decision *looked* to the world so much more coherent and rational than, in fact, it was. I recall many times reflecting, as the Administration "shook down," that democratic government enjoys an odd favor from the nature of mass communication. The daily press, radio and television *has* to make an intelligible report on national affairs, even though the matters reported may have been handled in a most unintelligible way. Journalistically, it is most difficult to report the details of confusion in an unconfused manner. Thus, at the end of a day of administrative disorder in White House or State Department, there was an almost tonic effect in reading, in the evening's news columns, a most tidily organized account of all that had happened. And it was a particularly reassuring experience, for example, to scan a thoughtful commentator's analysis of the subtle reasons why the Administration shrewdly avoided or deferred certain action—when anyone within the government might have been naïve enough to have thought it a simple case of someone failing to finish his work.

The lapses in "Republican efficiency," in any event, were not slow in coming. One of the earliest in my memory dealt with one of the most sensitive matters of the moment—the execution of the Rosenbergs as Soviet spies. Late one February afternoon in 1953, the President made public his decision not to grant pardon to the condemned. The fever of world sentiment against the decision, systematically fanned by Communist propaganda, had already mounted high, and the Department of State was deeply concerned with both the substance of the presidential decision and its proper handling by American propaganda, especially on the Voice of America. Yet the entire State Department (physically separated from the White House only by the narrow passage of West Executive Avenue) had been left wholly unconsulted on the decision—to read of it in the morning papers. With the staff of the Voice of America as surprised by the news as Radio Moscow, one State Department officer quietly lamented to me the next day: "Not a fatal case, I admit, but it would help if we didn't have to meet these things with a crash program."

Months later, just before the Supreme Court's rejection of the Rosenbergs' final plea, there took place the only extended exchange that the case provoked in a Cabinet meeting. This occasion reflected no lapse in communication between departments, but something else—the frequent haziness of communication between the President and a Department head. In this instance, Attorney General Brownell had reported both the imminence of the final Supreme Court decision and the resolve of the Department of Justice to proceed with the execution. And there followed this exchange:

President—"I must say I'm impressed by all the honest doubt about this expressed in the letters I've been seeing. Now if the Supreme Court decides by, say, five to four or even six to three, as far as the average man's concerned, there *will* be doubt—not just a legal point in his mind."

Brownell—"Well, who's going to decide these points—pressure groups or the Supreme Court? Surely, our first concern is the strength of our courts. And in terms of national security, the Communists are just out to prove they can bring enough pressure, one way or another, to enable people to get away with espionage. . . . I've always wanted you to look at evidence that wasn't usable in court showing the Rosenbergs were the head and center of an espionage ring here in *direct* contact with the Russians—the *prime* espionage ring in the country."

President—"My only concern is in the area of statecraft—the *effect* of the action."*

And after a brief discussion—and dismissal—of the notion of a "white paper" explaining the official view of the Rosenberg case, the matter was dropped on this inconclusive note.

It did not, however, require matters of life, death, or world propaganda to consume the time—and trouble the illusions—of all the men who had set to work so briskly straightening out the "mess" of government. The most seemingly routine issue—an innocuous message to the Congress—could suffice to do this. I recall the first such message to come, in draft form from the Bureau of the Budget, to my office for editing and clearance. This concerned the conversion of the Federal Security Agency into the Cabinet-level Department of Health, Education and Welfare. A matter of semantics required the labor of the better part of a day to resolve. So anguished—it seemed—were some Republicans by the sound of the word "welfare" that Budget Bureau experts feared the defeat of the bill unless the Department designation were "Health, Education and Social Security." Logically, of course, the department could have been plainly labeled the Department of Public Welfare. A suggestion to this effect,

* Cabinet meeting, June 19, 1953.

however, brought warning cries from the Budget Bureau: such nomenclature not only underscored the word most offensive, but it also deleted the most palatable, "health." As it was mordantly explained to me: "Health—this is what has sex appeal. Any time a congressman dies of a disease, the Congress can be counted on to appropriate millions to discover and conquer the microbe." And so HEW came to be circumspectly christened.

Other legislative messages of far graver moment often seemed to throw the shiny new decision-making process into still more confusion. Of these, none was more memorable than the first Eisenhower message requesting appropriations for Harold Stassen's Mutual Security Agency.

This was a cause to which the President felt—and remained—deeply committed. He not only viewed it as vital to national security, but he also rejoiced in it, in the words of his oft-repeated appeal, as "the most defense we can get for the least money." Secretary Dulles frequently made the same point still more graphically to the most frugal and skeptical of his Cabinet colleagues: "Consider for a moment the cost of obtaining bases in Turkey—if we had to get them by a military invasion." And so, when the banner of Mutual Security fluttered aloft over Administration deliberations, it rather became the most rare of all pennants of its time—the standard saluted with equal respect by those most preoccupied with foreign policy and those most obsessed with domestic economy.

All this made the more remarkable the disorder and dissension that erupted one Monday early in May of 1953. On the morning of this day, I had edited the text of the message, prepared in Stassen's office, containing the President's request for $5.8 billion. The full flavor of what followed, in the afternoon, may best be suggested by reverting directly to my diary record of the day . . .

On returning to my office from lunch, I find a huge hassle on. The issue, boiled down: does the Administration *really* want $5.8 billion —or would, say, a billion dollars less do just as nicely? Incredible—but no one has made a decision. And I quickly gathered a few other incredible facts. *One:* The State Department had neither seen the message nor knew its contents till this noontime. *Two:* Joe Dodge at the Budget Bureau likewise had not seen it. *Three:* State thinks the message is too weak, asks for not enough. *Four:* Budget thinks the message is too strong, asks for too much. *Five:* Neither Dulles nor Adams can be reached till the end of the day, for they are locked in a conference of state governors in the old State Department building. *Six:* Committee hearings on the request—whatever it turns out to be— start on the Hill at 10 A.M. tomorrow morning.

It took a while—and maybe a dozen phone calls—to piece together a coherent picture of all this incoherence. On one side, Douglas MacArthur at State lamented to me: "I'm terribly worried about this. There's no water in the $5.8 billion figure, and if we don't get all of it, we're in *real* trouble." (And Dulles somehow sent me a note, perhaps by carrier pigeon, from his closed conference with the governors —to the same effect). From the other side, came the voice of Joe Dodge: "Nonsense! State's going to have to have a lot of unspent funds at the end of this year. I just don't want to see the President getting out on a limb asking for so much money as a *must* when he may damn well take a licking on the request." To compound confusion, Herb Brownell somehow learns of the clash, shows up in the White House, and corners me in the corridor to back Dodge vehemently, adding: "What the hell, if we do need more money later, we can always ask for it then." A remarkable theory: call it "Planning for Yesterday"? Finally, to cap all, Jerry Persons emerges from the President's office, vaguely reporting this and other business, to advise that the President wants Dodge to be the deciding voice. At best, this seems odd, for I'm sure no one had briefed the President on the substance of the disagreements.

After some hours of this nonsense, and running between the White House and State, carrying the crumpled message-draft—by now it is beginning to have the feel of a battered and half-unfeathered shuttlecock—I decided to get Adams out of his conference. As he glowers kindly at the interruption, I tell him: "This is all too damn serious to be decided in a series of side-of-the-mouth corridor conversations. We just have to hold it till the morning when we can get to the President directly and quietly." Garrulously, he grunts: "Okay."

The circus continues after sundown. I finally locate Stassen, Stassen heads for Dodge's office, and after some three-way phone-negotiating we all reach agreement of a sort on the message language—roughly close to original, with the dollar figure intact. No sooner is this compact contrived than Dulles' office phones to suggest to me still stronger language in the request. Arbitrarily I decide to put it in and leave it to State to so advise Dodge and Stassen.

We come full circle next morning, when Adams and I see the President. He buys "strong" message as I've written it, even though we report both Brownell's (political) and Dodge's (fiscal) aversion to it. With marvelous disregard of his nomination of Dodge yesterday to be deciding voice, he shrugs off such reservations. Message swiftly typed in final form and rushed to the Hill.

How reassuring it would be to all governments of our allies around the world—if they could see the disciplined and dedicated way we plan and provide our economic assistance!

For all one's sense of dismay over such official proceedings, there was little in any of this, of course, significantly different from the conduct of business under almost any national administration. The relentless rush of public affairs, the sheer size of major programs, the capriciousness of internal communication, the impossibility of a thoughtful reconciling of divergent views in a few hours—all rather pitilessly defy any attempt to make the decision-making process a thing of nice symmetry, measured rhythm, or constant sobriety.

The discovery of all this, however, astonished and dismayed those who had thought that life and work in Washington would be a lot the way it had been back in the offices in Cleveland or Detroit.

4

The political education of the leaders of the Eisenhower administration had yet a more jarring turn to take. It was sad enough to feel forced to wonder if a certain amount of "mess" might not simply belong, ineradicably, in the processes of democratic government. But it was sadder still to begin to fear that, far from diminishing the amount, one might be adding to it. Unfortunately, this soon enough proved to be the case. And the proof was most plain in one sphere of government where disarray was least wanted and most costly—in and around the Department of State.

The innocence of inexperience accounted for some sins of more than venial consequence. With congressional cries about "loyalty" and "security" tormenting both State Department and Foreign Service, for many months past, there had stirred, in all more rational sectors of national opinion, some hope that a Republican Secretary of State would blunt such Republican attacks. In a matter of weeks, however, the hope died with the news of the appointment of the department's new chief security officer, a former FBI agent by the name of Scott McLeod. A loudly aggressive superpatriot, he was summoned to his new office from his post as an administrative assistant to New Hampshire's Senator Styles Bridges, a stout ally of McCarthy in the prolonged assault upon the State Department. The implications of the appointment were chilling, for it threatened the effective opening of all departmental security files to the capricious use of McCarthy, Bridges, and their aides and agents. And a further inference, widely drawn throughout Washington, concluded that the Secretary of State had deliberately embarked on a course of planned appeasement of his party's ultraconservatives—for could so extraordinary an appointment have been a matter of chance?

The bizarre truth, however, was precisely this, and Dulles had no more to do with designing the event than Eisenhower. The Under Secretary of State for Administration, Donold B. Lowrie, had come to Washington, from the presidency of Quaker Oats, with somewhat less preparation for the political scene than Charles E. Wilson. A serious and conscientious citizen, Lowrie had known virtually not a single citizen in Washington prior to his appointment. Idly conversing with a neighbor in Chicago, who happened to be an ex-FBI agent, he had picked up the name of Scott McLeod. The name came to mind again, as he settled into his Washington office. He called McLeod. They lunched. He liked him. He gave him a new job. And he conscientiously spent a large part of the next months mourning his own folly.*

The more serious damage done at this time, however, resulted from neither naïveté nor inexperience. Rather did it take the form of what subsequently came to be known in Washington as "the planned mistake." This was no brash act or hasty decision, but a policy thoughtfully deliberated, fastidiously calculated, precisely drafted, and boldly built—upon wholly false premises. For a number of Republicans, including John Foster Dulles, believed certain things about the nation's foreign policy that simply were not facts. Thus, for example, Dulles braced himself for problems within the State Department in a manner that succeeded only in fostering what he most feared. Although he enjoyed only a rather limited personal acquaintance with the Foreign Service, he darkly suspected most of its officers of secret Democratic allegiance, personal devotion to Acheson, and strong distaste for himself. There was probably nothing he could have done better calculated to provoke this distaste than publicly summoning—as he did—all who worked in foreign affairs to display "positive loyalty" to his new policies.

From a still deeper source—the mythology and demonology of the party's view of world affairs—came the inspiration for the vast and wasteful labor of smiting down the fancied threat of

---

* One consequence of this appointment, particularly humiliating to the White House, never became public. When McCarthy launched his fight against the nomination of Charles E. Bohlen as Ambassador to the U.S.S.R., there was reason to suspect that McLeod, either voluntarily or under subpoena, would testify vaguely to sharing McCarthy's view. For days, someone on the White House staff had to be assigned to making sure that the State Department's security chief was kept "secure" from any public place where a subpoena might be served on him.

"secret agreements" sealed by the preceding Administrations. For a period of many weeks, this exercise consumed an astonishing amount of the time and thought of the leaders of both parties. It was a quixotic ritual for an Administration dedicated to "efficiency" and horrified by "waste." And it served to remind all who witnessed it that even the most avowedly practical and pragmatic are given to respect certain idols before which they pause, genuflect, ponder, and let time—and history—slip by.

This particular ritual began with Eisenhower's first State of the Union message. "I shall ask the Congress at a later date," he declared, "to join in an appropriate resolution making clear that this Government recognizes no kind of commitment contained in secret understandings of the past with foreign governments which permit . . . enslavement [of any people]." The utterance had evoked wild applause from the Republican side of the aisle —almost as if in relief and thanksgiving for the sudden assurance that the dire "secret agreements" did, in fact, exist. The language and substance had been dictated by Dulles, who sincerely believed (or so *I* believed) that he would shortly discover the "secret" texts in some obscure vault in the Department of State. I had presumptuously modified his proposed language, however, in one respect: he had wanted to "repudiate" these agreements. Since all that anyone knew of such agreements was that their existence was far from certain, I had stricken this verb in favor of more ambiguous language. The precaution proved fortunate. Four days after the State of the Union was delivered, both "Chip" Bohlen and Assistant Secretary of State Thruston B. Morton were telephoning me from the State Department to inquire what the passage meant, since they had to draft the congressional resolution of "repudiation." Assistant Secretary Morton candidly confessed to being "red-faced" when I explained that he would have to ask his Secretary, who had prescribed the admonishing text.

A fortnight later, a semantic crisis was in full flower. Thruston Morton had spent painstaking hours in persuading Lyndon

Johnson and other Democratic leaders of the wisdom of a unanimous Congressional vote generally lamenting the Soviet enslavement of East European nations. They, in turn, had responded with the acquiescent spirit of men profoundly weary of being publicly punished for what they had not done. There had emerged, therefore, the odd but intriguing prospect of Democrats joining Republicans in resounding disavowal of things unsaid and compacts unsigned. But other departments within State, however, had meanwhile prepared texts, of both a congressional resolution and a presidential letter of transmittal, calling for flat and righteous repudiation of "past agreements committing us to such enslavement" of Soviet-occupied territories. On the basis of his pact with the Democratic leaders, Morton phoned me on the very morning when the presidential message was to go to Capitol Hill, to be sure that this language had been modified, since Democratic legislators could hardly be expected to join in posthumous excoriation of Franklin Roosevelt for acts he had not committed. By the time I got to the President's office, I found that he was with Dulles—and that they both had already approved the documents as drafted. The President handed them to me. A little frantically, I demurred: "But, Mr. President, I really don't think that we can talk about past 'agreements' as committing us to the 'enslavement' of other nations and expect Democrats to vote for the denunciation." Startled, the President said: "Does it say *that?*" I handed the papers back to him. And a few moments later both he and Dulles had agreed on the blurred language: "We would not feel that any past agreements committed us to any such enslavement."

There remained a small irony to close the whole episode. Confronted with the resolution, many Republican senators bitterly demanded a "stronger" attack upon the "betrayals" of the past. The majority of the Democrats, at the same time, found themselves stoutly defending the temperate language of the Administration, offering no direct offense to the memory of FDR. And by the time that this absurd point was reached, it seemed scarcely credible that the whole tortuous plot initially had been conceived to awe the Soviet Union.

In all this unsmiling parody of serious politics, there was more to cause concern than the merely ridiculous. For the duel with the phantom of "secret agreements" carried echoes of a more serious struggle. To Dulles and many other Republican leaders, this exercise had been but one more device to "repudiate" the diplomatic past, thereby boldly underscoring the promise in the State of the Union message of "a new, positive foreign policy." In the careless process, the Secretary of State began to sound, at times, as if he were reading lines written only to win applause from Senator Joseph McCarthy. And thus the shadow of the Wisconsin demagogue came to fall darkly across the path of all men and policies concerned with the nation's role in the world.

There is a nightmarish quality to even the memory of McCarthy's storming through Washington at this time—promptly after the election of a Republican leadership supposed to neutralize him politically. Day upon day, he seemed to rant through the front pages of the press—denouncing the Voice of America, demanding censorship of American embassy libraries overseas, inflaming public libraries across the country to purge their shelves of "subversive" literature, isolating government officials for inquisition, exploiting the malicious allegations of disappointed government employees, flailing at Bohlen as "worse than a security risk," and directly assailing the President for refusing to cleanse the State Department of "Acheson's architects of disaster." While these ugly sounds echoed through the chamber of the Senate, McCarthy enjoyed his alliance, at the other end of Pennsylvania Avenue, with the State Department's newly appointed security chief, whose private suggestion in the Bohlen case had been to demand a lie-detector test of the President's nominee. And finally—across the seas—there occurred the vulgar farce of McCarthy's audacious aides, Roy Cohn and G.

David Schine, hunting through American embassies for signs, names, and faces of traitors.

One small personal incident, expressive of the shame of it all, still stings in my memory. It came with a visit to my White House office, one spring afternoon, by a crippled German friend whom I had known years earlier in Berlin. The young man had almost blown himself to pieces with a grenade during World War II—in the course of making one of the anti-Nazi underground's several vain attempts upon Hitler's life. And both anger and anguish trembled in this man's voice, as he spoke of the only matter he could discuss. "You have just sent us, you Americans, two visitors—two new-style American ambassadors, I suppose you call them," he said. "Whatever fantastic harm they have done elsewhere, can you imagine their impact in Germany—and on Germans still looking a little skeptically at free government? *You* are supposed to be models for all us authoritarian-minded Germans. Tell me, my friend—*what* do I say to my German friends, when they gape at Messrs. Cohn and Schine, and then ask me: 'Is *this* what you call democracy?'"

The senatorial "architect of disaster" from Wisconsin responsible for all this, I gradually came to believe, possessed only a crude and confused conception of what he actually was about. He never devised any grand design or cunning scheme for attaining political power. To fear him as a potential dictator—I believed at the time—was rather absurd: he lacked the steel and stamina to stay fast on any course. To perceive him as a fascist was equally fanciful: he knew and cared nothing of political philosophy, good or evil. Essentially, the only kind of political life that he knew and relished was a wildly flailing show of knees and elbows, knuckles and nails. Often when he caused the most spectacular hurt or harm, he had merely closed his eyes and blindly swung. He knew and understood no political tactics but the most primitive—reflex and impulse, improvisation and revenge. As one member of the Administration who had watched him closely for many years described him to me: "He's strictly a counterpuncher. When he feels pushed around—or pushed aside—he snarls back. He knows that he's loathed in the White House and cursed in private. He plans nothing—not a damn thing, even from week to week, maybe not even from day to day. Many a time when he goes to preside over one of his own committee sessions, he hasn't even any notion of who or what is coming before it." At his punitive worst in 1953, McCarthy whirled and fired the guns of his invective in exactly this brash and frenzied way—first at the Foreign Service and the State Department, then at the Central Intelligence Agency, finally (and, at last, fatally) at the Army. And through it all, striking out with the cruel zest of a child, he bore far less resemblance to Huey Long than to Studs Lonigan.

Inevitably, then, the methods of both McCarthy and Roy Cohn often displayed nothing so much as mere pettiness and foolishness. Such was the case, for example, with their frantic and exhausting efforts to find preferential treatment for David Schine, when Schine was drafted into the Army as a private. No appeal—for an Army, Navy, or Air Force commission, or for simple relief from kitchen duty—was too degrading for them to direct to the highest official level they could reach. They invented and proposed a bizarre variety of special assignments for their ex-associate—from a civilian-clothes post in New York to a job at West Point as censor of Army textbooks. They even turned to the Under Secretary of State, General Walter Bedell Smith, to urge him to find a position for Schine in the Central Intelligence Agency; and they displayed no trace of embarrassment when Smith icily pointed out the impropriety of McCarthy soliciting a favor from an agency that he was supposedly investigating at the same moment. And on a wholly different front, Cohn conducted a perhaps even more laughable campaign. He sensed, quite accurately, the distaste with which he was viewed by a number of liberal Jewish organizations. Distressed by this, he sought to improve his repute in these quarters, and he singled out for courtship—of all organizations—the Anti-Defamation League. His technique proved even more remarkable than its object, for he chose to prove his affinity for the group by giving it advance information on the identities of "who we're going to go after next in this Administration." Practicing this strategy of charm, he confided that the three names highest on McCarthy's list for inquisition, as "dangerous liberals," were Bedell Smith's, C. D. Jackson's, and mine. Not surprisingly, his listeners failed to grasp the logic by which Cohn construed all this as establishing his credentials for association with the Anti-Defamation League.

The sum of political damage finally inflicted on the nation still eludes precise measure. But its size was not small. As Dulles seemed to reel back before the onslaught, the professional officers charged with conduct of America's foreign affairs felt more than a loss of morale: they felt an estrangement from the Administration—edged with an intellectual aversion—that would endure, subtly but stubbornly, throughout the 1950s. One career diplomat, a distinguished veteran of a half-dozen ambassadorial posts who had never been personally touched by any of McCarthy's thrusts, grimly confessed to me on one occasion: "If I had a son, I would do everything in my power to suppress any desire he might have to enter the Foreign Service of the United States." When Dulles' aides, bowing to McCarthy's strident demands, dispatched a directive to all American embassies to shun any "Communist" material in their local propaganda operations, the gratuitous exhortation was read with sickening disbelief by ambassadors around the world. From the embassy in London, there came back a cabled inquiry crackling with sarcasm. The cable posed two questions: (1) Could the Ambassador, in a forthcoming speech already drafted, make a point that depended upon citing a direct quotation from Stalin? (2) As the Department's directive aimed its strictures at material described as "Communist, fellow-traveling, etc.," would the Department kindly instruct the Embassy on its definition of "etc."?

Throughout all this—and on through the climactic episodes of McCarthy's humiliation of Army Secretary Robert T.

Stevens and his own senatorial censure—Eisenhower tenaciously held to his public posture of silent, passive resistance. He commonly repelled all pleas to take the offensive, most ardently made in the White House by C. D. Jackson or by me, with the gruff and often loud retort: "I just will not—I *refuse*—to get into the gutter with that guy." Such conduct was dictated by many qualities of the man, some of them deep within him and bespeaking much more than personal fastidiousness. His political behavior already had demonstrated his angry aversion to any kind of *ad hominem* word or gesture, as well as his equally strong distaste for the direct retort in political life. Both these attitudes now were reinforced by his sense of the dignity of the presidential office. And both, in turn, were but parts of a larger view of the world of politics itself. For Eisenhower, this was a world in which lines were sharply drawn only by the impulsive or the intemperate, the shallow or the selfish. It was a world in which truly constructive and creative political activity called for quite the opposite manners and methods—all the restrained words, expansive gestures, and healing deeds that could accomplish a long labor of conciliation.

This lofty and sanguine view had, as its corollary, a political strategy that, at times, proved apt to his purposes and disconcerting to his critics. Thus, for example, the patient courting of the more conservative Republican senators did win such rewards as Taft's willingness to lead the fight in support of Bohlen's Senate confirmation. As for countering McCarthy, the President—along with Dulles—believed the most effective retort could never be a political or forensic thrust across the line between the Executive and the Legislative. The Wisconsin senator's power would have to be rolled back gradually *within* the Legislature—in particular, through his increasing isolation from those Republican conservatives who were his closest political neighbors—until, at last, he would be left to stand alone. There seemed no doubt, in short, that a Taft rather than an Eisenhower could wound

McCarthy deeply, especially with McCarthy's own popular following.

Such a strategy, for all its sensible elements, could hardly be swift, and its slow working exacted a high price in the mutilation of reputations and careers. Nor did even such a strategy on the part of the President require that Dulles seem to flinch at every jab McCarthy aimed at the State Department. The Secretary of State would have done no violence to Eisenhower's general concept if he had forthrightly met almost any of McCarthy's initial charges with the cold dismissal that they deserved—including one honestly indignant assertion that the new Secretary's own concern for national security needed not at all the inspiration of public sermons by the senator. A Dulles who had done this could have enlisted both the professional respect and personal loyalty of the career officials in his department. But the Dulles who shied from doing this impressed his subordinates as a man suffering such painful preoccupation with congressional relations —and so chronic a personal anxiety to spare himself the sniping and harassment suffered by Acheson—that even human sacrifices would be offered to assuage and deter potential enemies. And this tepid performance, in the arena closest to his own office and person, seemed dismayingly incongruous—from the glowering foe of all appeasement on the world scene.

An Executive Branch wrenched and torn by such emotions naturally found its own behavior ambivalent, its own criteria confused. Thus, for example, the fight for the Bohlen nomination struck the public as a show of firmness, particularly from Dulles. Yet precisely when this fight was raging most dangerously on the floor of Congress, I was astonished, one Saturday morning in Dulles' office, to discover the Secretary pondering the possible desirability of withdrawing Bohlen's name. He evidently found himself in one of those precarious moments of irresolution when the first strong voice to reach his ears could propel him in one direction or the opposite. I exclaimed my incredulity and heard no further hint of doubt. And yet another sign of ambiguous

Administration judgment came a few weeks later. This occurred in the White House, when "Jerry" Persons confronted me with what he viewed as decisive proof of the value of conciliation toward McCarthy. "On the Bohlen case, for instance," Persons explained, "McCarthy had two speeches ready to use in fighting us. Both were pretty rough, but one was *real* dirty. So he went to Dick Nixon to ask which he ought to give. So Dick told him —and he didn't use the real *dirty* one." Such were the shadowy rewards of compromise.

As weeks and months slipped by, the cost, if not the dishonor, of temporizing became ever more apparent, but the specific occasion for throwing McCarthy on the defensive seemed elusive. On the occasion of a Dartmouth College commencement, Eisenhower spontaneously delivered some acid remarks about "the book-burners." A little later, I seized on a request for a presidential message to the annual conference of the American Library Association—to draft for the President another blunt warning on the ugliness of McCarthyism. But these were relatively abstract and ineffectual gestures—until, at last, McCarthy made a blunder. The director of his committee's investigations, J. B. Matthews, emerged as author of a magazine article whose opening salvo was: "The largest single group supporting the Communist apparatus in the United States today is composed of Protestant clergymen."* And, defying the instant public outcry stirred by this charge, McCarthy seemed to stand by Matthews' side. Suddenly, the Wisconsin senator was vulnerable to direct attack on an unclouded issue.

There followed for two days—a Wednesday and Thursday in early July—a feverish and somewhat comic little drama, suggestive of how much in government may have to be achieved by indirection. I was joined in preparing a seemingly appropriate scheme by Deputy Attorney General William Rogers, who was also urged on by two mutual friends of ours in Washington journalism. No anti-McCarthy zealot, Rogers nonetheless sensed

* *The American Mercury*, July, 1953.

the need for curbing the senator and further assured me that Vice President Nixon concurred. He also rejoiced that the Matthews case provided a fine political occasion: "With all the Protestants up in arms, even a buddy of McCarthy's like Karl Mundt on his committee can hear the Lutherans screaming back in the Midwest." So on this particular Wednesday, sitting in my office in the White House, we decided to encourage a telegram of protest to the President from the National Conference of Christians and Jews in New York—to which the President would respond in strong censure of McCarthy and his chief investigative aide. We also agreed on the need to move swiftly, since McCarthy was too astute not to realize at almost any hour that Matthews had become a dangerous liability who would have to be dismissed. Accordingly, while our mutual friends outside government spurred the National Conference in New York, I hastened the same day both to get the agreement of Adams to our plan and to draft the President's reply to the message we still awaited. By evening, all seemed ready.

The next day provided a minor study in chaos. The morning hours passed without receipt of any message of protest from New York, and a barrage of long-distance phone calls finally produced the intelligence that the message was, in fact, resting on the desk of the White House Special Counsel, Bernard M. Shanley, who had been asked by the Conference for renewed assurance that the protest would not embarrass the President. Uninformed of their whole scheme, Shanley had planned to discuss the matter with me "in the next day or so." By the time all signals were at last cleared, afternoon was upon us; the President, not yet even advised of what was afoot, was closeted with important visitors; and the rumor was racing across Capitol Hill that McCarthy was about to dismiss Matthews and publicly invite applause for his own fair-mindedness. Soon I began to get increasingly frantic phone calls from Rogers on the Hill: "For God's sake, we have to get that message out fast or McCarthy will beat us to the draw." Adams swiftly approved my text and agreed with my suggestion

95

that he take it in to the President without me in attendance, since the President tended, by now, to discount the heat of my own feelings about McCarthy. Minutes passed with agonizing slowness and with more cries for speed telephoned from the Hill. At last Adams reappeared with the message approved but slightly modified, so that the stencil for the mimeographed press release had to be recut. As I stood in Hagerty's office watching both this process and the news-ticker that would carry a bulletin on any action by McCarthy, there came a final near-desperate call from Rogers: "I'm in Dick's office, and Mundt and McCarthy have been meeting and are on their way here right now with, I'm sure, Matthews' resignation." I told him to keep McCarthy and the press away from each other for ten minutes, and *we* would be on the news-ticker. We finally were. Only some minutes later McCarthy finally got his news of Matthews' resignation to the press, but it was too late to escape the blistering presidential statement. As Rogers later told me of the incident's bizarre last minutes on the Hill: "McCarthy wandered into Dick's office just after I put down the phone from talking with you the last time. Dick and I kept on and on asking him all kinds of thoughtful questions about how he was going to investigate the CIA. He even looked a little puzzled at our sudden interest. As he was rambling on, of course, your message got to the press, which he had no way of knowing. So as he headed for the door finally, he said with a big grin, 'Gotta rush now—I want to be sure I get the news of dumping Matthews to Fulton Lewis in time for him to break it on his broadcast.' "

It was easy to wish, at times such as these, that a number of high government officials could have devoted full and trying days to more exalted matters. Yet this one small, almost thwarted exercise did contrive the only notable reverse suffered by Mc-Carthy in a period of more than a year. And there would be no other until the political climax of the Army hearings and his Senate censure.

All such labyrinthine ways of getting "business" done in

national government made seem fantastically remote and distant the time—only a few months earlier—when Republican campaign orators had been stirring themselves, if not the multitude, with their fervent public vows to "straighten out" and "clean up" life in the nation's capital.

I recall deciding, somewhere about this time, never to forget one obvious inference from it all.

The opportunities for creating a "mess" in Washington are so unlimited—the chances to make bad matters worse are so inexhaustible—that no administration should ever underestimate its capacity to surpass the folly of its predecessor.

CHAPTER FOUR

The Eisenhower Leadership:
Thrusts and Tremblings

The qualities that make for historic greatness in a democratic leader spring from spheres of the human spirit so gray and distant and secret that they do more than confound most politicians. They elude the historian. And they perplex the philosopher.

The philosopher must face a disconcerting and dismaying fact: within a man, the humane and the politic appear, alarmingly often, to stand at pitiless odds with one another. As a sophisticated strategy of politics rarely evolves merely from a pristine premise, so the great political conquests quite commonly are won by weapons less than noble—guile or force, threat or bluster, deception or ambition. And the converse is true: the virtue of the person may seem transmuted, by obscure and cruel alchemy, into the sin of the leader. The honest word can seem—and can be—the foolish word. A self-effacing act may prove the self-destroying deed. And the lack of a sense of self may loom, not shiningly but bleakly, as mere lack of a sense of purpose.

The historian does not find the matter more easy. Scanning the whole panorama of an age or a decade or a year, he seeks to weigh forces and circumstances of majestic size. He strives to appraise them with the dispassion of a physicist and the cunning of a prophet. And he ends, so often, by finding the meticulous calculation wholly upset by the most puny but decisive matter—a prejudice of a man's heritage or an eccentricity of his temperament, the quantity of his energy or the eloquence of his tongue, the death of a friend or the ferocity of an enemy, a fatal flaw in his convictions or a fatal accident in his arteries.

All ruthless intrusions of chance aside, the truth would seem to be that the man who would lead his people, boldly and democratically, must perform—perhaps even *live*—an almost endless series of marvelous conjuring acts. By these feats, he strives to neutralize and to pacify the crude contradictions of political life. He must proudly know and profess principle—yet sometimes keep his greater purposes from being blunted by his lesser scruples. He must summon his people to be with him—yet stand above, not squat beside, them. He must respect the opinions and the powers of others—but not too much. He must question his own wisdom and rightness—but only a little. He must appease the doubts of the skeptic and assuage the hurts of the adversary— sometimes. He must ignore their views and devise their humiliation—sometimes. He must be aggressive without being contentious, decisive without being arrogant, and compassionate without being confused. He must respect ideas—without adulating them as substitutes for acts. He must respect action—without unharnessing it from thought and reason. He must respect words—without becoming intoxicated with his own. He must have a dramatic sense of history that inspires him to magnify the trivial, fleeting event to serve his distant goal—and to grasp the gravest crisis as if it were the merest nettle. He must be pragmatic, calculating, and earthbound—and yet know when to spurn the mean arithmetic of expediency for the act of utter courage, the sublime gamble that holds no hope beyond the audacity of his own imagination.

The democratic leader possessed of *all* such qualities would achieve, as he would merit, whatever might be the political equivalent of beatification.

99

Their sum implies, of course, an unattainable standard for any leader—or for any President.

They prescribed a difficult one for Dwight David Eisenhower.

2

There came one day in March that seemed to shine through much that was murky. The day itself made no public history. Yet I noted it in my diary as "memorable." And so it seemed —for its intimate and explicit evidence of probably the most moving of all qualities of the President: his passion for peace, for all humankind. The cynic might retort: this is neither an original nor a complex desire. The truth remained: the force and purity of this fervor in the man, in his long groping for the ways of peace, refreshed and inspired.

The immediate prologue to this day had seemed much less clear and auspicious. On March 4, the news from Moscow of the illness of Stalin quickly excited, and soon obsessed, official Washington. As the capital began rather loudly to speculate on what might follow within the Soviet Union, it also soon started, a little uneasily, to whisper to itself the question: what, if anything, did the United States propose to do, as the crisis of transition gripped Soviet rule? In fact, the American response to the reasonably predictable occasion ignited no flame that could be seen a foot away.

The Cabinet had met, two days after Stalin's death, in a session impossible to describe as inspiring. Harold Stassen discoursed on the need for lower tariffs; Henry Cabot Lodge reminded all present of congressional sensitivity on the subject; Charles Wilson related a procurement problem; Joseph Dodge lamented the slowness with which departments were suggesting reductions in their next budget. The President, sparked by mention of some business before the Atomic Energy Commission, launched into one of his sharp disparagements of those who counted—witlessly, he felt—upon American atomic power to solve the world's divisions and fears. "Any notion that 'the bomb' is a cheap way to solve things," he exclaimed, "is awfully wrong. It ignores all facts of world politics—and the basic realities for our allies. It is cold comfort for any citizen of Western Europe to be assured that—after his country is overrun and he is pushing up daisies—someone still alive will drop a bomb on the Kremlin." And then he turned to the fact of Stalin's death and its portent. His remarks were short and acid. "Ever since 1946, I know that all the so-called experts have been yapping about what would happen when Stalin dies and what we, as a nation, should do about it. Well, he's dead. And you can turn the files of our government inside out—in vain—looking for any plans laid. We have no plan. We are not even sure what difference his death makes."*

The following days fast revealed no lack of prophets and dreamers, alarmists and zealots, eager to fill this void. One of the most celebrated leaders of American industry wrote the President an urgent and elaborate proposal. The President, according to the famous industrialist's impassioned letter, should ask the government of the Soviet Union for thirty minutes of unjammed air-time to present "a plan for peace"—its terms unspecified—and the author solemnly guaranteed that this initiative would constitute "the greatest effort for world peace and mean more to the world's people than any event since the Prince of Peace came two thousand years ago." On a less celestial level, meanwhile, an *ad hoc* group of government experts in "psychological warfare" prepared memoranda much more long and explicit. These were, however, hardly less fanciful. One recommendation of this group soon became widely publicized, though I confess to thinking it a joke when a White House correspondent first told me of his hearing rumor of it. This was the offer by the United States Government of a one hundred thousand dollar reward to the

* Cabinet meeting, March 6, 1953.

first Soviet MIG pilot who would defect to the West. It seemed difficult to decide on which count the notion was more shabby and distasteful—for the invitation it issued to Soviet propaganda to mock Western capitalism for trying to "buy" its "freedom-lovers," or for the insult it implicitly conveyed to those who might flee Soviet sovereignty for reasons other than cash. At the same time, other proposals urged massive American propaganda programs beamed to the Soviet Union and the Far East to report with relish all signs of stress between Moscow and Peiping—a psychological technique almost perfectly designed, of course, to hasten the healing of any existing breaches. But all such urgent and varied memoranda converged and concluded on one recommendation—a "rip-snorting" presidential speech. None suggested its content.

I now came to appreciate again the curiously strategic value of being the source of presidential words that must be persuaded, somehow, to flow. I resisted and evaded all exhortations to prepare some compelling rhetoric for the occasion. For the moment, I believed, this could amount only to a shallow kind of verbal improvisation, in lieu of serious national policy. In the State Department, Bedell Smith and Bohlen thoroughly agreed, counseling some salutary silence until we had collected our facts, along with our wits. Meanwhile, I found it possible to check the enthusiasm of most advocates of "a big speech" with a basic question: "You have to decide first, at the least, *to whom* you propose to address this, politically. Will it be aimed at Soviet satellites, to stir their insurrection? Or quite the contrary: will it be aimed, over their bowed heads, to Moscow, to bring the Soviets into a field of East-West negotiation? It cannot aspire to *both*." And this simple dilemma sufficed to temper the ardor of many for some days.

And the particular day I appreciatively recall finally came. Late one afternoon in mid-March, I went in to the President's office to discuss some routine speeches, and we soon found ourselves resuming a relaxed, continuing exchange that we had been having about possible major statements of foreign policy in weeks ahead. On this occasion, however, he grew more excited and intense. He began talking with the air of a man whose thoughts, after a permissive spell of meandering, were fast veering toward a conclusion. And—as always when he became intellectually stirred—he began to pace the oval room, in a wide arc around me. He spoke slowly, forcefully . . .

"Look, I am tired—and I think everyone is tired—of just plain indictments of the Soviet regime. I think it would be wrong—in fact, asinine—for me to get up before the world now to make another one of those indictments. Instead, just *one* thing matters: what have *we* got to offer the world? What are *we* ready to do, to improve the chances of peace?

"If we cannot say these things—A, B, C, D, E, F, G, just like that—then we really have nothing to give, except just another speech. For what? Malenkov isn't going to be frightened with speeches. What are we *trying* to achieve?"

He stopped in his long, slow strides about the room, to punctuate his rhetorical question. I waited and watched the familiar features: the head martially high, the strong mouth tight, the jaw set—and the blue eyes agleam and intent, staring through the tall windows to the long southern lawn, as if some distant tree secreted a response, or might nod encouragement, to his blunt inquiry.

He wheeled abruptly toward me and went on . . .

"*Here* is what I would like to say.

"The jet plane that roars over your head costs three-quarters of a million dollars. That is more money than a man earning ten thousand dollars every year is going to make in his lifetime. What world can afford this sort of thing for long? We are in an armaments race. Where will it lead us? At worst, to atomic warfare. At best, to robbing every people and nation on earth of the fruits of their own toil. . . .

"Now, there could be another road before us—the road of disarmament. What does this mean? It means for everybody in the world: bread, butter, clothes, homes, hospitals, schools—all the good and necessary things for decent living.

"So let *this* be the choice we offer. If we take this second road, all of us can produce more of these good things for life—and we, the United States, will help them still more. How do we go about it? Let us talk straight: *no* double talk, *no* sophisticated political formulas, *no* slick propaganda devices. Let us spell it out, whatever *we* really *offer* . . . withdrawal of troops here or there by both sides . . . United Nations-supervised free elections in another place . . . free and uncensored air-time for us to talk to the Russian people and for their leaders to talk to us . . . and concretely all that we would hope to do for the economic well-being of other countries.

"What do we say about the Soviet Government? I'd like to get up and say: I am *not* going to make an indictment of them. The past speaks for itself. I am interested in the future. Both their government and ours now have new men in them. The slate is clean. Now let us begin talking to each other. *And let us say what we've got to say so that every person on earth can understand it.* Here is what *we* propose. If you—the Soviet Union—can improve on it, we want to hear it.

"This is what I want to say. And if we don't really *have* anything to *offer*, I'm not going to make a speech about it."

The excitement of the man and the moment was contagious and stirring.

And yet—fervently as I felt his essential rightness—I felt, too, an unhappy need to speak some warning reminder of how far all this stood from the temper and attitude of John Foster Dulles. For only the day before—just twenty-four hours, almost to the minute—I had had a long meeting alone with the Secretary in his office, and I had then pressed my own anxious question as to what our immediate national purpose and intent were at this diplomatic moment. I had even narrowed the issue down to the specific case of Korea, with the direct question: "Would we be glad—or sorry—if *tomorrow* the Communists *accepted* the

Indian compromise for a settlement?" And Dulles had replied unequivocally: "We'd be sorry. *I don't think we can get much out of a Korean settlement until we have shown—before all Asia—our clear superiority by giving the Chinese one hell of a licking.*"

The chasm between the President and his Secretary of State could hardly have appeared more starkly shown.

Now, speaking to Eisenhower, I briefly pointed to it.

He stood very still for an instant, then he snapped out the words . . .

"All right, then. If Mr. Dulles and all his sophisticated advisers really mean that they can *not* talk peace seriously, then I am in the wrong pew. For if it's *war* we should be talking about, I *know* the people to give me advice on that—and they're not in the State Department. Now either we cut out all this fooling around and make a serious bid for peace—or we forget the whole thing."

I could only cheer the President's stout retort and hope to serve his initiative. Immediately I suggested that a small group of us meet the following morning—with the prior order from him to think toward specific actions to fit the spirit of his intent. Agreeing, he commissioned me to call the Secretary of State, his brother Allen Dulles, Director of the Central Intelligence Agency, and C. D. Jackson to come prepared to such a meeting the next day.

Before I withdrew from the room, however, he was back to his pacing the floor. He stopped abruptly, as if in mid-thought. And he turned, a little sadly, frowningly. There was about him that familiar, almost palpable sense of humility—an unafraid but slightly dismayed awe, before the matters confronting him. And the fiber of his voice was gentle and soft, as he said slowly: "You know, it is *so* difficult. You come up to face these terrible issues, and you know that what is in almost everyone's heart is a wish for peace, and you want so much to do *something*. And then you wonder . . . if there really *is* anything you can do . . . by words and promises. . . . You wonder and you wonder . . ."

The meeting the following morning in the oval office followed a predictable pattern, but the general spirit of the President prevailed. I had held no illusion that our gathering would produce specifics of a "peace plan." But I was eager that the President convey his feelings to others, with all the intensity of his initial fervor, undulled by elaborate counsels of caution to the contrary—for I was learning the practical truth that "policy," in the profoundest sense, can be decisively shaped by such intangibles of the moment and the mood. John Foster Dulles, when I had phoned him the President's call to the meeting, had murmured coolly: "What all this gets down to is the question of whether we are ready to start negotiating directly. The President hasn't seemed to feel this way, in his various exchanges with Churchill. But perhaps he's changed his mind." Prosaic as was the response, Dulles could not fairly be criticized, on this and a few similar occasions, for his caution in reacting to such surges of presidential resolve: they were prone to arise suddenly and somewhat surprisingly. In any case, the sum of the Secretary's contribution to our meeting amounted to a dry and dubious acquiescence that we try to draft such a speech as Eisenhower proposed. Allen Dulles reacted a little more warmly to the mood of the President, and even submitted a memorandum of some random and tentative "proposals" to consider. These included such gestures as offering to hold the next United Nations meeting in Moscow, or—drastically, indeed—considering a proposal to the Soviets to enter a joint program to supply Communist China basic economic assistance.* Most cool and critical of all was C. D.

---

* The mere fact of Allen Dulles proposing initiative of any substantive kind in foreign policy—even at the invitation of the President—stood out as a remarkable exception to his general conduct as Director of CIA. With a stern scrupulousness, in all dialogues with the President that I ever attended, he insisted on confining himself to the neutral role of dispassionately reporting intelligence. He refused to advocate a line of national policy, or in any way to trespass on his brother's official province—even

Jackson, who sharply argued that the leaders of the Soviet Union, in his opinion, were most unlikely to be mollified in their global ambitions by "genial, bourgeois talk about schools and hospitals for the ignorant and the sick." To this, the President offered the rejoinder: "Damn it, I don't know that you're right, basically. I remember that in one four-hour session I had with Stalin, damn near all he talked about was the essential things his people needed—homes and food and technical help. When he talked about seven people to a room in Moscow living quarters, he seemed to me just as anxious as you or I would be in looking at an American slum problem. Hell, these boys *have* to think in material terms. It's all they believe in."

Even throughout the diffuse and hesitant discourse of that morning, I felt the simple truth to be that the President was dreaming a quite splendid—and sensible—dream. It would not wither under the fire of technical or tactical objections. A month was left to us, before his scheduled appearance on April 16, before the American Society of Newspaper Editors, to put the dream into words. And this meant, most critically, to guard it from the ambushes of policy debate and bureaucratic scrutiny through which it would surely have to pass.

I could foresee and avoid most of these perils by largely limiting all discussion of the text to the President and myself, with only occasional copies of a rewritten version dispatched to the Dulles brothers and Jackson. Every day or two, the President would find a few hours to review with me in detail our latest version, each redraft incorporating changes of substance or style agreed on at our previous meeting. I lost count of these multiplying drafts after the number passed a dozen, but they all retained a basic structure that, from first to last, scarcely changed. Its elements were: (1) an appeal to the Soviet Union to look for its own security elsewhere than in its own amassing

on some occasions when I knew him personally to hold quite specific views. All this reflected simply his austere definition of the proper duty of a chief of intelligence.

of force, inevitably provoking counterforce by the West; (2) a specification of the cost of arms, in the waste of the goods and benefits of peace and prosperity; (3) a call for explicit Soviet signs of good faith on such matters as an Austrian peace treaty and a Korean armistice; (4) a set of five principles for disarmament, covering limitations upon conventional forces, production of strategic materials, atomic and other modern weapons of mass destruction; and (5) a look at the peaceful fruits to be gained from such disarmament. In all these areas, both Eisenhower and I knew the need to reach broad decision on both substance and language *before* submitting a text for exhaustive study by the State Department. It would have been an exercise in futility, for example, to have opened discussion with the State Department on possible disarmament proposals merely by inviting departmental attention to a blank piece of paper. So notoriously nervous were the technical experts on disarmament, so hesitant to commit themselves to almost any proposals, that the paper would be returned immaculately untouched. And so it was barely a week before the speech was to be delivered that the President was sufficiently satisfied with our text to warrant my starting detailed consultation with the department.

A most fortunate event followed. The department assigned Paul H. Nitze, the successor to George F. Kennan as chief of the policy planning staff, to work with me on the speech in its final, critical phase. A veteran of years of service, in both the Defense and State Departments, Nitze quickly displayed a rare combination of a sense of history, a flair for diplomacy, and a care for language. We spent long and painstaking hours struggling—page by page, word by word—to strike and to hold, in the speech, the most delicately balanced tone: confidence without a show of truculence, conciliation without a trace of weakness. Carefully we filtered out of the text a number of possible proposals either too complex or too trivial. These included, for example, a suggestion for a neutral zone along North Korea's border, a presidential offer to travel abroad to meet Malenkov, an exchange of American and Soviet air-time to allow the leaders of each nation to address the people of the other. In so basic a document, the matters to omit demanded quite as much thought and definition as the matters to state. And high on this list of omissions were any allusions to "liberation" of Eastern Europe or "unleashing" Nationalist China.

The political moment and environment in Washington, however, superficially appeared most inhospitable for such an endeavor as ours. While press headlines of these days were reporting McCarthy's rage against the Bohlen appointment, Republican Senator Styles Bridges was groaning to all who would listen that the Moscow Embassy should go to "a deserving Republican— there are several millions of them." Also in these same days, a formal dinner at the Chinese Embassy had been highlighted by Republican Senators Joseph McCarthy, Styles Bridges, and William Knowland rising and joining in the shouted Nationalist toast: *"Back to the mainland!"* And all such displays of unreason lent both background and encouragement to something more serious—the delicately muted opposition to the President's speech by John Foster Dulles.

Only obliquely to the President, but plainly to me, Dulles murmured his distrust and dislike for the whole project, almost to the end. Initially, he voiced concern on the basis of some new signs of a Communist "peace offensive," such as Chou En-lai's initiative for a Korean prisoner-exchange and Soviet agreement with the West to support Dag Hammarskjold's nomination at the United Nations as Secretary-General. "I grow less keen about this speech," Dulles cautioned, "because I think there's some real danger of our just seeming to fall in with these Soviet overtures. It's obvious that what they are doing is because of outside pressures, and I don't know anything better we can do than to keep up these pressures right now." The reasoning was characteristic of Dulles' penchant for viewing "his" and Soviet foreign policy almost as if the two were opposing attorneys, engaged in cunning and intricate maneuvers in a majestic courtroom. Nor could I even glimpse the nature or the shape of the "outside pressures" that he apparently thought the West was applying with such telling effect. So I confessed to him that I felt differently: "If the Soviets *are* embarked on a 'peace offensive,' Mr. Secretary, I see only one way of wresting the initiative from them. This is not by turning to race in the opposite direction—but by publicly leaping several steps *ahead* of Soviet proposals, to a prepared position where we take *our* stand and summon the Soviets to come to *us*."

This brief exchange signaled a conflict of views—a distance between two profoundly distinct attitudes toward all the politics and the history around us—that stood hopelessly beyond reconciliation. The Secretary's view was eventually to color and mark almost the whole of the foreign policy of the Eisenhower administration, until his death. And it would assure the defeat of the hopes of all who believed differently.

The watchful, not too aggressive, opposition of Dulles to the President's speech persisted. Ten days before the address was to be given, he was again lamenting to me—but without protesting to the President—that we were "falling in with the Soviet scheme of things." His final comment, shortly thereafter, was left in writing, as he departed for vacation, and it read: "Reference to ending of wars in Asia gives me a little concern *lest it commit us to end the Chinese civil war* and again to 'neutralize' Formosa." My own response to this was at least as heated as Paul Nitze's, when I showed him the secretarial caution: "Damn it, if we mean peace, we mean *peace*—and not another civil war in China." Nonetheless, for Dulles, his concern with Nationalist China's aggressive military potential was obviously further buttressed by his lingering conviction, as he had voiced it to me, that a display of American military "superiority" in Korea was necessary.

A final crisis in the course of the speech awaited us, just five days before its scheduled delivery, and this arrived from a wholly unexpected source. The Paris and Bonn Governments had approved confidential résumés of the proposed text, sent them by the State Department, but there now suddenly came a personal message from Prime Minister Churchill to the President. From a point of view precisely the *reverse* of that of Dulles, Churchill questioned the wisdom of the speech. The same Soviet initiatives that so dismayed Dulles gave Churchill, as he cabled, "great hope." While he applauded the actual text of the presidential speech as "grave and formidable," he thought the political moment a propitious one in which to "bide your time," while further Communist overtures might unfold. With characteristic Churchillian aptness of phrase and plausibility of argument, he observed that the present moment called for remembrance of the tale of Napoleon, napping in his chair as a prolonged military engagement began, and saying: "Wake me when their infantry column gets beyond the closest wood."

Suddenly summoned to confer with the President, along with Bedell Smith and Milton Eisenhower, I found myself now alone in pressing the argument to go ahead with the speech. One point in Churchill's message, I thought, could properly be met —a suggestion to delete any too specific references to terms for a Korean settlement. On the main question, however, I felt —and on this there was general concurrence—that Churchill's deep, unspoken concern was to guard and reserve for himself the initiative in any dramatic new approach to the Soviet leaders. To my dismay, however, Bedell Smith, while repeating the State Department's warm collective approval of the actual text of the speech, nonetheless felt obliged to report Dulles' general doubt as to the "need" for *any* speech. Milton Eisenhower—addressing himself only to Churchill's particular viewpoint and totally disregarding the quite contrary concerns of Dulles—suggested that the speech should, perhaps, completely eliminate any challenges to the Soviets and "simply say what we are willing to do." This, of course, would have upset all balance in the "grave" declaration. And impatiently, with that air of resignation which at times seemed almost to engulf him, the President broke in:

"Well, maybe Churchill's right, and we can whip up some other text for the occasion." In what I felt was a desperate appeal, I recalled my own opposition to a premature speech; I argued that now there was sufficient clarity to the Soviet temper to allow us to address it with some precision; and I warned finally against greeting all recent events merely with impassive silence. As minutes passed, the conversation slowly, almost imperceptibly, began to revert to the substance of the speech, not the question of its delivery. Finally, the President summoned his secretary to dictate a cable to Churchill and Foreign Secretary Anthony Eden. He invited their specific suggestions on the text and explained that American opinion, watching the worldwide rush of change, needed some clear official reaction and guidance that would be "more than just a jumble of platitudes."

A last editing session, the next day, brought Smith, Nitze, and me to the President's upstairs study. And I recall the occasion as one of the very few instances when I heard Eisenhower acknowledge specific disagreement with Dulles. Churchill had cabled back one particular suggestion: the address, he urged, should contain a frank expression of hope for general pacification throughout Asia. This view conflicted head-on, of course, with Dulles' anxiety to avoid even the hint of such a "neutralization" of force. Dulles, at one point, even had urged Nitze and me to make plain in the speech that American signature of a Korean armistice would be *contingent* on restoration of peace in Indochina. We "forgot" this suggestion, for it seemed outrageously illogical to insist upon such a condition while, simultaneously, excluding as irrelevant the matter of Nationalist China and Formosa. Now, while the President seemed receptive to Churchill's suggestion, I felt obligated to remind him, in Dulles' absence, of the Secretary's diametrically opposed opinion. The Eisenhower retort was crisp and pointed: "Well, I know how he feels, but sometimes Foster is just too worried about being accused of sounding like Truman and Acheson. I think he worries too much about it."

And so—at last—"The Chance for Peace" was delivered in Washington on April 16, 1953. The force of its substance and words had survived the ordeal of weeks reasonably well. . . .

Every gun that is fired, every warship launched, every rocket fired signifies, in the final sense, a *theft* from those who hunger and are not fed, those who are cold and are not clothed. . . .

The cost of one modern heavy bomber is this: a modern brick school in more than thirty cities. . . . We pay for a single fighter plane with a half million bushels of wheat. We pay for a single destroyer with new homes that could have housed more than eight thousand people. . . .

This is not a way of life at all, in any true sense. Under the cloud of threatening war, it is humanity hanging from a cross of iron. . . .

We care only for sincerity of peaceful purpose, attested by deeds. . . . Even a few such clear and specific acts, such as the Soviet Union's signature upon an Austrian treaty or its release of thousands of prisoners still held from World War II, would be impressive signs. . . .

A world that begins to witness the rebirth of trust among nations *can* find its way to a peace that is neither partial nor punitive. . . .

The first great step along this way must be the conclusion of an honorable armistice in Korea. . . . We seek, throughout Asia as throughout the world, a peace that is true and total. . . .

The fruit of success in all these tasks (of ways and provisions for disarmament) would present the world with the greatest task, and the greatest opportunity, of all . . . a declared, total war, not upon any human enemy, but upon the brute forces of poverty and need. . . .

This Government is ready to ask its people to join with all nations in devoting a substantial percentage of the savings achieved by disarmament to a fund for world aid and reconstruction. . . .

We are ready, in short, to dedicate our strength to serving the *needs*, rather than the *fears*, of the world. . . .

What is the Soviet Union ready to do? . . .

There is, before all peoples, a precious chance to turn the black tide of events. . . .

[We] aspire to this: the lifting, from the backs and the hearts of men, of their burden of arms and of fears—so that they may find before them a golden age of freedom and of peace.

The impact of the speech—like the President's own courageous initiative in its creation—was rather memorable. The New

York *Times,* the next day, editorially assured that "this magnificent and deeply moving" declaration by President Eisenhower had "obviously undertaken to seize the peace initiative from the Soviets." The fervently Democratic New York *Post* saluted "America's voice at its best." And years later Sherman Adams, in his memoirs, recalled it as "the most effective speech of Eisenhower's public career."* One of Washington's most acute journalists, Richard H. Rovere, analyzed the occasion in greater depth. Saluting the speech as "an immense triumph" for Eisenhower, he went so far as to conclude: "It firmly established his leadership in America and re-established American leadership in the world." Too optimistically, however, he inferred that "the Eisenhower administration had cleared up most of the questions about the policies it hopes to pursue between now and 1957." But —for all this history of the 1950s—his most notable comment was the observation that the speech "revealed a greater desire for a flexible and adaptable diplomacy than that shown in the latter-day speeches of President Truman and Mr. Acheson, who, toward the end of their tenure, increasingly tended to answer criticism by showing that they could be even more hard-boiled and militant than their critics."†

This appraisal recalled precisely what had seemed the crucial and lofty hope in Eisenhower's election in 1952. It was a flame soon to be nearly smothered, to flicker now and again, in 1955 and 1956. And—too late—it would flare forth in the closing months of the Eisenhower Years.

As for Secretary Dulles, shortly after his return to Washington, he summarized in a formal address his own memory and view of the events and decisions leading up to the President's speech. There had been rumors throughout Washington of some dissension about the speech in both White House and State Department. Naturally, the Secretary assured the press that there had been not a moment of disagreement. The President, he said, had

* *First-hand Report,* p. 97.
† *The New Yorker,* May 2, 1953.

done no more than lead the nation calmly into "a planned stage" of American policy. This had been "determined upon without regard whatsoever to the recent Soviet moves." And the world should know this: "The words which President Eisenhower uttered might have been uttered at any time during [these past] ninety days."*

3

There is one process in national government, as I came to realize, that works with some speed and remarkable thoroughness. This is the process that somehow contrives, almost always, the dissipation of much of the force behind the most bold thrusts of initiative. As elusive as it is effective, this process seems, at various times, to assume different shapes and to suggest many images. It is the silent defense-in-depth against the new act. It is the curse of Sisyphus, newly designed for modern democracy: the mountain whose steep scaling assures the eventual, breathless exhaustion of the energy of—an idea. And, for the individual daring to defy it, it reserves a kind of slow anesthesia which deadens, at last, the exhilarating pain of vigorous and original thought.

Sometimes this process begins to work almost instantaneously and mockingly. This occurs when the men who presume to challenge it themselves betray flickering signs of inner doubt or imperfect awareness of what they are doing. And these were the signs marking all that followed—and all that failed to follow —upon the most important speech of Eisenhower's eight years in the presidency.

The political world outside the White House—from Washington cocktail parties, to West European chancelleries, on to the editorial rooms of the Indian or Brazilian daily press—chattered with excitement and anticipation over the fresh invigoration of American foreign policy. New, explicit, and eloquent acts

* New York *Times,* April 19, 1953.

—to translate words into deeds, in language meaningful to all peoples and in all tongues—surely seemed to be in the making, at the highest levels of American government.

Within the White House, in fact, the day after the President's speech, Eisenhower and Adams were absent. They had retired for some needed rest to the golf course in Atlanta, Georgia. But urgent national business had to proceed. And it was discharged, this day, in two official meetings. The first was the regular morning meeting of the White House staff. And the second, a few hours later, was the Cabinet.

I recall both these meetings well.

The White House staff meeting stirred with delight over the press reaction to the President's speech. The group did not waste time or emotion on the substance of the declaration, its implications for our practical diplomacy, its demand for further acts to prove its intent—or its possible portent of the final outcome of the critical but ambiguous conflict, in views of the world at large, between Eisenhower and Dulles. Instead, the talk was of more immediate matters. And it went like this:

A.—"This speech is just what this Administration needed—in fact, we were needing it goddam bad. It really gets us off our backs—and off the ground."

B.—"The problem's more than that. Now that we've gotten this lift—how do we *stay* up?"

C.—"I think it's pretty obvious what we need. One speech isn't enough. We got to follow up. We need *another* speech. Only this one has to do for us in *domestic* affairs what we've just done in *foreign* affairs. If we could just get the same sex appeal into this other speech as there was in yesterday's . . ."

A.—"All this just brings us back to an old question. We can see now how much *can* be done with a speech like this. We have to be doing it all the time. And we need professional help for this—as a lot of us have been saying. We simply have to get into our setup a really first-class *public relations* man. If we had that kind of help, we'd not be sitting around wondering—we'd *know*—the answer to, where do we go from here right now?"

The Cabinet met a couple of hours later.

The session was called "special." This fact helped to quicken popular and press expectation that major decisions, in the sphere of foreign affairs, might be expected shortly. In truth, however, the session bore the designation of "special" only for the technical reason that the President was not present to preside. And in his absence, the meeting was chaired by Vice President Richard Nixon.

The first order of business involved general agreement, in rather desultory spirit, that the problem of tariffs was, politically, quite a difficult problem. The Republican protectionists in the Congress were displaying all the intransigence to be expected of them. There was a general nodding of heads in the consensus that nothing more could be extracted from this session of the Congress, in the way of liberalizing tariff policy, beyond simple extension of authority for reciprocal trade agreements. And there was further agreement that it might be a politically good idea to set up a committee, simply to study the whole problem of tariffs.

The main order of business for this Cabinet meeting was stated and discussed at length by Vice President Nixon. "The time, the right time," he declared with sincere urgency, "to start winning the 1954 elections is right *now*." Articulate and forceful, as he almost always appeared at Cabinet, Nixon then delivered a short speech on a seeming heresy of politics: the "dangerous" notion that a lot of the President's program in the Congress was eliciting more support from Democrats than from Republicans. The Vice President did not address himself to the question of whether this suspicion was true or false. He stepped past the matter thus: "There's been some talk that the President could work as well with the Democrats in majority. But let's not have any illusions about that. The support he is getting from them is purely *expedient*, and they will go after him just as soon as they think they can." Some of us on the White House staff could not help thinking that it would be nice if the Republicans in Congress approached the program of their own President with a little of the same sense of "expediency." But Nixon's message was addressed to the men sitting around the table with him, and for them he had a program. "What can the Cabinet do? First, it matters most, of course, to have a really good program in your departments. But—secondly—do not get your public-speaking schedules all crowded with engagements in congressional areas where there will be no contest next year." *

The final part of this Cabinet discussion was dominated by Postmaster General Arthur Summerfield. His worries were both political and departmental. On the first, he reported "a desperately serious situation"—in Michigan. This consisted of the threat to the Senate seat of Republican Homer Ferguson by Democratic Governor G. Mennen ("Soapy") Williams. And Summerfield warned: "We've simply got to be thinking of ways to help Ferguson. Give him a good bill to carry in the Senate. Or something." As for his departmental problems, Summerfield seemed to discern that the Cabinet had nothing more important on their minds this morning, so he recited to them, in exquisite detail, the perennial dilemma of his deficit. He saved for the long last, however, one fresh suggestion. "Let's get thirty-four million dollars out of our budget right now," he happily proposed, "by having each department in the Cabinet *pay* its *own* mail bills." Summerfield, with this jab, sharply summoned back the wandering thoughts of his colleagues, but they betrayed, without exception, a predictable lack of enthusiasm.

In the confused mumble of dismay that ensued, the Cabinet adjourned. The meeting had succeeded in avoiding any mention of any aspect of the President's initiative in foreign affairs. And I closed my diary notes of the day, observing: "I suppose a lot of people thought we spent this day in the White House talking about the peace of the world."

There remained for my learning, in these events following

* Cabinet meeting, April 17, 1953.

upon the President's speech, a more ironic lesson. While major matters might easily get stalled or lost in government machinery, the trivial matters—so it appeared—could move swiftly and unimpeded through the process of decision and action. It seemed, at such times, as if the very structure of government were like an infuriatingly ingenious filter—so fine as to allow passage only of the small or the petty.

The instance here concerned the man who had so notably helped to make possible the President's speech, the State Department's Paul Nitze. The personnel policies of the Administration, but especially of the State Department, reflected their somewhat tortured views of political reality around them. Nitze was a life-long Republican, first prominent in Washington service in the Defense Department under Secretary James V. Forrestal; his career, one of consistent competence and distinction, later had carried him to the State Department, there to contribute notably to shaping the Marshall Plan; and by the time Acheson and the Democratic Administration departed from the scene, Nitze had succeeded George Kennan as chief of State's Policy Planning Staff. These facts were sufficient to rouse Dulles to suspicion—the gnawing half-fear that a man, even a Republican, of Nitze's long record in government, might not be "loyal" to the new Republican Administration. Such fear was inflamed, and even a little rationalized, by the fact of so many Republican leaders on the Hill constantly complaining to Dulles and other department heads: "Hell, we still see coming before our committees the same old tired faces we watched under the Democrats. Can't you find some new fellows to give your testimony for you?" Finally, this was a time when, as Bedell Smith used to lament to me, "Dulles is still dreaming his fancy about reactivating the civil war in China." The cool intelligence of Nitze could not be heated to encourage Secretarial illusions of this order. And after some months, Dulles—with the hapless and impatient air of a man viewing the mere presence of another as an unsettling kind of intellectual challenge—suggested that Nitze pursue his career elsewhere.*

Enter Charles E. Wilson. The bluff self-assurance of the Secretary of Defense gave him, at times, a refreshing capacity for the unorthodox. Knowing of both Nitze's abilities and his dismissal, Wilson called upon him to serve as Assistant Secretary of Defense for Foreign Affairs. Correctly, Nitze cautioned Wilson that his appointment, requiring Senate confirmation, would annoy some Republican leaders in the Congress. With a flourish of disdain for such ignoble politics, Wilson insisted that Nitze start work immediately. Within a week, however, he sheepishly summoned his unconfirmed Assistant Secretary to his office to hear the humiliating confession: Senate Majority Leader Knowland had, indeed, "blackballed" Nitze. All Republican archconservatives were raging at the durability in office of "Acheson's architects of disaster." And the Secretary, sorrowfully, felt that he did, after all, have to bow.

There occurred a postscript to this incident—the only

---

* Dulles unfortunately persisted in worsening his own personal repute with career officials in the State Department and the Foreign Service by handling such severances of unwanted staff members in a manner so abrasive as to seem rude. The most flagrant instance was his conduct—precisely in these same weeks—with regard to the resignation of George Kennan. The parting of Dulles and Kennan was not, in itself, surprising, for Kennan had publicly expressed dissent from some of Dulles' views before the new Administration took office. But (as I learned only by accident) Kennan, in late June of 1953, had waited some two months for acknowledgment of his resignation from either the Secretary or the President. By this time, it had become clear that Dulles intended to deny him the courtesy of any reply—to close out decades of duty in the Foreign Service—and to merely employ a device normally reserved for dismissal of incompetents: a Foreign Service regulation terminating an officer who receives no new assignment within three months of the completion of his last assignment. When I investigated, I found that (1) the State Department protocol office had no knowledge of Kennan's resignation, and (2) it had been filed in the Secretary's office—where embarrassed efforts would be made to "locate" it. When it finally reached the White House four days later, the resignation was covered by a memorandum from Dulles suggesting, indeed, that it be left to become "automatic." A report of the facts to Adams enlisted his support, and we arranged that a respectful and warm presidential letter promptly leave the White House to the retiring Kennan.

occasion when I ever directly reported in anger to the President on a personnel matter unconnected with my official duties. While the loss of Nitze to government service was an accomplished fact, I wanted to be sure that the President personally was informed on its inglorious details. When I related them, he pounded his fist on his huge desk in wrath against "those damn *monkeys* on the Hill." He even invited me to instruct Adams, on his behalf, to find a place for Nitze on the White House staff, loudly exclaiming: "I simply will not have those monkeys telling us what we can and cannot do." I did not pass on his message to Adams, however, since I knew the exercise would be futile, if only because Nitze would never accept so transparently artificial an assignment. Thus the man who had so significantly helped the President to "seize the peace initiative" left the service of his government—to return in 1961 with the Kennedy administration to the same office in the Defense Department from which Wilson had let him be driven these many years earlier.

Enter—at this precise time—Robert Frost.

The poet and Sherman Adams had long been warm personal friends, and Frost chanced now to pay one of his occasional calls upon Adams at the White House. As Adams afterwards told me, the two men talked at length, with the candor of New England friends, of the state of the nation—and of the Administration. Frost acknowledged some good in what he saw. He appreciated and respected the capacity of Eisenhower to stir the people, the obvious purity of the President's highest political intent, the force of some of his words. "But I sense," the poet confessed, "from around the country, something troubling. It comes from the young people especially. It is one fear and one want. It is—*a lack of decisiveness.*"

The President, in fact, had increasingly seemed to me rather distracted in the months following his show of initiative in foreign affairs. I found myself often remembering one personal detail of that day of his speech in April. Throughout its delivery, he had looked ashen and ill, for he had painfully suffered from food poisoning since the night before. And as so much time passed without his giving sign of reverting to the spirit or the promise of that occasion, the wry thought occurred that he almost acted as if the event itself had left some unpleasant aftertaste. More seriously and obviously, other current and complex problems—like the futile campaign to induce the French to ratify the European Defense Community pact—were heavily pressing on presidential time and patience. In Cabinet, one also sensed, in subtle signs impossible to document, a far more important fact—a growing assurance in Dulles, a bolder show of force in discussions, and a firmer resolve to summon back the President's attention from the loftier sphere of peace-making to the more mundane and immediate troubles of daily diplomacy. Accordingly, some months later, Henry Cabot Lodge, upon returning from a trip through the western states, could report, as he told several on the White House staff: "I heard everywhere one major criticism—that promises of action in the foreign field don't seem to have been kept. There's just a widespread feeling of no follow-up to the sweeping declarations of last April."

And so it seemed—as, in truth, it would be—that, from all the initiatives that had recently flashed through Eisenhower's mind, as he boldly scanned the whole front of world disarmament plans and world economic policy, only one stout impulse would endure. And this would be a readiness, in the cause of peace, to travel to any place on earth.

4

The doubt softly voiced by Robert Frost probed, gently but keenly, to the heart of the question of presidential leadership and the very nature of the Eisenhower administration. In an editorial reviewing a full six months of the President in office, the Washington *Post* could only conclude cautiously: "The picture still lacks clarity."* The appraisal further noted, quite accurately, that "Senator Knowland does not seem able to separate Administration objectives from his own pet phobias." And, as any member of the White House staff might have added, the senator from California also never wearied of forcing upon the President hours of argument in advocacy of his own favored schemes for remaking the world, notably by a bold American naval blockade of the coast of Communist China. As the *Post* warned: "There still exists the danger that by compromising too far the President will abet the very extremist elements he abhors." And indeed, for all witnesses to the Eisenhower administration, this fast became the focus of honest and critical concern: the President's view and conduct of his relations with the Congress.

There may have been no aspect of Eisenhower's presidency misunderstood so widely—and so understandably—as his whole behavior toward the Congress. A public image of Eisenhower, more and more sharply etched by criticism through the passing years, purported to explain the political facts simply, vividly, personally. The man, according to this caricature, was merely too lazy to lead. Or, he lacked both the interest and the ingenuity to work with congressional leaders. Or, he really was intimidated by the archconservatives with the loudest voices in his party. Or, he was a helpless amateur ringed by professionals far more tough and determined. Or, he simply was slack of spirit and tired in body. And all such images—at times, most plausible inferences—were oddly, but profoundly, false.

Far from reflecting either acquiescence or abdication, the conduct of Eisenhower's congressional relations bespoke a most deliberate intent, firm from the outset and—for better or for worse—consistent to the end. Anyone working close to the President heard him, not once but many times, make his sharp and spontaneous speech on the matter. Provoked by almost any passing criticism or lament upon his handling of the Congress, he would

* Washington *Post*, July 20, 1953.

push back his leather chair, grimace tightly, vault upright, and start his march-to-rhetoric around the oval office. . . . "Now, look, I happen to *know* a little about leadership. I've had to work with a lot of nations, for that matter, at odds with each other. And I tell you this: you do not *lead* by hitting people over the head. Any damn fool can do that, but it's usually called 'assault'— not 'leadership.' . . . I'll tell you what leadership is. It's *persuasion* —and *conciliation*—and *education*—and *patience*. It's long, slow, tough work. That's the only kind of leadership I know—or believe in—or will practice."

He would stop in his striding, on such occasions, to note bitterly some suddenly remembered disparagement of his "lack of aggressiveness." And he would surge on, firing his furious words at the critical, anonymous "them." . . . "*They* talk and write and prate about leadership. And they'd be happy and cheering—if I knocked some congressional heads together. Well, I *won't*—not even the thickest heads in my own party—not if I can possibly avoid it. For that will not be leadership, and I'll tell you *why*. In the first place, you don't 'lead' a man by yelling at him in public or forcing him to say publicly, 'Yes, it's true—I've been voting like a damn fool ever since I came to Congress twenty years ago.' In the second place, if I forced some of these fellows to go through that kind of public penance and conversion—how long do you think they would *stay* converted? I'll tell you—long enough to get off their knees, run a short distance, and curse me for humiliating them. And in the third place, when Senator X or Senator Z does something I think is just deplorable, more than half the time that means he's a Republican—*supposed* to be helping me, not working against me. So if I tell him off in public, what am I accomplishing? Just this much: I am yelling to the world, 'Please come and look, all of you, at the knucklehead I have representing me and my party and my program on Capitol Hill.' "

And this heated declamation would end, almost invariably, on a softening note, as his voice slowly attuned and yielded to the sense of personal humility and personal responsibility. . . . "Look," he would almost implore, "I know how good I could make *myself* look. Everyone who's yapping now would be cheering . . . if only I would do my 'leading' in public—where they could *see* me. . . . Well, I can't do that. I will spend the hours here, quietly, in this office, staring out these windows, sometimes a little hopelessly—with Dirksen or Millikin or Knowland here, to tell me what industries I have to protect with higher tariffs—or how the folks back home don't like these big bills for Mutual Security—or how to put Chiang Kai-shek back in Peiping. . . . So I'll listen. And I'll answer. And I'll try to get them to understand, to *give*. I'll try to get them to give not everything, but—a little here, a little there. And I'll hope that maybe something I say *does* get through—and stays with them." And finally he would end with the candid confession, murmured not meekly but firmly: "I don't know any other way to lead."

There shone in these words and perceptions—so I believed—qualities even more substantial than manifest sincerity. There was full awareness, here, of the harsh dilemma tormenting any President at deep odds, in critical areas, with some of his own party's most cherished traditions and comfortable postures. There was honorable willingness, too, to accept a formidable task, even though possibly underestimating its immensity: the direction of government and the leadership of party, while simultaneously striving to inspire this party both to renovate its structure and to renounce its prejudices. All the seeming simplicity of the President's words, in short, was deceptive, for they actually described some of the most tangled and complex political knots that can be tied by the democratic process itself. And I often later wondered if the hands of any leadership, sharing Eisenhower's purposes but restricted by his methods, could have unsnarled these particular dilemmas.

He held and he spoke some high hopes—in this first while. These hopes were strong enough to withstand, for example, the gales of criticism assailing his refusal to do direct battle with McCarthy. He never doubted either the rightness of his shunning that encounter or the inevitability of the Wisconsin senator's final frustration and fall. He knew well the more angry and impatient view of the matter, too, for he read his mail with all the care and thought that he withheld from the daily press. And apropos of these cries for action, he took the occasion of one Cabinet meeting to emphasize the general resolve that would rule his posture toward the Congress. "My position," he told the assembled, "is simply this: our *long-term* good requires that leadership on the Hill be exercised *through* the party organization there. This is the key to success, in the long run, and we all will just have to bear with the wrath of our critics for a while. I want all of you to help in this—in all your work with Senator Taft, with Knowland and Millikin and the others. We have already come a good long way, and I think the difference in atmosphere there on the Hill is almost revolutionary."*

To support this sanguine view, there did occur, from time to time, encouraging flickers of light in the dark battles in Senate and House—aside from the prudent mollifying of a Robert Taft. An Everett Dirksen, unflattered and uncourted, would never have committed the political act of tearing up years of speeches in opposition—to lead the fight for Mutual Security legislation. And there were quite a few Republican congressmen who occasionally marveled a little at their own audacity in rebelling against their own voting records. Any one of them might have made the humorful phone call that came to the White House, from a Midwesterner in their group, one early summer afternoon: "Hello, put me through to Persons. This is *internationalist* Allen speaking—*brand new* internationalist. Damn it, I just voted for Mutual Security for the first time in my life."

But to have sewn such patches of success into a prevailing pattern—so I came to fear—would have demanded herculean effort,

---

* Cabinet meeting, March 27, 1953.

limitless time, masterly persuasiveness, saintly patience, and incredible luck. From the outset, the score of failures and disappointments was impressive, too. Not long before his fatal illness, Taft himself almost shattered one of the President's weekly meetings with congressional leaders by spluttering and shouting his defiant scorn for the President's requests for defense appropriations. "The country and the people" he cried, "simply won't stand for it." This harangue was delivered despite the Administration's cutback on previous budget estimates and despite its public promises—not among Eisenhower's loftiest—of "more defense for less money." Still later, the modest accomplishment of winning extension of the Trade Agreements Act, covering reciprocal trade treaties, proved possible only at the price of allowing some special protectionist legislation to be pressed on the House floor by Republican leaders. To all White House appeals to compromise on tariffs upon Australian wool, Colorado's Senator Millikin retrieved from the nineteenth century his cold retort: "Australians don't vote here." And the years would pass thus: as late as 1958 Eisenhower would find himself still waging the same battle, still warning that the nation could not "cower behind new trade walls," still finally settling for mere renewal of reciprocal trade agreements.

Nor did the strategy of conciliation and education prove much more effective on other fronts. The President had hoped, for example, to attest the "humanity" of this "business" Administration by formally establishing the Department of Health, Education and Welfare at Cabinet level. But Republican congressional leaders, grudging enough toward new titles, felt even less generous about new appropriations. The department was barely christened before Republican congressmen set to slashing its moderate requests. All the while, Indiana's Representative Charles A. Halleck could cast a pall over almost any of the President's weekly meetings with the legislators, with the tireless incantation: "Education is a business for the states, not the federal government." And Knowland—even after succeeding Taft as Senate Majority Leader, supposedly serving as the President's key aide on the Hill—showed ponderous and determined lethargy in support of so critical a part of his President's program as Mutual Security funds. The California senator's portentous head-shaking over the costs of both foreign aid and national defense at one weekly meeting with the legislators, finally exasperated the President to the point of snapping: "My God, you just can't sit back and assume the nation is safe from all harm because the Republicans won the last election!"*

The President's own response to such conflicts, however, became somewhat blurred by his own highly personal interpretation of the relationship between the Executive and the Legislature in recent American political history. Quite frequently, he would murmur that Franklin D. Roosevelt had "usurped" powers of the Legislature and that the Congress understandably had felt "deprived" of its "rightful role" for two decades. From this, he inferred a sense of obligation, as President, to redress matters by "restoring" some power to the Legislature. And upon this benevolent vision of Constitutional politics, there intruded no harsh awareness that—from the time of Congress's rebuff to Roosevelt in the historic fight over the Supreme Court—the Executive had never been able, in fact, to move much beyond frontiers guarded by an essentially conservative coalition within the Legislature. Such Presidential solicitude plainly implied a sense of the *separateness* of the two branches that forbade any political trespassing. And by this process of self-denying logic, Eisenhower could and did face the prospect of a Knowland becoming the Republican party's Senate Majority Leader by virtually insisting upon the rightness and the justice of this burden. As he quite sharply told his Cabinet: "I want to say with all the emphasis at my command that this Administration has absolutely *no* personal

* President's meeting with legislative leaders, July 7, 1953.

choice for new Majority Leader. *We* are not going to get into *their* business."*

There probably never existed much chance for a truly creative partnership between Executive and Legislature, under the terms of such a view of their proper roles. Any such hope as there might have been would have called for the frequent wielding of either or both of two weapons. One of these was the raw power of patronage. The second was the frankly personal appeal to the people. And Eisenhower could contemplate either exercise only with reticence, if not repugnance.

As a party man, Eisenhower, of course, was not without his zest for victory, his thrill to the clash of forces in the open national arena, and—above all—his dream of a reborn Republican party. This dream inspired his constant preoccupation with youth in the party. I recall being in his office one day, for example, when Adams came in with a routine slip of paper for his initialing. The matter concerned a minor appointment in the Department of the Interior. The President took a moment to glance through the appointee's presumed credentials, then turned to Adams with the appeal: "Okay, Sherm, but I wish these minor jobs would not always go to old men. I know the veterans have to be rewarded and all that—and you can't trust them with jobs that are too important. But this lower level is also the place where the *young* can break in. You're not going to have much of a government—or much of a party—without them." And over the years Eisenhower tirelessly repeated this call to all party leaders.

But precisely the clean conscientiousness of this concern for the party's future impelled him to spurn the more crude and swift uses of patronage. I recall another instance, early in the Administration, when Adams reported to the President a surge of sentiment on Capitol Hill for the Administration to find a respectable job for an ex-Senator whose financial dealings had recently

* Cabinet meeting, July 31, 1953.

come into some public question. Coldly, Eisenhower refused: "I don't think he's interested in a damn thing but using us to give him a job so he can wave it publicly as a clean bill of health. Can't see it. Let him suffer a while." On another occasion, the President enlivened a Cabinet meeting with some blunt remarks to Leonard W. Hall, Chairman of the Republican National Committee: "One of your committeemen told a Secretary in one of our departments that he wanted an appointment for a man even though he knew him to be a member of the Ku Klux Klan. And when the Secretary refused, he said he was coming to see me. Don't let him, Len. If he does, he'll get thrown out of here so fast he won't touch ground this side of Pennsylvania Avenue."*

Such remarks exploded out of an impatience that Eisenhower seemed to reserve for Hall and for all discussion of patronage at Cabinet meetings. Hall attended several such meetings, in the course of the first year of the Administration, and he always entered with the air of someone slightly astonished at being admitted, slightly fearful of peremptory dismissal. There was a nervous and hesitant tone to his appeals for "cooperation with the National Committee" in rewarding the political helpful with departmental posts. Squirming unhappily in his chair and perspiring profusely, he would half-implore, half-lecture his listeners. . . . "Our first job is to build the Republican party into a true majority party. This not only takes a program but real reorganization. Now there are somewhere between two thousand and four thousand removable political appointees in Washington— and so far, after four months, we have replaced fifty or sixty. We haven't made *one* appointment that can directly help to win *one* congressional seat in 1954. We haven't appointed a single Italo-American—or a single Polish American." Then—in the rushed and anxious voice of an advertising agency's account-executive talking against the clock in a sedate board of directors meeting—he tried to beguile the "businesslike" Cabinet: "Now,

* Cabinet meeting, May 8, 1953.

I've got my own new team. They're no political hacks. With just one exception, they are all from business corporations. So we won't be recommending hacks to you." At last, desperately: "We want to be able in the future to rely on our own organization, not running for help to the President all the time. But—forgive me for being blunt—if we don't get your cooperation, and get jobs for more than fifty people named by us, the morale of the party will be gone."* Some quality—or lack of it—in this appeal so exasperated the President that he would snap, as on this occasion: "Quit apologizing for what you're saying—and tell us what you want." And with such almost petulant expressions of distaste, Eisenhower tended almost always to show his contempt for the power of patronage.

As for using the power of his own personality in direct appeal to the people—to summon support, to bestir the Congress, or to rally the party—Eisenhower felt and practiced the same constraint and diffidence. Any President, of course, enjoys unique and unsurpassed ways and occasions to command national attention, and Eisenhower used most of them at one time or another. But he never employed such resources in any coherent and sustained campaign. Rather did he restrict the use of each device almost to the minimum that his advisers would tolerate. For weeks before and after his first Inauguration, he grumbled and argued against even the necessity of press conferences, deploring their establishment by Roosevelt as a fixed form of presidential communication; and it required the persistent persuasion of Hagerty to have him hold his first such conference, almost a month after he took office. When he did yield to the need for some nationally televised appeal, he tried tenaciously to break away from the formula of a direct address to his audience, in favor of informal "discussion," with Dulles or other Cabinet members joining in a "presentation." And his reasoning turned upon the same lament, repeated again and again: "I keep telling

* Cabinet meeting, May 8, 1953.

you fellows I don't like to do this sort of thing. I can think of nothing more boring, for the American public, than to have to sit in their living rooms for a whole half hour looking at my face on their television screens."

The most conservative Republican leaders of the Congress, as they came to sense this remarkable disposition of the President, greeted it as a fact almost incredible but vastly reassuring. They found it incredible since, as Adams sardonically remarked of *them:* "There is not a senator or a congressman on the Hill who does not spend some good part of the night, lying awake in his bed, thinking how in hell he can possibly get *his* name in the papers within the next twenty-four hours." And they found it reassuring, of course, by virtue of the automatic equation they made of all such matters: any effacement of presidential power signaled a direct enhancement of their own. It is doubtful if any of them had felt, ever in their political lives, so genuine a sense of respect and thankfulness for the modesty of another man.

A perhaps fair measure of the failure of Eisenhower's strategy with Congress came, ironically, with the senatorial vote condemning McCarthy for conduct unbecoming a senator, at the end of 1954. As the most hostile of all senators in Eisenhower's own party slipped, protesting loudly, toward this humiliation, he fired a last salvo at the President: he issued a public "apology" for having supported Eisenhower in 1952. After this act of malice, it might have been expected that the Senate's Republican leaders would, at least, take the occasion of the condemnation vote to signify some belated regret for the sniping that their own President had so patiently endured. With the single exception of Massachusetts' Leverett Saltonstall, all Republican Senate leaders —Knowland, Dirksen, Bridges, and Millikin—voted for McCarthy.

Through all such trials and disappointments—and all the years of his Administration—there remained one conspicuous personal object on the President's large, neat, almost bare desk in the oval office. This was a gift from his economic adviser, Gabriel Hauge. It was a small block of wood, bearing a brief inscription.

The President obviously viewed the legend as symbolic and pertinent. In Latin, it enjoined simply: "Gentle in manner, strong in deed."

For Eisenhower, these words proclaimed his view of the meaning and nature of political leadership. As plainly as the presidential record of eight years, they recorded his personal belief that the two matters—"manner" and "deed"—were, in political life, distinct and unrelated. They were—quite like the Executive and the Legislature—*separate*.

The history of many things, for all the decade of the 1950s, would have been quite different, if the President had faced, each morning upon entering the handsome oval office, a different memento. This probably would have been a thing of steel rather than wood. And it might have borne the stark warning of T. S Eliot . . .

> Between the idea
> And the reality
> Between the motion
> And the act
> Falls the Shadow.

5

The Cabinet provided perhaps the supreme occasion, both practical and symbolic, for the voicing and the enactment of Eisenhower's concept of government. Neither his predecessor nor his successor engaged in any such elaborate exercise: this was peculiar to his approach to the processes of governmental decision. It reflected his trust in experts and specialists—a confidence reaffirmed throughout his Administration by every new naming of a special committee, an *ad hoc* commission, or a study group. It translated into political terms his military experience with a staff system, with its promise of work and responsibility lucidly defined, divided, and delegated—so that the commander in chief could confidently expect, from each appropriate aide, either information or action in nicely prescribed spheres of competence. It signified once again, therefore, the faith in the analogy between military and political experience—quite akin to Charles E. Wilson's confusion of business acumen and political skill. And, above all, it expressed the President's basic assumption that many heads are always better than one—especially one's humble own.

A historian of a decade hence, however, reviewing an exhaustive filmstrip with sound track of all the years of deliberations by Eisenhower Cabinets, would find the narrative punctuated with remarkably few decisions. And the scholar's focus of interest would quickly become, in all probability, the small and simple insights, so abundantly offered, into the personal temper and mental habits of the men most conspicuous in this ritual. And he would note their constant marks and mannerisms . . . the judicious interventions of Nixon, crisp and practical and logical: never proposing major objectives, but quick and shrewd in suggesting or refining methods—rather like an effective trial lawyer, I kept thinking, with an oddly slack interest in the law . . . Dulles gradually more confident and more didactic, his speech slow and humorless, yet never wholly blurring the internal rigor of his tactical logic . . . Adams rarely murmuring a word, but, when so doing, swiftly crystallizing some discussion about to become unbearably diffuse . . . Benson, uncompromising and conscientious, deploring any political temptations to extend federal programs in almost any area of national life, and reporting either farmers' distress or drought in the Southwest with remarkable equanimity: "We're doing all we can—we just need rain."

And presiding—not just by force of office, but by quality of personality—was the President. Grim and harsh, or grinning and jesting, he shifted moods with the news or harassments of the particular morning. More than occasionally, he would slip and forget to ask Benson for the opening prayer, Dulles would murmur a reminder, and he would blurt almost boyishly: "Oh my gosh! And I really need all the help we can get from *up there* this morning. Ezra, please . . ." And when the heads had been raised again and as the voices began rising in discussion, the President, more often than not, would go to work on the little white pad beneath his hands—slowly, concentratedly, meticulously sketching a face or profile, with a loving attention to detail suggesting an anxiety that this labor, at least, be completed by the time for adjournment. But while his eyes focused downward, his ears seemed never to leave the discourse around him. His interjections were sudden, sometimes sharp or even explosive. And at such times no hostile caricature of the man seemed more ludicrous than the image of him as meek and soft and self-doubting, encircled by stern and aggressive advisers pressing their fixed resolves upon their abject leader.

Diffuse as were these Cabinet discussions—often as inconclusive as academic seminars—they held a crucial place in Eisenhower's scheme for governing. They fixed the occasions for exchange of facts and views between a President and department heads who, in the majority, had little other opportunity to see and to hear him. Again and again, the President would seize on some particular matter of legislation or administration as spark for a warm homily on his most personal views—the world need for freer trade, or the practical necessity (and "cheapness") of programs of mutual security, or the need to temper austere "businesslike" administration with signs of serious concern for "the little fellow," or the "unthinkable" dimensions of nuclear warfare. For almost all the persons present, these fervent sermons carried an authority almost scriptural. And they tempered, if they did not alter, some of the Cabinet's own generally more conventional predispositions.

Moreover, while these presidential interpolations often might seem to border on the banal, they took on added force because of the repeatedly proven range and specificity of the President's knowledge of the matters confronting the various departments. Practically and detailedly, he would comment on technical procurement problems in Defense or aberrations of the parity laws in Agriculture, the economic impact on New York Harbor of the projected St. Lawrence Seaway or the economic plight of Massachusetts' textile industry, the collapse of zinc prices or the worthlessness of Bolivian tin—and on from there to the warmth of his friendship for Harold Macmillan or his tolerance of the idiosyncrasies of Charles De Gaulle. To a Charles Wilson or a George Humphrey, not to mention an Arthur Summerfield or a Douglas McKay, such a range of acquaintanceship with things and with people seemed no less than dazzling.

Aside from these presidential opinions or perceptions, the men assembled in Cabinet often found the room excitingly filled with facts of life from all over the world. Thus Dulles would report to them, in the meeting of June 5, 1953, his efforts to impress upon India's Prime Minister Nehru the warning, for transmittal to Peiping, that a failure in armistice negotiations in Korea would mean "a bigger war." And two weeks later the Cabinet's scheduled meeting fell on the day of the ominous news from Korea that President Syngman Rhee had brashly upset the agreement on exchange of prisoners—of war—by releasing thousands of anti-Communist North Korean prisoners. As Dulles and Eisenhower commented on the crisis imperiling all hopes of a Korean armistice, and as messages of alarm cabled from Korea were rushed to the Secretary of State, all members of the Cabinet became rapt eyewitnesses to one of the classic nightmares of diplomacy—the I-can-attend-to-my-enemies-but-God-protect-me-from-my-friends situation. From the first moment of this crisis, Eisenhower was poised and determined to force Rhee back to rationality—as he shortly did—and he even greeted the perilous situation with wry humor: "Well, we can all relax and start understanding the British in Iran a little better. Now we have *our* Mossadegh." But the reckless folly of Rhee gradually enraged him to exclaim: "This thing is so foolish as to be fantastic."* He always retained a gift for somehow conveying—with

* Cabinet meeting, June 19, 1953.

most eloquent wrinkling of brow and bulging of eyes—an astonishment akin to awe when forced to gaze at a spectacle of dramatic and aggressive stupidity. And he would display this amazement again, in 1956, as he wonderingly watched Great Britain and France join Israel in their attack upon the Suez.

On other occasions, the Cabinet was treated to general reviews of foreign affairs by Dulles. Most often, these dissertations reflected Dulles' curious capacity to sound, at one and the same time, glowingly optimistic and darkly belligerent. An event like the dramatic fall of Beria, in July of 1953, sufficed to impel him to expand happily upon "Soviet weakness." One practical spur to such talk was the need that he felt to combat "economy" drives threatening to cripple American foreign policy. Quite deliberately, he sought to blunt such attacks by dangling before the eyes of his Cabinet colleagues some all-too-bright vision of immediate diplomatic triumph—as if inviting them to enter the future prospect on mental ledgers, to offset the current price tags on defense and mutual security programs. An almost evangelical fervor, however, often seemed to propel him beyond such pragmatic intent, and he would declaim: "This is the kind of time when we ought to be *doubling* our bets, not reducing them—as all the Western parliaments want to do. This is the time to *crowd* the enemy—and maybe *finish* him, once and for all. But if we're dilatory, he can consolidate—and probably put us right back where we were."* Such impassioned words seemed to imply an extraordinary amount of national strategy and world history to be geared to even so dramatic an event as the fall of Beria. And at these times I could not help feeling—a little uneasily—that, for the Secretary of State, all the world of nations threatened to become a little like a secret chessboard, whose pieces moved through elaborate and mysterious gambits, fully witnessed and shrewdly influenced only by himself.

And the Cabinet served, too, as an arena for conflict, however

---

* Cabinet meeting, July 10, 1953.

muted, with the issue of domestic economy vs. world responsibility threatening to trouble the surface of every session. Few men
present felt greater distress than Henry Cabot Lodge at the
threat of deep cutbacks in expenditures vital to supporting foreign policy. As he heatedly exclaimed to me on one of his weekly
visits from the United Nations to the White House: "We are
just too damn worried about Taft and the leaders. They don't
carry as much weight as they dream—even in the Senate—and
they don't matter a *damn* in the country. We won one election
despite them, and we can go on winning. Besides, they have *nowhere* to go but to be with *us*. And the one thing we can *not*
afford to do is to hand Symington and the Democrats a nice major
issue like the charge that 'big business' ideas are shortchanging the
nation's security." It was pithily said. But such sentiments seemed
smothered in the kind of reviews of the budget that Humphrey
impressed upon the Cabinet. One typical and striking exchange
came with a Cabinet meeting late in May, as Humphrey lamented
that his mathematical projection to 1955 forewarned of a $9.5
billion deficit. So bleak a prospect, he declared, "takes us right
back to Truman." And then . . .

Humphrey. "I'll tell you what this means. We have got to get
our budget down to between $60 and $62 billion in 1955. And
to justify *tax cuts*, at all, we have to get $12 to $15 billion *more*
out. In other words, we've just scratched the surface. We have
to do a hell of a lot more. We've got to revise whole programs.
And this means *surgery*."

Wilson. "That means you want at least $10 billion more cut out
of Defense and MSA."

Humphrey. "Charley, that's right. You just got to get out the
best damn *streamlined model* you ever did in your life. And you
have to do it in six months, not three years. This means *a brand
new model—we can't just patch up the old jalopy*."

President. "Well, there are two horns to this dilemma, you
know. Charley's being attacked right now for not spending
enough."

Dodge. "What all this boils down to is this: unless we do something drastic, as George says, we'll be in the same position at the start of 1955 as we were at the start of this year."

Humphrey. "It's *just* like reorganizing a whole *business*. It's got to be done from top to bottom."

President. "Well, there's one particular reason why we can't delay in facing up to this. If we should see that it *can't* be done —just as soon as we see that—we have to be absolutely honest, and say as much to the country, and not go on kidding them and ourselves."

Humphrey. "Well, I believe it *can* be done. I'm expendable, and I'm glad to go out on a limb and say I believe it, because we have to have something to shoot at."

President. "My God, when you think of the pressure and the pressure groups . . . the bills for the farmers . . . and the veterans . . . my God . . ."

Lodge. "Well, look at them—why can't a lot of this saving come from any place else other than Defense?"

Dodge. "This is why, Cabot. Out of $23 billion in *non*-defense spending, more than half of it—debt servicing, social security, veterans, and so on—is really untouchable. So what have you got to work with?"*

As the Cabinet was a remarkably true mirror to the whole political life of the Eisenhower administration—and all its attitudes and prejudices, convictions and conflicts—so, inevitably, its surface did not merely reflect sharp and vivid images. It clouded, again and again, with the film of irresolution and vacillation. And it bore, too, the dark fleck-spots of the half-acts and the broken gestures, the halting assertions and the hesitant rebuttals —all befitting an Administration in painful quest of its true identity.

There were two somewhat serious, somewhat comic, issues continually plaguing the first score or more of Eisenhower

---

* Cabinet meeting, May 22, 1953.

Cabinet meetings. Their protracted discussion was tortuous and typical. One of these matters entailed a procurement dilemma confounding Defense Secretary Wilson. And the other involved the Bricker Amendment.

The unsuspecting Cabinet was first introduced to Wilson's procurement problem at an early March meeting. Initially, the dilemma did not seem appallingly intricate. The Department of Defense, having invited bids from British as well as American firms for generators for the Chief Joseph Dam, had been disconcerted to receive one British bid as much as 12 percent lower than its nearest American competitor. Under the law, the Secretary had discretion in such matters, so long as the protected American bidder did not exceed his lowest foreign competitor by 25 percent. What should the Secretary do? On the one hand, Wilson observed that American industry wanted this contract badly; maintenance was easier on American rather than foreign equipment; and might not a war erupt, in the course of the next two years, to bar delivery of the British equipment? On the other hand, as Wilson uncertainly posed his quandary to the Cabinet, there was the President's known concern for freer commerce within the Western world. Moreover, the high cost of "protection" for American industry was rather troubling to an Administration frantic for ways to save money. Wilson concluded with a simple: "Well, Mr. President? . . ." After some diffuse general discussion, the President murmured: "Well, just shooting from the hip, I'd say to give the order to the British."*

The unreassuring vagueness of this response was to cost both President and Cabinet months of meetings almost never free from reversion to the unresolved matter. And the high price of procrastination, in session upon session, was to be recorded thus—in my notes of the time . . .

* Cabinet meeting, March 6, 1953.

March 13 . . . President is prompted to talk ardently on subject of freer trade—by specific pressure to raise tariffs on Italy's briar pipes. (Can't be done, at least not with Italian elections soon, and he will reject urgings.) He thinks there ought to be "a continuing body like the National Security Council" to prepare in advance the meeting of such tariff and trade questions. Oddly, however, there is no *specific* reference back to the problem of Wilson's generators—still unresolved.

March 27 . . . Toward end of meeting, Wilson brings up his generators—and says he will give contract to American firm even though it will cost Defense $1 million. Bedell Smith, sitting in for State in Dulles' absense, reports that London is intently watching this episode as serious test of whether Eisenhower means what he says about freer trade. Wilson admits a lot of senatorial pressure on behalf of Westinghouse. President asks: "But I thought they had just about all the business they could handle, no?" Wilson answers: "Yeah—but they wouldn't mind at all having this, too." He admits decision is "close call" but "thinks" verdict is for Westinghouse. No one seems happy. No one dissents.

April 3 . . . News of prospective snubbing of British bid on generators has gotten out, and item is on the Cabinet agenda. President has had strong note from British Ambassador on case, and Dulles speaks up: "If the *Executive* doesn't show a strong lead in these trade questions, how in the world can you expect to get the *Congress* to go along with knocking down trade barriers?" Wilson replies that so many senators are urging an American firm on this contract and that accepting the British bid might lead them to turn their fire on the whole business of renewal of the Trade Agreements Act. Nixon sides briefly with Dulles. President adds nothing. And Wilson finally murmurs—as debate dissipates toward nothing—that he wants to double-check specifications to be sure British will produce "same quality" product as Americans. Transparent evasion.

April 10 . . . Unpleasant sound of whirring generators again. Wilson reports he's decided to start all over with a call for new bids. Steely, Dulles leans forward in front of President to say directly to Wilson, on other side of President: "I have an increasingly strong suspicion that the British are never going to get this contract." Wilson slides off into disquisition on engineering complexity of objects in question: "You gotta be sure they're all putting the same amount of copper into these things." President seems to acquiesce: "Well, all right, Charley. But let's be sure the new specifications are really on the level—and not drawn so that *only* an American firm can meet them." This provokes some titters of amusement—till Adams suddenly leans forward for one of his most rare interventions. And this one is acid: "Would it not be more straight to send new and detailed specifications *only* to the original lowest bidder—if it really *is* a question of his fully meeting the specifications? Otherwise, this all looks like a rather diabolical way of getting foreign bidders to tip their hands and letting American companies have a second chance to undercut them." The logic is so elemental it imposes on all assembled a full ten seconds of rather embarrassed silence. Discussion fogs and closes. Wilson leaves, free to play with new bids.

May 22 . . . A belated postscript of the Chief Joseph generators—the contract for which ended, to no one's surprise, by going to American manufacturers. Wilson now has another dam—another set of British bids—another irresolution. He makes an honest thrust at avoiding repetition of such situations with suggestion of an arbitrary 5% "bulge" he would allow the American competitor: any larger margin of saving in a foreign bid would dictate its acceptance. But the President, noting that the criterion is technically arbitrary, demurs that "we can't bind ourselves to a fixed rule." When one Cabinet member begs for "at least a clear direction to our policy," President surprisingly shies back: "Well, I'm not even sure about that. Our policy must depend, for example, on the level of employment here at home." Finally, fatuity sets in. Humphrey contributes: "Our only fixed yardstick can be whatever's in the best interest of America." President closes discussion with philosophizing: "Yes, but the problem is to determine what that interest is."

These few specific exchanges may suggest why—for all the sporadic zeal displayed over the years by the President in championing of freer trade—his Administration would end with so modest an achievement in so crucial a cause.

The tale of the Bricker Amendment, as symptom and as portent, proved monotonously identical. For Eisenhower, this question fast became "a damn thorn in our side." For a full year, he and the Administration scratched and picked at it, tried needles and poultices, and finally had to lance it with direct action. All the tedious while, however, it reflected two kinds of constant Administration travail: the intellectual contortions through

which so many Republicans suffered in order to try to "repudiate" the Democratic past, and the political contortions through
which the Administration struggled in order to try to appease its
own party's congressional leadership.

The amendment, introduced by a resolution of Ohio's Senator
John W. Bricker a few days before Eisenhower took office,
sought so drastically to limit presidential treaty-making power,
and to enhance congressional control of the conduct of foreign
affairs, that it would have virtually stripped the President of
authority to make even routine executive agreements. Thus it
struck another blow at the specter of "secret agreements" darkly
attributed to Yalta and Potsdam. And thus, too, it snared even
Dulles a little, for—resolutely as he was to fight the amendment
now—his own past critiques of Democratic foreign policy had
actually paid the amendment some courteous tribute. This was
embarrassing enough, but the Democrats were cheerfully making it more so, as Dulles glumly noted in Cabinet: "They're
being damn smart. They're casting themselves in the role of
Eisenhower supporters, just the way they played it in the declaration of Yalta."* Obviously, no one could accuse the Republicans of being stingy with the opportunities—for advantage or
amusement—which they were pressing upon their opponents.

The President spent pained months—and the Cabinet hours
beyond number—trying to avoid what Eisenhower glumly
called "a head-on collision over this darn thing." One week,
the Cabinet merely groaned at the dilemma; another week they
pressed on George Humphrey the vain expedient of trying to
deter his friend and fellow-Ohioan in the Senate; yet another
week, they schemed of getting some philanthropy to set up a
study group to be called the "Bricker Commission"—in the hope
the President was right that "all Bricker wants is something
big in public with his name on it." At one point the President,
listening to the latest accounts of trying to appease Bricker, cried

* Cabinet meeting, March 13, 1953.

in anguish: "I'm so sick of this I could scream. The whole damn thing is senseless and plain damaging to the prestige of the United States. We talk about the French not being able to govern themselves—and *we* sit here wrestling with a *Bricker* Amendment."* Yet a few weeks later his own impulse to conciliate could not be suppressed, and the President personally tried to work out with Bricker some compromise wording on an "innocuous" declaration. He did this despite the sensible caution from Dulles that, in Constitutional terms, no future decision of the Supreme Court could be expected to interpret and construe a *new* amendment as intended only to *reiterate* the original intent of the Constitution. When Bricker's continued intransigence, even on language, spared everyone this dilemma, the President returned to crying impatiently: "If we can't get thirty-three senators to vote with us, what kind of a *team* is this?" But, after six months of trying to persuade Senate Republicans not to humiliate their own President, Nixon still felt he had to caution the Cabinet: "Well, there's just no doubt there's a lot of public support for this amendment. You take a fellow like Lyndon Johnson. He says he doesn't think it's wise at all, but he's going to vote for it. And you ask him why, and he says simply: 'Because all my people in Texas want it.'" At this, the weary and unhappy Dulles exclaimed sharply: "We just have to make up our minds and stop being fuzzy on this."†

And thus the issue droned on—until its dreary climax the following year. The senator from Ohio was cheered on, all the while, by the Chicago *Tribune*, the Daughters of the American Revolution, the Vigilant Women for the Bricker Amendment, and an ex-President of the American Bar Association whom

* Cabinet meeting, April 3, 1953.
† Cabinet meeting, July 17, 1953. At this particular point in the discussion, Eisenhower said tartly to Dulles: "I haven't been fuzzy about this. There was nothing fuzzy in what I told Bricker. I said we'd go just so far and no further." And in a rare show of exasperation with the President, Dulles retorted just as sharply: "I know, sir, but you haven't told anybody else."

Eisenhower bitingly described as a man bravely determined "to save the United States from Eleanor Roosevelt." And Bricker marched to the Senate floor, waving aloft a favorable report on his amendment from the Senate Judiciary Committee. So, finally, the President had to hand to Knowland a letter containing a flat declaration: "I am unalterably opposed. . . . Adoption [of the Amendment as drawn] would be notice to our friends as well as our enemies abroad that our country intends to withdraw from its leadership in world affairs." Even so solemn a warning swayed but a few of the President's own leaders on the Hill. The amendment was defeated by only a narrow margin. And a substitute amendment, slightly tempered, missed passage by only one vote, while it received the support of Knowland himself.

The image of government process and presidential leadership, as caught and reflected in the mirror of the Cabinet, was thus no brightly shining sight, constant and clear.

Yet, time and again, something on the shadowed surface would glint . . .

It could start from the mention of an isolated fact—like the overexpansion of the tin mines of Bolivia. From there, the President would begin, wanderingly, to allude to the precarious state of so many one-product national economies, almost helplessly scattered through Latin America. And rather suddenly, something more meaningful would be on the minds of men present, as Eisenhower warmed to the subject . . .

"You know, we sit here and talk, all too rarely, about one commodity in one country, out of all the American republics. Yet when we speak of the affairs of Europe, we talk on a totally different level. Unity, unity, unity: we say it over and over. And we think back to Charlemagne, and we try to plan or lead ahead toward something better and stronger for Europe as a whole.

"But what is true for one continent should be just as true for another. We have to begin and look at all of Latin America— and look at *it* as a *whole*. We, with all our urgings to the nations of Europe to achieve some kind of unity—I don't know why *they* have not chided *us* long ago about this Western Hemisphere. Why are we not thinking and planning a design for unity here?"*

In the air of the Cabinet room, such a question floated, hovered a moment, then vanished in the silence. Yet for such instants, whenever they came, one caught a glimpse, through the tall glass doors of the Cabinet room facing southward, of a world wider and larger and grander than the long soft green slope of the White House lawn.

6

A witness to the men and the councils and the events of these times had to sense, within himself, doubt and debate.

I knew there was much here to mourn, even to ridicule. There were the narrow and shallow beliefs about the structure of government, the play of politics, even the world crisis for freedom itself. There were the frayed prejudices and the worn clichés of an almost obsolete partisan vocabulary. There were the elaborate rites performed, the solemn incantations uttered, the political superstitions perpetuated—in the name of Republican orthodoxy. There was sadly much, indeed, that seemed laughable.

Yet merely to jest or to grieve—or to despair—was too facile and too simple. For the evidence seemed mixed, and even its portents seemed confused. I felt a certain envy, at times, for those brisk and confident critics who saw the whole scene bathed in the glowing light of their own certitude. Theirs appeared a delightfully lucid vision: all facts and persons, all forces and problems, drawn up in martial array—like toy soldiers upon a neat field of felt—with a clean, open space between to divide all things right from all things wrong, as befitted two little armies

* Cabinet meeting, July 3, 1953.

in precise and direct confrontation. And yet, one could not, for long, covet the beholding of such a simplified vision. For it, too, was laughable.

There were times when I wrote, to friends or in my diary, of the inner debate. Doubt and ire alternated with compassion and hope. And so I could optimistically contend on one occasion, writing to critical friends:

On the world scene, there is still reason to feel that the perspective of an Eisenhower will prevail over the view of a Dulles. The fact is that even the first year is marked by an end to the Korean War—despite Dulles' ambiguous approach to the fact—and by at least a fervent affirmation of intent both toward disarmament and toward more direct encounter with Soviet diplomacy. As for the national scene: the man in the White House is engaged in the most complex of political tasks—nothing less than the rebuilding of a national party, so that it can be a healthy and responsible instrument of American democracy. This transcends partisan objectives: it is a *national* necessity that there be a vigorous and thoughtful second party. He has had to begin with a party so remote from the real-life exercise of responsibility that only one Republican alive in the Senate has ever known the simple experience of serving under a Republican President. So the labor is going to take time and skill and prudence and patience—lots of patience—maybe more than you or I will be able to bear.

Other moments bristled with their own bitter retorts to this calm counsel. And thus, in quite different temper, I wrote harshly in my own notes, after one Cabinet meeting:

Dulles reported with spontaneous self-congratulation on his meeting with Foreign Ministers Bidault and Salisbury which ended three days ago. *Most* gratifying (to him) was final declaration's pledge of concern over "true liberty" for East European peoples—which he hails as "the first time to my knowledge that London and Paris have been willing to embrace this principle."* Does he really believe such

* Cabinet meeting, July 17, 1953.

147

words are going to free anyone, any people? . . . *Next* most gratifying (to him) was the very heavy pressure we brought to bear on "the
French" to ratify EDC. Maybe he can succeed—but does he really
think lecturing Bidault here in Washington will swing many votes in
the French National Assembly? . . . Looking back to the beginning
—and asking, how far have we really come?—I cannot see the distance
as reason for anyone's pride. So little has been done. Worse still is the
amazing infatuation of so many with the sound of their own voices—
as if, for example, *speaking* of an event like Beria's fall or internal
crisis in the Kremlin amounts to having *caused* such things. I was
stunned just yesterday to hear O. [an aide in Dulles' office] orate on
the phone: "Well, this is the time for us to *talk it up*—remind people
how our policy has been getting results right on down the line. *Anyone* can see, with this business of Beria, that we're accomplishing
everything we *said* we could with a *dynamic* policy." The sheer fantasy of it! The raw truth is that Washington has been confronted with
rare political *opportunities* in these months—Stalin's death, the uneasy
Kremlin triumvirate, the heroic revolt of East Berliners, the Beria crisis
—and I defy anyone to show how *American* action has imaginatively
capitalized on a single thing that has come to pass.

The churning debate within one's self thus went on and on,
now veering toward a hesitant verdict of hope, now swerving
toward the final indictment of despair. In the swirl of all un-
certainties, one fact alone stayed firm and clear. And this was
the towering fact that all things would totally depend upon one
man.

This fact carried one, however, not a step toward the comfort
of greater assurance. I had come to know the man, better and
better. Yet the man himself so often seemed a little like a debate
come to life.

His image and profile seemed superbly clear and sharp—from
a distance. For *was* he not a simple man—a man as personally
uncomplex as he was politically unsophisticated? Was he not,
beyond doubt, an individual of immense good will, great warmth
with people, slight interest in politics, paltry regard for ideas,
no sensitivity to words? Even his diversions seemed appropriately conventional: much golf, some painting, a little reading of

light fiction. A man whose temperament must be as sunny as his smile, he would be expected to preside placidly and gently over the more rugged and forceful men around him. No man to incite the great passions—either fervent admiration or angry hostility —he was a man with whom to be *comfortable*, was he not? No man to nourish lusty ambitions, either for his person in politics or his nation in the world, he was a man to trust. Surely, above all, he was a man to *like*. And this was precisely how the many millions of his people hailed him.

Thus did Eisenhower appear—from a distance.

To come closer was to discern the greater complexity.

His mere mood of the day was unpredictable and volatile. The more anxious White House aides watched even the color of his suits, as he appeared of a morning in his office, fancying that they here discerned a cipher to warn them of the emotions ahead. (Brown clothes, so some insisted, foretold black moods.) As warm and winning as his smile were his frequent gestures of appreciation for help given and work done. But an unwelcome report of some baseless criticism or some unfinished labor or some blemished performance could ignite an explosion of temper almost fiercely physical. His voice would shout, his cheeks flame with rage, his arms wave threateningly. And I recall one of his oldest White House associates murmuring, after witnessing one such scene: "My God, how could you compute the amount of adrenalin expended in those thirty seconds? I don't know why long since he hasn't had a killer of a heart attack."

He was the genial and gregarious man whose face glowed with pleasure before cheering political throngs, as he raised both arms high in salute—stretched out far, as if he would embrace all who were so fond and generous in their acclaim. The thrill of such moments was real and deep. But so, too, was the private distaste for "the killing motorcades" and "another yowling mob" and "the unattractive lot" of local politicians. And, in almost exactly matching paradox, he could turn either eagerly toward the word of approval—or contemptuously—from the word of dissent. He would chew his lips with nervous anger, on hearing certain kinds of criticism, especially charges of lax leadership or confused foreign policy; and he could smile broadly in appreciation of a compliment to the contrary. Yet he stubbornly refused to pay even passing heed to daily editorials or columns or telecasts, and he would burst forth impatiently if a member of the Cabinet even casually alluded to any such source of comment: "Listen! Anyone who has time to listen to commentators or read columnists obviously doesn't have enough work to do."

No less anomalous were his displays of care—and disdain—for words themselves. In press conferences or extemporaneous speeches, he conveyed an appreciation of syntax and grammar roughly comparable to George Humphrey's regard for Fabian socialism, deficit spending, and runaway inflation. Yet he would edit a speech draft with a penetrating sense of the structure of an argument and a precise concern for the balance of a sentence, the tense of a verb, or the force of an adjective.

Paradox, too, seemed to mark many of his personal views of the nature of the world itself. Perhaps no adjective figured so prominently in his political vocabulary as "spiritual," and his spontaneous speeches were rich with exhortations on America's "spiritual" strength. Yet his personal concern with either religion or philosophy appeared casual at best. He enrolled in the Presbyterian church in Washington after his election in a spirit suggesting merely that he viewed the act as vaguely appropriate to the presidential office. And the ritual of the Cabinet prayer was performed with the same perfunctory air. Beguilingly and characteristically casual was his offhand remark to the Cabinet one morning: "Saw a really fine film on Luther last night. I suppose some Catholics might resent it, but—what the devil—it was all four hundred years ago anyway, wasn't it?"[*]

His breadth and sensitivity of view in international affairs were attested by oft-repeated convictions. The drive for West European unity, the need for freer world trade, the crucial impor-

---

[*] Cabinet meeting, May 22, 1953.

tance of the Anglo-American alliance, the indispensability of mutual security programs, the wisdom of greater rather than less economic contact with the Communist world—all these concepts were firmly anchored in his thinking. Yet the man whose mature life had been so largely shaped in the international world, and the man who repeatedly affirmed his eager readiness to "travel" anywhere in quest of peace, could sometimes blurt out to the Cabinet such anachronistic laments as: "This idea of the President of the United States going personally abroad to negotiate— it's just damn stupid. Every time a President has gone abroad to get into the details of these things, he's lost his *shirt*."* This, nonetheless, was the man who was more intellectually at home in a meeting of NATO than in a meeting of the Republican National Committee; a man who knew Harold Macmillan not merely as a foreign dignitary but as a trusted comrade from wartime North Africa; a man whose sense of friendship—and sense of history—bound him closer to a Winston Churchill than to a Robert Taft; and a man whose discernment made him far more tolerant of the grand egoism of a De Gaulle than of the petty vanity of a Knowland.

At this intersection of the personal and the political, there occurred other curious encounters. His sense of personal loyalty, like his sense of personal integrity, was alert and lively, expressing itself in warm and kind gestures that seemed the surface signs of deep attachments. Yet he *had* been able to perform in 1952 the act of self-censorship to erase publicly his tribute to General George Marshall—who had picked Eisenhower for the wartime North Africa campaign, had defended him in Washington against all critics, and had nominated him as Supreme Commander for the Normandy invasion. Even the memory of this bleak event seemed erased from his mind, like the words left unspoken. At the peak of the outcry for some presidential retort to McCarthy's assaults on American foreign policy, Eisenhower could review recent political history with a human inclination to

* Cabinet meeting, July 17, 1953.

revise it conveniently, as he assured the Cabinet: "Back in the campaign, we compromised with this fellow not at all. We set our course, and we didn't deviate an *inch* from it."*

The unexpected and the contradictory did not flare merely in some sudden crisis or hasty response: they seemed threaded through his whole social and economic philosophy. The instinct for frugality was strong and swift to find voice—whether he were tartly mocking the expense of maintaining military attachés in embassies or shouting after George Humphrey, as the Secretary of the Treasury excused himself from the Cabinet to join talks with a visiting French delegation: "Please save us a few billion, George!"† His frequent homilies on "free enterpise" and "private initiative" were underscored by dire, vague warnings on the dangers of "regimentation" and "the barrack state." And he singled out the Tennessee Valley Authority as a symbol of monstrous federal violation of the "freedom" of the economy, exclaiming to one Cabinet meeting: "By God, if ever we could do it, before we leave here, I'd like to see us *sell* the whole thing, but I suppose we can't go that far."‡ *And yet* . . . another Cabinet meeting could hear the President excoriate the House of Representatives as "fools" for slashing appropriations for HEW's Office of Education—a classic target for Republican budget-cutters. "If any of those darn fools were running for re-election right now," he cried, "they'd lose the vote of every *liberal* in the country—and that includes me."§ And his views on tariff and trade *were* liberal enough to outrage most Republican leaders.

A soldier, then—in attitudes and responses? Yes, in many ways—and in others, not at all. His daily speech often slipped into military vernacular. His methods of work even more emphatically reflected his training: a reliance on oral briefings, a shunning of copious documents, an appreciation of the terseness

* Cabinet meeting, March 13, 1953.
† Cabinet meeting, March 27, 1953.
‡ Cabinet meeting, July 31, 1953.
§ Cabinet meeting, July 3, 1953.

of a memorandum. And still more obvious, of course, was his reliance upon the staff system that essentially left to others the initiative for both information and execution. Nowhere did the lack of civilian experience so betray itself as in this system's cheerful assumption that, once the Chief Executive had pointed in a certain political direction, the full force of government would move in that direction, in concert as precise and as massive as battalions and divisions wheeling through field maneuvers. *And yet*—there were some strikingly unmilitary qualities to his political behavior. He coldly scorned the vanities of ostentatious command, all the paraphernalia of martial arrogance. While the force of his presence and personality assured his authority in Cabinet or conference, he actually presided over all such meetings with a laxness hardly conceivable in an army command post. And below the surface of mere procedure, at the deeper level of his political self-awareness, he forever stayed serene and firm in his disinterest toward his opposition—his profound conviction that he must see himself, and speak for himself, in detached and absolute terms, never in relation to a foe or a critic. No military campaign ever was conceived in this spirit that wholly ruled his political campaigns. And indeed some of the most crucial of his political beliefs and practices—the self-limiting view of the Executive's relationship to the Congress, or the self-denying concept of leadership by gentle indirection—almost seemed born of some deep, secret resolve to abjure all habits of thought and behavior born of a military experience.

And if there were signs of deliberate reticence or withdrawal in his political behavior, they were hardly less marked in his personal relations. With the trophies and tribute of World War II all around him, yet he could turn as shy, in the face of a direct compliment, as a young officer hearing his superior's first commendation. He could extend and convey appreciation with a gentle clap on the shoulder, a slight smile, and a half-broken phrase; but he could bestow a complete, resounding compliment no more easily than he could receive one. And thus his daily demeanor stayed singularly barren of full and open expressions of inner thought and direction. Typically and significantly, the decisive political comradeship of his regime, so slow in forming through the months and years, would be his association with John Foster Dulles. Yet the sealing of this bond would be marked by no visible testimonials, no evidence more apparent than the gradual modification of the President's initial display of simple boredom.

He was not, then, exactly a simple man.

He bore some marks of character and temper beyond doubt or qualification: a formidable honesty, a rare humility, a sense of dignity, an abhorrence of pretense, a distaste for all self-seeking, a tireless will to conciliate, a speechless horror of war, and a restless hope for peace.

The rest, so it seemed, was unresolved.

The gregarious man was shy.

The man deeply stirred by demonstrations was undemonstrative.

The man with the glowing smile had a thunderous temper.

The internationally minded leader of the Western world was a frugal Kansan.

The soldier shunned and renounced the trappings, even the weapons, of political command.

The man whom the throngs cheered and *liked*—with a warmth extended to only one other President in more than a generation . . . the man toward whom they seemed so eagerly to reach, as one akin to themselves in feeling and manner and speech and countenance . . . this man was, singularly, a man who stood alone.

And one could not but wonder at times if he were not, too, a lonely man.

CHAPTER FIVE

The Scene from Afar

There came now a kind of intermission, personal and political, that shifted the focus and range of my own vision as a witness. This interlude offered the perspective of distance, with its chance for a few new insights. And these had some relevance to the story of the unfolding Eisenhower Years . . .

For the greater part of 1954 and 1955, following my resignation from the White House staff to return gladly to journalism, I found myself far from the Washington scene and once again a foreign correspondent, crisscrossing Europe from Moscow to Madrid, from Athens to London. During these months, all the great political issues summoning one's scrutiny seemed almost equally ambiguous and uncertain: the slow-forming profile of European unity, the restless enigma of Soviet Communism, and the blurred shape of American foreign policy. In my own traveling and searching, I visited occasionally, and watched thoughtfully, a Mendès-France, vaulting out of, and tumbling back into, the whirlpool of French politics . . . in England, an aging Churchill in the statelier ceremony of sadly passing on his power to an aspiring Eden . . . and in Germany, an Adenauer, disdaining all surrenders of power, ceremonial or convulsive, and merely threatening with magnificent stubbornness to become a political immortal. Between all journeys to see such men and their political environs, I lived in Rome. And, as the months passed, I came to accept the fact that most things in the world, as viewed from the edge of the Tiber, looked remarkably as they had when scanned from the shore of the Potomac.

A great deal of all that one saw or heard in Europe, throughout this time, amounted essentially to reflections or echoes of the world of Washington. There stirred in every Foreign Office the questions about Eisenhower, phrased with mingled affection and anxiety: why was he the kind of a leader he *seemed* to be—and exactly what kind *was* this, anyway? There persisted everywhere the nagging European doubt and distrust toward Republicanism: were its leaders still secretly a little addicted to the drug of isolationism—some still growling that Europe meant nothing to America but debts and dangers, others still hailing Chiang Kai-shek as freedom's sword and savior in Asia? And—above all—there carried through the official circles of all West European capitals the wonderment about John Foster Dulles: what *did* he have in mind with all his rhetoric about "liberation"? And did he really regard the notion of "negotiation" as such a diplomatic indecency?

Shrewd and caustic and searching as were its questions, however, the Europe of these years, in mood or in resolve, could itself lay no serious claim to offering or inspiring the leadership that seemed wanting in America. For this continent, broadly, was a place of more prosperity than pride, more complacence than ardor. The memory of war still hurt and haunted, so that the challenges of peace were numbing rather than rousing. This Europe cherished all new and healing comforts of commerce and abundance. It wished to turn its face from any ugly omens of the future. Most of all, it wanted to stuff its ears against any exhortations, warnings, sermons—shouted from an ocean away—that might command it to shoulder arms, lower tariffs, raise taxes, and shake fists at Moscow. It was a place—and a time and a spirit—easy to indict for want of honest passion or militant principle. Yet it was equally easy to indict a Washington for apparent ignorance of the kind of audience upon which it was wasting its harangues.

The American presence in Europe—the *official* presence—bore, more plainly than all else, the marks and scars of Washington. In particular, it showed the raw wounds of McCarthyism. The American ambassadors outraged by the seeming timidity of their Secretary of State, the lesser Foreign Service officers frightened into purging their reports of critical candor, the American loss of pride in confronting foreign critics left aghast (or maliciously amused) by the vulgar spectacle of vilification in Washington—all these were hidden costs to the nation, never entered in the books of the Eisenhower administration, as it reckoned the practical value of appeasing Republican congressional leadership. Perhaps less stark but no less baleful was the effect of the autocratic kind of leadership that Dulles had imposed upon State Department and Foreign Service. To ambassadors in the field, the Secretary's decisions seemed imperious and his communications negligent. The American ambassador to West Germany told me of relying upon his airmail editions of New York newspapers for insight into policies concerning Germany, as these might be forming in Washington. The ambassador to the Soviet Union was instructed, on one occasion, to advise the Soviet Foreign Minister of an imminent and important presidential speech—but the ambassador himself was not allowed to know the essential content of the speech even for his own information. And the rigid and doctrinaire quality of Dulles' whole concept of world diplomacy made still a third ambassador exclaim to me: "We are engaged in the deadliest possible encounter of will and wits with the Soviet Union. It simply is not possible to conduct such a duel with one's shoes nailed to the floor."

While these were the somber facts to be faced in Western Europe, there were other truths as pertinent and as urgent to be learned—so I believed—to the east. I found my own journey to Moscow at this time, in fact, impelling me to look back thoughtfully—and to write back earnestly—to the White House where I had so recently been. Some whim of Soviet bureaucracy made me the first American correspondent to receive a Soviet visitor's visa in the post-Stalin era, and I was most swiftly impressed by one obvious truth of Russian life. This was the fact that Soviet domestic concerns ruled Soviet policy, more directly and more compellingly, than theoretical Leninist designs for world conquest. Already, early in 1954, the Soviet scene showed sure signs of change, as the tight reins of Stalinism began to loosen. Authority and austerity, in their Stalinist extremes, were fast slipping from fashion as "the new *bourgeoisie*" of Soviet bureaucracy both sighed with relief at the curbing of secret police powers, and sighed with longing for more decent consumer goods in stores and homes. The basic temper of all Europe's peoples thus seemed to defer to no limit of national boundaries or ideological curtain—as Moscow shared with Rome and Paris and London a pacific and self-indulgent mood, stubbornly resistant to political exhortations to sacrifice.

All this made me question more deeply than ever some premises of American policy. And as my thoughts went back to the White House, so also went some gratuitous observations written to the President . . .

There was one dominant thought with which I left Moscow. . . . If the Soviet Union is politically and psychologically geared for major aggressive war, then we're living in the sixteenth century—and I'm Martin Luther.

It must sound frivolous to utter so dogmatic a conviction . . . but —aside from the manifest seriousness of the economic shifts going on within the USSR—there is a *sense* of things, a simple but compelling intuition, which I suspect is as often right in such matters as the most labored statistical analyses or hush-hush reports from frenzied military attachés. And there is one thing I think it necessary for us all to remember: the colossal Soviet peace propaganda—while it has its obvious self-serving purposes in foreign affairs—is just as real, just as insistent, just as ubiquitous in *domestic* life. The Russian people today are being told with drumbeat insistence not only that their sweetly benevolent government *wants* peace, but also that it will *bring* peace.

If this is the way to gear a poorly fed, poorly housed, warsick people for the savage sacrifices of a major war—well, I'm back in the sixteenth century again. . . . The fact is that the shape and drift of Soviet policy today . . . means that the years immediately ahead are going to be fought in . . . terms of peripheral political warfare. And to this our energies and imagination must be directed.

The President, only a week later, replied with a courteous acknowledgment of this brief analysis. He accepted it as one with which "I have long been in agreement." And I believed this to be quite true, if not always apparent.

We had a yet more full and frank exchange of written beliefs at just this moment. For I found that the burden of political doubts with which I had left Washington did not ease with the passage of time or the remoteness of Europe. It could find some relief, or so I felt, only in an open confession of my anxieties to the President. And accordingly I presumed upon his time and patience to submit a quite explicit catalogue of my concerns . . .

There are a great many ways by which the Administration in the next six months can invite and deserve defeat . . . [in the mid-term congressional elections] and again in 1956. Some of these ways are:

(1) By trying to live off the sins and errors of the past. . . . Any effort to conduct future campaigns by running against Harry Truman will deserve no better—and get no better—than the Democratic effort to run against Herbert Hoover in the last election. . . .

(2) By confusing *public* opinion with *congressional* opinion—and, in such grotesque confusion, assuming that the obstacles and impediments thrown up willfully by members of the Congress are really *popular* restraints and reservations . . . This is not to be contemptuous of a branch of government that should be genuinely co-equal with the Executive. It *is* co-equal. But that status does not demand that another branch of the government be, daily and abidingly, *solicitous*. . . . Public opinion—the kind that is nationwide, that is stirred only by great deeds or great failures—simply does not break down into congressional districts.

159

(3) By forgetting that the seal of victory in 1952 bore, for the American people, the initials DDE and *not* GOP. . . . Deference to the party, with however high a motive, means deferring to a group that the people neither fully know nor fully trust. . . . [In] transferring to the party the confidence that *you* command . . . the full and firm assertion of *your* leadership must come *first*.

(4) By forgetting that the deed—however simple—counts in politics for more than the word—however eloquent. I felt around Washington at times an electrically charged version of [the idea] . . . that "public relations" was about all there was to worry about. . . . To rely on a speech for some kind of triumphant substance is, of course, nonsense. . . .

(5) By assuming that successful political performance consists of placating everyone and alienating none—forgetting that leaders and governments are judged perhaps as much by the readiness to make the right enemies as by their ability to hold good friends. . . .

(6) By forgetting that the *humanity* of government is infinitely more important than its machinery, for the cheapest, smoothest, tidiest government that does not *demonstrate* its heartfelt concern for plain people will get what it deserves—a very short life. . . .

(7) By indefinitely allowing the air of the American capital to be choked with the sickening poison of personal slander, coldly (and stupidly) calculated to destroy men and win elections. . . .

(8) By appearing—on any critical front of our national life—irresolute and indecisive. . . . Through all of this run these words: resolution and decision. In innumerable ways and in innumerable persons, these qualities are present in fact. But in the total impact—the sweeping impression conveyed to whole people by a whole program—they are not yet clearly seen. Good will and virtuous intent, yes. Bold deed and solid achievement, no. . . .

To act with such force is to enable people—at home and abroad—to say: "At last I can *see* the clean, clear lines of this government—nothing blurred or fuzzy about this—*now* they're going to work." . . .

And as for those who think of a growing, revitalized Republican party . . . *this* is the way this party will grow: with noise and bluster and brawling, as well as all the patient behind-the-scenes work that no one hears of. Unity? Of course—but based on principles, not on the lowest common denominator of opinion. . . .

The President had a remarkable reply to all these exhortations and appeals to leadership. It did not come some weeks later—but within ten days. It did not bridle at by bluntness—but warmly welcomed it. And his letter was neither brief nor perfunctory—but six long pages of personal reminiscence and revelation.

For he did not answer in contemporary political terms at all, but in vivid remembrance of the moving and historic moments of his own military life. And through them all he traced the fine, strong thread of one supreme and compelling lesson. . . .

He went back to December of 1941, when he had been summoned to higher command at the War Department in Washington. He recalled the strident cries, in public press and public forum, for dramatic action: anything less was "un-American." He remembered the cries of alarm over the lost garrison on Bataan and the impudent Nazi submarines off the Florida coast. And he remembered, above all, the denunciation of the military leadership of the nation as too cautious, too hesitant, too deliberate.

He went back to November of 1942 and after—following the landings of a great Allied armada in North Africa. Wryly, he recalled the urgings of his own staff that he "personalize" his operations by formally christening "Eisenhower's Headquarters." His officers wanted him "out front" with headline-catching gestures, postures, and pronouncements. Characteristically, he refused.

He went back—next—to the pressures and strains of the months following military victories in North Africa and Italy, when the critical clamor now called for Operation Overlord to rush the invasion of the European mainland. His headquarters were in London, of course, but the cries for bolder leadership sounded as shrill as they had two years earlier in Washington. He bided his time, tended to his preparations—and continued to disdain even reading the newspapers.

The inference from all of this was far from arrogant. He was not exclaiming that he would shortly hurl back all the political challenges before his Presidency, in rout as memorable as the

flight of German armies from Normandy. Rather did he conclude—and passionately insist—that his patience was tested and
strong, in pursuing the kind of leadership that shunned all bluster
of deed and bloating of self. His faith in such leadership had
been proven right before. Why would it not be so again—in
this new arena?

Finally, he surveyed this new arena briefly, with some realism
but with no despair. He acknowledged the burden of the tradi-
tion-bound leadership of the Republican party—a party, as he
conceded, that had viewed the electoral victory of 1952 less as a
threshold of new challenge than as a chance for new jobs. Yet he
saw signs of progress, defying party inhibitions, even on the domestic economic front—with new programs for federal housing
and vast enlargement of unemployment insurance. Above all,
he saw spirit and strength in the "teams" around him—both
the Cabinet group and the Legislative-Executive alliance. And
what could be more welcome to a man seeking to inspire political
change far more deep, far more enduring, than the influence or
the ingenuity of one mere individual, who happened to be President?

Such were the grave and humbling truths of politics, as he
saw them and as he fervently wrote of them.

One could not greet such fervor with a shrug.

One might sigh—with doubt.

And one could only pray that beliefs so decent—by some saving
marvel—would not be held in vain.

2

The Washington scene, then, never slipped far from mind or
view, as one watched, from Europe, the stumbling march of
events on both sides of the Atlantic through these middle months
of the decade . . .

The year 1954 had begun with Dulles' proclamation of the

doctrine of "massive retaliation" by nuclear weapons against any aggressive Communist thrust, and the year ended with Eisenhower's assertion, widely shared, that the danger of war somehow had clearly receded. In the span of time between these two appraisals, there did occur a gradual, perceptible lessening of East-West tension. The Dulles doctrine notwithstanding, a nuclear stalemate was in the making, with America no longer enjoying an H-bomb monopoly. In the running score of the conflicts 'round the world, there were gains and losses for both sides to record and to ponder. The United States could point to successful covert intervention in Guatemala, dispelling a threat of Communist sovereignty there, and to conclusion of a Trieste settlement, checking the danger of strife around the Adriatic. The more grandiloquently proclaimed purposes of American foreign policy, however, did not fare so well. In Europe, summer found the French National Assembly profoundly untroubled by Dulles' threat of an "agonizing reappraisal" of America's role in European defense: the Assembly rejected any French role in the European Defense Community. In the Far East, spring had already witnessed the French disaster of Dienbienphu, and July brought truce and partition in Indochina, now as sundered as Korea. The Western retorts to these reverses were mixed in meaning and efficacy. In the Asian arena, Dulles brandished two pieces of paper. Both were more pretentious than substantial: the signature by eight nations upon the alliance establishing the Southeast Asia Treaty Organization, and the formality of a defense pact with Chiang Kai-shek. In Europe, Eden contributed something more solid: a pledge of British ground forces to Europe's continental defenses.

To provide dubious diversion from the moves and countermoves on the world scene, there was more graphic, if less historic, drama on the Washington scene—notably, as Senator McCarthy and the United States Army entertained millions of television viewers with their fantastic duel. The year ended with the condemnation of the senator, and since the year had begun with the belated, narrow defeat of the Bricker Amendment, the Administration's strenuous work on Capitol Hill could not be counted a total political loss. But while the Congress laboriously fashioned such bizarre footnotes to history, the Supreme Court had briskly written a memorable chapter—with its decision declaring racial segregation in the nation's public schools unconstitutional.

On the partisan political front, one watched—from great distance but with little surprise—a number of predictable occurrences. Nixon, tirelessly campaigning across the nation in support of a Republican majority in the Congress, displayed anew his gift for polemical extravagance. This time his strident campaign charged that Adlai Stevenson and other critical Democrats were senseless servants of Communist propaganda, for they were suggesting to the American people that Soviet economic progress was threatening to pose new and grave challenges to America. The fitting enough reward for such rhetoric was the Democratic recapture of the Congress without much difficulty—but also without much sign that they knew, in foreign or domestic affairs, quite what to do with their victory. Meanwhile, the prospect of diminishing electricity in the international atmosphere, along with more and more Soviet murmurings about "peaceful coexistence," had begun to disturb Senate Majority Leader Knowland. Despite Eisenhower's greater optimism, Knowland warned darkly against the "Trojan horse" of coexistence, and he scowled with disapproval at quickening talk of disarmament in the halls of the United Nations. Exactly one week after these utterances, the politically renowned Soviet envoy to the United Nations, Andrei Y. Vishinsky—presumably unwounded by Knowland's arrows but by natural causes—died.

Viewing the posture of American policy from the far edge of the Atlantic, I felt increasing dismay over its seemingly stiff and sluggish response both to Western Europe's temper and to the Soviet Union's strategy. In London, when Dulles arrived for the Conference of Foreign Ministers called to patch

Western defense designs after French rejection of the EDC, I presumed to ask an hour of his time to hear my lament. This, in essence, amounted to the fear that the United States seemed frozen in a position of hostility toward any diplomatic confrontation with the Soviet Union—a position politically unnatural, diplomatically unfruitful, and impossible to maintain indefinitely. While he confessed that there might be reason for some such concern, he plainly viewed the matter as, at most, a minor question of psychological overtones, or "public relations," rather than of serious substance. So, shortly thereafter, I found myself again writing to the President to describe sorrowfully the growing image of American policy. The words were rather harsh: ". . . a political face of stone—unyielding, unsmiling, and quite without imagination." And there seemed to me a critical choice to be made swiftly by American policy:

There are two different postures we can take whenever the issue of conference with the Russians comes up. The first effectively says: "This is dangerous, these men are insincere . . . and everyone had better keep a tight hand on his wallet." The second says to the world, in so many words: "We have no illusions, but neither will we ever give up hope that reason will finally rule. Conference? All right: we shall do our best. If the Soviets really want to start building for peace, the world and we shall gain. If the Soviets only want to haggle, harass, and divide, then we shall—diplomatically—beat their brains out. Bring 'em on!"

Again, the President's quite prompt reply signified more than his habitual courtesy: obviously, he still preferred close scrutiny of his private mail to even casual scanning of the public press. His words were typically cordial, and appreciative. He lamented the insistent rifle-fire of crises, grave or petty, around the globe, always conspiring to distract Executive attention from basic and enduring issues of war and peace. He deplored, too, the sluggishness of the Europeans, especially the French, in their progress toward military and economic unity. But he spoke no direct response to the matter I had sought to stress—the need for an open, challenging, and unafraid diplomatic posture toward the Soviet Union. And the prospect of some such diplomatic encounter at the "summit" of world politics, I still recall, stirred in my own imagination a vision as crude as a cartoon: the grimacing President, like an alpine climber, scratching and clawing his way toward the peak with one hand—while the other hauled behind him the protesting Secretary of State, one fist protesting furiously and both feet wildly kicking in air. A little too brisk a caricature, I kept cautioning myself, but the fancy would not fade. . . .

The year 1955 saw all these currents of change deepen and widen toward a profound shift in the world struggle, both in strategies employed and in areas contested. After the February fall of Malenkov and the institution of the Khrushchev-Bulganin regime, the thrust of Soviet policy moved quietly but conspicuously away from the military sphere—ruled by atomic stalemate —toward the political and the economic. The shift seemed even more strongly accented by its seeming contrast to the loud belligerence of the Chinese Communists, again threatening assault on Quemoy, Matsu, and Formosa—to which Washington retorted with the congressional resolution authorizing presidential discretion in the use of American forces to defend the offshore islands.*

The Soviet Communists, moreover, seemed to be not only accepting a military stalemate but also inviting a political stalemate on the European front. Thus, in unmistakable succession, there came sudden Soviet concurrence in a treaty recognizing Austrian sovereignty, the resumption of amiable Communist relations with Yugoslavia's Tito, and the establishment of diplomatic relations with Adenauer's West Germany.

---

* There was some irony in the Eisenhower administration's use of the device of this "Formosa Resolution"—in view of the President's solicitude for congressional prerogatives. At a time of international crisis, the risk of encouraging Chinese Communist aggression—by voting against, or even seriously examining, the Resolution—quite effectively deprived the Congress of any chance to speak its own somewhat divided mind.

Soviet attention to its world-design was not lapsing, of course, but merely directing its sights toward "peripheral" areas of the Middle East and South Asia. Thus, just as Great Britain began final withdrawal from its traditional position of power in Egypt, there began the flow of Communist arms to the Egyptian Government. This furbishing of Arab weapons was also well calculated, of course, to help aggravate the new French tragedy beginning in North Africa. And to southern Asia there went not mere weapons but the astonishing presences of Khrushchev and Bulganin themselves, there to blow on the still smoldering embers of anti-colonialism the fiery breath of their denunciations of all Western "imperialists" and "warmongers."

The most memorable diplomatic event of the year, however, occurred at the center of the European stage. In Geneva, in July, there took place the summit conference of the Big Four chiefs of state: Eisenhower and Eden, French Premier Edgar Faure and the Soviet Union's Nikolai Bulganin. It was the first of the Eisenhower administration's direct encounters with the Soviet Union—in the series that would end in Paris in 1960, vainly and dismally, with the fury of Nikita Khrushchev heralding the end of hope.

I had but one brief contact with Eisenhower during these particular days, and this took an oddly personal turn, suggestive of the warmer qualities of the man. In the weeks before the Geneva Conference, I had made a number of visits to Winston Churchill, recently retired to his Chartwell estate in Kent, where he was finishing writing (and I helping to edit for serialization) his *History of the English-Speaking Peoples*. During these lengthy visits, he would, on occasion, summon his thoughts back from Saxons and Normans to speak of Americans and Soviets, or leap from Plantagenets and Tudors to Eisenhower or Adenauer. On one of these visits, only some ten days before the Geneva meeting, the old man could not suppress great emotion as he contemplated the imminent conference. He had so ardently hoped for the meeting to occur during his last months as Prime

Minister, to mark a climactic initiative for peace. And now his pale blue eyes welled with tears, as he looked back upon the unhappy timing of his resignation barely three months earlier. "I did not want to leave," he explained. "But I think the people realized that I did it for the general good, do you not believe?" For days thereafter I could not erase the memory of the sad face and the blinking eyes, watching history—at long last—move pitilessly past, to leave him behind to gape. Hastily, I wrote to the President an irrepressible suggestion that he might send a note to Churchill at this time, to assure the old statesman that his stubborn quest for peace was proceeding even in his absence and stirred by his spirit. From Geneva, on the very eve of the conference and amid all the frenzy of its arrangements, there came a reply from the President—just to assure me that he had written to Churchill before leaving Washington. It seemed the act of a man hardly ever too busy to be kind.

The diplomatic value of the Geneva Conference quickly came into dispute. The event was easy to disparage as a ceremonial conclave whose only explicit achievement consisted of an agenda of unresolved issues for future meetings of foreign ministers to leave still unresolved. Less harshly appraised, it was widely understood to signalize, without articulating, the acceptance by the major powers of the common necessity to shun recourse to nuclear war. And the most generous appraisal was one voiced by Foreign Secretary Harold Macmillan months later: "What struck the imagination of the world was the fact of the friendly meeting between the heads of the two great groups into which the world is divided. . . . I cannot help thinking that . . . [it] was not a vague or sham affair."*

There seemed to me at least two reasons for inclining toward the more sanguine estimate of Macmillan. In the first place, the Eisenhower proposal of "open skies" aerial inspection over American and Soviet soil—although it was dismissed by many

* *Documents on International Affairs*, 1955, Royal Institute of International Affairs, Oxford, 1958, pp. 73–77.

sophisticates of diplomatic reporting as a mere "stunt"—entered the historical record as the first imaginative and specific sequel to the President's initial appeal for world disarmament more than two years earlier. And the impact of this proposal upon the European press and public was nothing less than dramatic, in its crisply eloquent proof of the American desire for peace. In the second place, the simple fact of the physical confrontation between West and East implied—so I dared believe—a renewal of a hope still rooted in the Washington scene: the hope of the gradual ascendancy of Eisenhower's view of the world, prevailing over the stern strictures of his Secretary of State. Vague and diffuse as were the immediate consequences of Geneva, they suggested that there still might be some quiverings of life in that prospect, born on the American political scene in 1952 and so nearly stifled—the prospect of a foreign policy freed from the snarls of domestic politics, personified by a national hero, and directed with suppleness and confidence toward true diplomatic engagement with the Communist world.

Such were the vagrant notions and reflections stirring within me as—living in Rome but looking toward Washington—I watched the approach of the midway point of the Eisenhower Years. They were speculations that still refused to surrender to the outnumbering host of disappointments. They spelled out a lingering kind of hope—even though, were the word itself to be written, the pen would have had to trail off in a final, faltering scrawl of doubt.

And such hope of the moment suffered, in fact, clear challenge from two sources.

The first was a fact—a sweeping fact—of world politics. The more patiently one analyzed the passing months of the global political struggle, the more striking seemed one historic reality, transcending the humble level of daily news. This was the fact that the Soviet Union, two years after Stalin's death, had effectively solved the riddle supposedly fatal to dictatorships: the transfer of unbroken political power. With the attainment, by whatever crude devices, of this political triumph, along with the military triumph of breaking so swiftly the American monopoly of advanced nuclear weapons, the world design of Soviet Communism now possessed a new force and vigor, already proven by the depth of its probings into the Middle East, Africa, and Southeast Asia.

The second shadowing fact was not intrinsically political at all. It was personal—and physical. And the news of it stunned and saddened, sharply etching in my memory the sudden instant of its learning.

The melancholy moment came as I was sitting over a leisurely Sunday breakfast at a café on the Piazza del Populo. It was an idle moment, serene and unguarded. The bright, late-autumn sun of Rome was warming, and I was casually turning to glance at the headlines of my morning paper. The dateline was Denver, Colorado, U.S.A. And the President had suffered a massive coronary thrombosis.

As 1955 ended, the import of the unborn new year, for the fate of free men in all the world, was no more masked in doubt than the strength of heart or length of life of Dwight David Eisenhower.

3

It was August of 1956 when I next found myself in Washington, to pay a courtesy call upon the President. A visit to the White House had not the least political meaning to me beyond this personal gesture. For I had no intention of returning to any official work with the Administration or to any service in the coming national election.

Three things contrived—in a matter of a couple of days—to change my mind.

First: even back in the nation's capital, I found that I could not suppress the haunting awareness that, in the shaping of

foreign policy over the *next* four years, Eisenhower still singularly *possessed* the *power* to lead toward the diplomatic initiatives
which I, rightly or wrongly, so urgently sought. I even gave
some credence—much too wishfully—to insistent Washington
rumors that a second term would see the Secretary of State elevated to the Supreme Court. And one basic political fact of 1952
still seemed to persist with undiminished force: no Democratic
President, under the verbal artillery of a Republican opposition,
could enjoy, even remotely, such political freedom to act, in
world affairs or in Soviet relations, as would Eisenhower. Still
quite fresh was the memory not only of the particular hope
stirred by Eisenhower at Geneva, but also the significant little
incident of his private correspondence with Soviet Marshal
Georgi K. Zhukov—and the President's bland and confident refusal at a press conference even to discuss its contents. Minor
though the episode was, this, too, sharply reminded one of the
luxurious diplomatic latitude enjoyed by Eisenhower, so beyond
the reach of any Democratic President. Nor, for that matter, had
the leadership of the Democratic party distinguished itself with
such trenchant or constructive critiques of foreign policy as to
promise that a Democratic President and Secretary of State
would be imaginative architects of new hope.

Second: I was seriously swayed by the counsel of some astute
and conscientious Democratic friends who had stayed watchful
on the Washington scene all the while of my absence. And they
had some seemingly paradoxical advice to offer. Their concern
centered strictly on the duration of the campaign ahead, for they
assumed that its outcome—wanted or not—would be an Eisenhower victory. But the din and stress of the campaign, in their
reasoned fears, might easily tempt the Administration to elaborate boasting of its fancied attainment of world peace. And they
argued persuasively that months of such unchecked self-congratulation might not only leave the governments of other free
nations aghast at such unrealism; it also might leave the embattled
Administration believing, at least a little, its own domestic politi-

cal propaganda. For these reasons—and as some check against these hazards—my Democratic friends earnestly urged me to return to work with the President for the duration of the campaign. It was one of those unexpected arguments that appear, so disconcertingly and so often, in the serious dialogues of a democratic people. And I found it hard to deny its sense and relevance.

Third: I visited with the President.

Once again, as four years earlier, I found remarkable the impact of his physical presence. Now the fact had new meaning, since I had not seen him since either his heart attack or his yet more recent intestinal surgery. His vitality seemed undiminished, the eyes as brightly alert and intense as ever, the excited stride around the office still as brisk and assured. Every gesture, every response, seemed to speak for a man astonishingly strong.

As the supposedly brief courtesy call rambled on, it became an unusual hour and a half of free and relaxed conversation. We found ourselves discussing significant places, problems, and persons without constraint. He spoke of Geneva and of Moscow—of the value he still attached to the first, of the fresh approaches he envisioned toward the second. He spoke in broad and affirmative, even aggressive, terms of more resolute and clear diplomatic initiatives, especially in the sphere of disarmament. He talked bluntly, almost belligerently, of applying far firmer presidential pressure in years ahead upon the Republican congressional leadership. He spoke incisively of the need to create "a new image" of Republicanism, worthy and capable of appeal to independents and liberals. And wherever he conversationally turned, he showed sheer zest for a second term.

Nor did he mute his judgments when they concerned specific individuals. Looking to the foreign scene, he voiced (as I shared) a respect for Eden conspicuously more warm and appreciative than Dulles' coolly condescending view of the British Prime Minister. Looking to the domestic scene, he spoke with equal warmth—but in disrespect—of Knowland's senatorial leadership.

172

No less plain was his dismay over the absence of what he called "fresh, young, new leadership" in the Republican party. This lack, he insisted, had played a vital role in his own decision to run for re-election. And this logically led to a candid commentary on his Vice President, Richard Nixon.

He avowed no sense of regret over Harold Stassen's then-raging campaign to displace Nixon from the 1956 Republican ticket. "I told Harold he should feel entirely free," he said, "so long as he did not purport to speak in my name, and I meant it." He recalled his own urgings to Nixon, earlier in the year, to transfer to a Cabinet post, such as the Secretary of Defense —"where he could get some executive and administrative experience." And finally he acknowledged: "Well, the fact is, of course, I've watched Dick a long time, and he just hasn't grown. So I just haven't honestly been able to believe that he *is* presidential timber."

We struck—in an hour and a half—not one troubling note of dissent between us.

As I departed, the President said he might be calling for "a little help and advice" in the campaign ahead.

I had no need to answer the offhand remark. But I knew that the request would explicitly come. And I knew that, with deep but silent reservations, I would respond.

CHAPTER SIX

The Second Campaign: 1956

"The campaign of 1956 was curious and special," a veteran of Democratic national politics mused, some weeks after the event, as we reviewed the many such struggles he had witnessed through the years. "It was nearly a classic of its kind. For it's almost impossible to recall anything you people did wrong—and nearly as hard to remember anything we did right. In fact, that makes *two* classics for young politicians to study up on in the future: how to plan a national campaign virtually without a mistake—and how to conduct one that looks as if nobody planned it at all."

To many witnesses, the 1956 National Election appeared almost that coherent and uncomplicated—comfortably after the fact. Yet it rarely *felt* so, not even for a day. For all the period throbbed with tension, from the first strategy meeting in Sherman Adams' office on September 3, until Election Night on November 6 and the liberating festivity of victory.

The tension did not turn upon any deep doubt as to the outcome. Very early—once the theme of the drama was defined, as it were, and the essential roles cast—this question was, for me, resolved. But the more subtle and elusive issue—the one that had

impelled me to take a part in these events—remained a suspense-
ful challenge: might the President actually win the *election,*
yet truly lose the *campaign?* The reverse phenomenon, of course,
was common enough in politics. Many a superior campaigner
has lost an electoral verdict at the polls to his less adroit or less
responsible opponent. In this instance, a host of factors, from
Eisenhower's popularity to the nation's prosperity, favored a
victory so probable and substantial that only great and perverse
ingenuity could dissipate such advantages. But what would be
the worth of such a victory, for Eisenhower, to crown a "lost"
campaign—a campaign marred by laxness in public debate with
his skillful opponent, ambiguity in his statement of public policy,
or slurring of the harsh truths of world affairs? At the end of such
a campaign, even the somewhat disenchanted and doubtful
citizen might well pay Eisenhower the hesitant homage of his
vote. Yet the man who would be President for the next four years
would need—for the sake of America's leadership in the world
and his personal leadership, even within his own party—the robust
confidence of his people. And thus the hope for four years,
so I believed, could critically turn upon the acts and words and
gestures, their wisdom or their folly, in the 64 days of this campaign.

No one sensed this matter more keenly than the President.
And no caricature of the man seemed more frivolous than the
image—fearfully held by some and zealously propagated by
many—of a spent and sickly President, prodded and goaded by
heartless "politicians" to forego the retirement that he needed
and coveted. Eisenhower's decision to run for re-election had
been completely personal, scrupulously pondered, and, at
thoughtful last, utterly unreserved. While the absence of Republican candidates qualified to take his place had weighed
heavily in his judgment, as he had told me, he had needed no
Republican politician to call his attention to the bleak fact. Far
from longing for retirement, his taste of it, through the gray winter weeks of convalescence at Gettysburg, had decisively sharp-

ened his desire for continued office. I recall Press Secretary Hagerty, who had grown so close to the President ever since his heart attack, reminiscing to me on this point: "I really don't know the exact moment when he decided to run again, but I *do* know that history was made sometime in those weeks at Gettysburg. It was then that he really faced the sheer, god-awful boredom of not being President."

The man's resilience, of course, awed everyone around him, and he seemed to find real therapy in the labors of the presidency. His recovery from his intestinal operation, only two months earlier, had dramatically shown this. As "Jerry" Persons related to me, just as the 1956 campaign was starting: "The Old Man was to go to Panama July 21, and that Friday before he left, he was a sorry sight. And he said to me privately, 'If I don't feel better than this pretty soon, I'm going to pull out of this whole thing.'" Persons marveled at what happened: "So he goes down to Panama, almost gets crushed by the mobs, meets God-knows-how-many Latin American diplomats, suffers through all the damn receptions—and Tuesday, *Tuesday* mind you, three days later, he comes waltzing back looking like a new man." And it seemed hard to conclude which fact was the more remarkable—the nearness of his withdrawal from politics in late July or the speed of his renewed resolve to run.

From my first quiet talk alone with him about the campaign on the third day of September, through the weeks ahead, rarely a day passed without our spending one hour or several hours together, and never did I see his vigor for the political conflict lag or fail. His sense of personal command seemed surer than ever. One of his first comments on the Republican National Committee's role in the campaign crackled with the familiar and lively disdain: "All machinery and no imagination. . . . They have a couple of great strategists over there, A. and B. Yes, sir, they can get any Republican candidate elected anywhere in the country—that is, in any solidly Republican district. . . ." And his looks forward, throughout these weeks, seemed as keen as his sideways glances. Thus, as he growled aggressively to me: "We're *not* going to go through this campaign slapping ourselves on the back and telling the nation how wonderful we are. We've done some damn good things—in the economy, especially, and overseas too—Iran and Guatemala and Trieste and the offshore islands. Sure, we have some successes. But we have got to do a *hell* of a lot *more* in the next four years than we've been able to in the last four." And the sturdy temper of such talk did much to ease my fear lest he "lose" the campaign by trying to turn a face of complacency to the electorate and to the world.

There was no assurance obtainable, however, on two other issues. Both would cast their warning shadows through the campaign, to its last hour. And quite simply, they were: health—and Suez.

As for the first of these, all the White House staff knew that the merest cold or stomach-ache, sending the President to bed for as little as a day or two, could cause instant political chaos. For this eventuality, the prudent Hagerty was braced, as he told me at the outset of the campaign: "If it happens, we'll call in only independent doctors, beginning with the head of AMA, if need be—*no* personal doctors, *no* Army doctors, *no* one who's politically suspect for having attended him before. We'll meet it head on."

As for the second shadowing issue, this was hardly so clear-cut but no less menacing. The noises of the Middle East crisis, ever since Egypt's seizure of the Suez Canal in July, had carried, like the soft and rhythmic ticking of a time bomb, into every serious conclave where Republican or Democratic politicians met in these months to weigh their chances and set their courses. An explosion could shatter most Republican pretensions in foreign policy, as well as validate much Democratic criticism of the strategy and behavior of Dulles. Reviewing the whole Middle Eastern scene with Dulles, the first week of September, I found him, understandably, both harassed and unreassuring: "I really don't know how much we can do. Every day that goes by without some outbreak is a gain, and I just keep trying to buy that day. I don't know anything to do but keep improvising."

Of the two threatening political ordeals, therefore, it seemed possible to make some advance preparation against only the first. Naturally—as should astonish no one in political life—the Administration would be confronted, in the end, only by the second.

2

The basic strategy of a national campaign is rarely simple, almost never symmetrical, and sometimes only a notch above the intelligible. So many imponderables and unknowables hover and threaten, throughout its course, as to turn the most sleek design, almost always, into a preposterous plot. No solemn deliberations seem finally to matter so much as agility in action, suppleness of argument, aptness of timing, and—above all—luck. And yet the 1956 campaign came remarkably close to following a logical and planned pattern.

The threads of this particular pattern were few, and the President and Adams and I discussed them, in the campaign's early days, on the basis of a brief memorandum that I had prepared. There were three key propositions. *First:* The President would hold his speaking to the minimum—despite all predictable pressure to the contrary—and, in particular, he would delay opening his campaign until well into September. This not only responded to Eisenhower's preferences, his distaste for "barnstorming" by an incumbent President, and a modest precaution against exhausting him physically. It also recognized the fact that Adlai Stevenson, already feverishly rallying rather dispirited Democratic forces, would be compelled to talk a great deal; and until his line of attack—and any weakness inviting counterattack—became clear, the President should hold his fire. *Second:* The severely limited schedule, which finally ended with a total of only seven major speeches before political rallies, would be kept flexible to the last moment, to allow for action fitted to unfolding opportunities. And this speech schedule would be supplemented, in the running political argument, by an occasional appearance from a Washington television studio and by formal written statements of policy to be released by the White House. The latter device would prove most apt in meeting the issues of nuclear testing and the military draft, as both became challenged by Stevenson. *Third:* Apart from clear exigencies of retort and rebuttal, the level and tone of all speeches would be grave and prudent—as far from self-congratulation as an Administration in office could reasonably sound. While a glance at the state of the world suggested such sober and circumspect attitude, so, too, did the political wisdom of pre-empting as much ground as possible from the critics. As I remarked to Adams: "There is no word in our political vocabulary more important than the word 'sacrifice,' and the President should use it—and call for it—from the first speech of this campaign to the last." And he did so.

The first phase of the campaign thus came to be marked by a kind of suspense—the suspense of silence. Throughout the first half of September, the nation's press grew more and more congested with news of Democratic activities, plans, slogans, rallies, and speeches. From Eisenhower, there came nothing. And this rather quickly began to disconcert and unnerve the Republican National Committee under Leonard Hall. The tone of the Committee's phone calls to the White House gradually moved up the emotional scale from curious, to concerned, to distressed, to anguished. To all their importunings, Adams responded with a laconic invitation to relax, as well as the bland advice that the President would not make his first speech till mid-September, that it would be a quiet studio "report to the nation" without the raucous drama of a rally, and that it would be a quite somber look at the world scene. All of this, naturally, chilled the National Committee.

In the rigorous subsurface logic of politics, the President's calm opening speech of the 1956 campaign, expressly abjuring "the noise and extravagance usual during a political campaign," played a role even more vital than his similar address to the Al Smith dinner in the 1952 campaign. Both speeches, by their very judiciousness, sparked no immediate excitement in public or press. But, precisely as the 1952 speech had caught and retrieved fast-slipping support in key sectors of educated opinion, so this opening speech of the 1956 encounter allowed the President to disarm many critics by stressing *his* grave view of the world scene. The speech contained its direct retorts to the two key proposals thrown out by Stevenson: a unilateral suspension of nuclear testing and a curtailment of the military draft. The President emphasized the necessity for "explicit and supervised international agreements" on nuclear testing, and he dismissed the suggestion of unilateral action as a "theatrical national gesture." He further stated "categorically" that any "hinting that our military draft might soon be suspended" amounted to careless advocacy of a policy that "would shock our allies who are calling upon their people to shoulder arms in our common cause." Sternly, the President told the nation: "We cannot, in short, face the future simply by walking into the past—backwards. We cannot salute the future with bold words—while we surrender it with feeble deeds." Beyond all this, the President—to the dismay and confusion of many members of the Republican National Committee—refused to describe the world in terms of a *Pax Republicana*. Instead, he warned of the growth of "a number of grave problems" across the earth. And he enumerated them: the revolutionary forces proclaiming new nationalism across Africa and Asia; the need for progress toward world disarmament ("the only way to win World War III is to prevent it"); the shift of accent in Communist aggression away from the military arena and toward the political and economic; and the skills and productivity of the Soviet Union, signaling "the rise of the first great industrial power to challenge the West." All these historic problems had to be wisely measured and met, the President concluded, to attain the kind of peace that "is no static thing, no passive mood. It is not a prize: it is a quest. . . . It inspires not relaxation, but resourcefulness—not stagnation, but stamina." There sounded here, in short, no trumpets to proclaim the attainment of world peace, but rather a warning roll of drums to give signal of coming perils.

Undramatically, even unobtrusively, this first speech of the campaign set and fixed, with uncommon rigidity, the lines of argument that would be pressed, almost without waver, to the end. The two challenges issued by the opposition were accepted as most welcome issues for debate. The President wholly escaped the danger of being charged—as so many Republican senatorial and congressional candidates quite accurately were charged— with a blindness to world crisis induced by chronic euphoria. Instead, he summoned national attention to ominous world dilemmas even before Stevenson had found time to mention them. And weary weeks later, as the campaign neared its end, one of the Democratic candidate's closest counselors sadly confessed to me: "The night of the President's first speech I decided to destroy six speeches I'd outlined for Adlai. Eisenhower *gave* the speech I had been trying to get our boy to give for weeks."

If the "interior" logic of the campaign was thereby firmly enough fixed, the outward, daily form of it presented no such smooth surface. The imposing doors of the White House, so it quickly became apparent, offered no serious barrier to the onrushing confusion and frenzy so well remembered from four years earlier. While I had easy and constant access to the President, and while Adams and I could always discuss any problems with dispatch, there were times when the official group as a whole seemed equipped to bear the stress of a campaign even less adequately than in 1952. For the regular and continuing demands of government upon the White House staff were hardly subject to a moratorium for the duration of the campaign. The tense race of typewriter against time began again and never relented. A document such as a presidential statement on nuclear testing required days of painstaking review with experts and officials, followed by nights of careful drafting. As a result of such pressures, the President would start upon the one extended trip of his campaign, the October 16–20 swing to the Far West, without a single speech written as the *Columbine* left the Washington airport. Once airborne, I would start dictating text to Eisenhower's secretary, the competent and devoted Ann Whitman; and on both our Seattle and Los Angeles stops, the process would continue even through the din of motorcades from airport to hotel. When the texts for press release were thereby drastically delayed, the speech was preceded—on the news-wires across the country—with remarkably detailed, and wholly inaccurate, stories of "deep policy debates" being "fought out" to the last instant. The simple and true explanation was too unexciting to be newsworthy.*

And the importance of all that the President did *not* say was underscored by bizarre drafts of proposed statements, from a variety of quarters implacably determined to be helpful. The more lofty of these suggestions would have put him through such implausible rhetorical exercises as quoting full paragraphs from Romain Rolland's *Jean Christophe*. Even more vigilance was invited by "notes" or "remarks" hastily staff-prepared for ad-lib delivery on brief occasions such as "prop-stops" at airports. These creations would propose hurling flabby insults at "scrambled eggheads" and "baby-sitting government," or they would admonish that "the opposition ought to wash its mouth out with soap." When such texts occasionally found their way to the President's desk, he would groan, and, with some self-directed humor, say: "Gosh, someone around here is always

---

* The slightly hysterical distress of last-minute labor was evidently as much a mark of Eisenhower's career as of political campaigns generally. As "Jerry" Persons related one day, with dry laughter: "The boss is the darndest man for this sort of thing I ever knew. At SHAPE in Paris, I remember when he was set to announce his decision to run in 1952. As he went down the hall to make his statement, Al Gruenther and I were still sitting in his office rewriting the last paragraph."

feeding me all these 'folksy' phrases. Hell, I'm folksy *enough* as it is, without their trying to make matters worse."

The hazard of some careless verbal slip by the President, however, was a matter of minute importance beside the question: who is watching what the Vice President is saying? The question was pertinent—and, in the White House, frequent. The relationship between Eisenhower and Nixon, at its warmest over the years, could never have been described as confident and comradely. While the first scars dated from the 1952 crisis over "the Nixon fund," a much more recent wound seemed to have been inflicted by Eisenhower's rather ambiguous performance, in the early months of 1956, in accepting Nixon as his running mate for a second time. The President, moreover, was well aware of the almost tense reticence, in many sectors of public opinion, that denied him support for fear of the danger of Nixon's succession to the presidency. And Nixon was aware that the President was aware.

Liaison between the two men, therefore, was imperfect. On the one occasion, during the second week in September, when I heard the President phone Nixon from the oval office, the remarks carried cautious overtones. Nettled by some sweeping Democratic charges of Administration "corruption," Eisenhower had thought that the answer ought to be given on the vice-presidential level. But the President's careful words were: "Look, Dick, we've agreed that your speeches generally in this campaign ought to be on a higher level than in the past. Still I think it's perfectly all right for you to pick up some of these wild charges and throw them back at the other fellow." Many in the White House nonetheless continued to worry—as the phrase went—about "Dick running loose through the country," unaccompanied by a tough-willed adviser to control and to censor his impetuous bursts of partisan oratory. Nixon's friend and deputy, William Rogers, and I discussed the danger in mid-September, but neither one of us could nominate such an escort. The matter dropped. So, too, did the level of an occasional Nixon speech—

183

such as one in late September gaudily suggesting to all American workers the prospect of a doubled standard of living and a four-day week. No further distress followed, however, until the campaign had almost finished when—at the height of Anglo-American tension over the Suez—Nixon cheerfully saluted his government's role in the crisis as "a declaration of independence," presumably rekindling the spirit of 1776.

The other man whose every word and movement the White House watched with keen interest was, of course, the Democratic candidate.

From the first, Adlai Stevenson suffered a tactical liability that bore the momentary and misleading aspect of an advantage. He had to talk too soon and too much. The volume of words—some sweeping and eloquent phrases, some witty and partisan jests—had begun to multiply back in August, as Stevenson zig-zagged across the nation to rally local, county, and state leaders. He had no choice but to go through this exhausting prologue, since important sectors of Democratic opinion had viewed his renomination with neither enthusiasm for his person nor hope for his victory. The lightning flashes of excitement provoked by his appearances did serve to lift party morale. But the price to be paid for all this was high, for the exercise consumed physical and mental time and energy that the candidate sorely needed to define the very premise of his campaign strategy.

This disability became apparent with surprising speed. On September 5, I was lunching in the White House "mess" when Hagerty came to report that Stevenson, addressing the American Legion in Los Angeles, had just highlighted his speech with a "dramatic" suggestion that the military draft might be cut back. I recall my own incredulity: I refused even to credit the report, until I went to the newsroom to watch the ticker click out the "takes" of the story. Actually, I had little reason for astonishment except my own assumptions as to the kind of critique that would mark Stevenson's whole campaign. These assumptions, inferred from the kind of campaign Stevenson had waged in 1952, suggested a clear, central line of attack—the erosion of American world power, hastened by both the rigidity of Dulles' foreign policy and the elasticity of expenditures for national defense, under constant budgetary pressure. And perhaps the most persuasive line of argument in this vein would have followed the proposals of General Maxwell Taylor, calling for *greater* commitment to national defense in terms of *conventional* forces. Such a critique would have (1) underscored warnings against "economy-minded" defense policies, (2) focused charges of "complacency" permitting such loss of capability for limited warfare, and (3) condemned the excessive reliance of Dulles' foreign policies upon "massive retaliation." Hence it seemed little short of fantastic that Stevenson was foreswearing this whole argument, in favor of the possible and superficial political appeal of *reducing* the burden of the military draft.

From the vantage point of the White House, it would have been impossible to have wished for a greater political gift. And the eccentric twist that this single event gave to the whole dialogue of the campaign had a much more meaningful consequence than mere partisan comfort or convenience. For it effectively erased any chance for Stevenson to develop the kind of serious critique that might have forced the Administration, more and more, to retreat into a shelter of false boasts and frivolous claims on the attainment of world "peace." Hence the nation was spared any drift in presidential argument toward such defensive distortions of reality. And the Administration, incidentally, was spared the towering embarrassment that would have afflicted it, at the end of a campaign of such boasts, when war flared forth in the Middle East.

From this quite fateful starting point, the Stevenson campaign seemed to steer, almost willfully, from one misfortune to another. Routine technical problems and confusions plagued the candidate constantly—from the official "kick-off" speech in Harrisburg, Pennsylvania, on September 13, when the vagaries of television lighting gave Stevenson a sadly spectral appearance, on to the traditional New York Madison Square Garden rally on October 23, with Stevenson again slipping into the habit of talking beyond his scheduled television time. But the true trouble seemed far deeper than such mechanical matters. There were telltale signs of hastiness or carelessness of intellectual labor. And a notable one was the blunder, in a speech on September 25, of blaming the Administration generally, and Milton Eisenhower specifically, for extending financial help to Argentina's Juan Perón—when the act in question belonged to the history of the Truman administration.

More serious still were repeated slips and contradictions in the argument made for the suspension of American nuclear testing. I doubted at the time the prudence of injecting such an issue into a political campaign. Whatever one's final position on the issue, it was clear that men both honest and competent could and did differ profoundly—even after elaborate education in the complexities of nuclear physics and the problems of national defense. And it seemed equally clear that the Democratic candidate had enjoyed no such education. As the White House stressed in two successive statements—prepared despite the President's great reluctance even to discuss the matter publicly—there were demonstrable misconceptions of reality in the Stevenson view. There was the implication, throughout his many speeches on the matter, that the proposed ban need apply only to "large" weapons, whereas the unmentioned fact was that many "small" weapons caused the greatest amount of radioactive fallout. There was extraordinary ambiguity with regard to the political action really proposed, as the suggestions seemed to range from unilateral American action, to "leadership" in collective Western action, to persuasive "initiative" toward the Soviet Union. Each of these courses of action stood at obvious variance with the others, but all seemed advocated with equal ardor. And there was, finally, the singular device of citing, as witnesses in support of the proposed ban, a number of world figures, from Pope Pius XII to Sir Anthony Eden—none of whom had done more than voice laments upon the general peril of a protracted international race in nuclear arms. In short, the most grave and intricate of issues was set forth in a manner that seemed oddly alien to the more statesmanlike Stevenson of 1952.

The almost designless pattern of the Democratic campaign prevailed to the end. As election-time neared, Stevenson kept pressing the two issues—the draft and the H-bomb—more and more insistently. Alone, either one seemed dubious at best and open to easy retort. Together, they conveyed an unreassuring negative quality—since they advocated the *not* doing of things, in the sphere of national defense, in terms of *both* nuclear and conventional forces. Meanwhile, as the candidate sought to quicken the tempo of his whole attack, all the adjectives grew more harsh. The charges of Republican "corruption" became more vehement, and the lurid vision of nuclear tragedy was expanded to catch horrified sight of the earth itself being knocked off its axis. The least graceful touch was reserved, however, for Election Eve. After a campaign of discreet silence on the matter, Stevenson concluded his months-long appeal to the people with the cold warning that—no matter what the electorate thought of the political issues—the medical facts plainly indicated that his opponent, the President, might not live long enough to serve out another four-year term.

The total impression was regrettable. Obviously, the Democratic "strategy" had started from an elemental assumption: since a more lofty political approach had failed in 1952, a more unsophisticated technique was required in 1956. But analogies in politics are always dangerous, and this one contrived an almost perfect *non sequitur*. The circumstances of the two campaigns were, quite obviously, very different. A reasonable inference, therefore, might have suggested some hope for a better result from the same political devices and positions. And I recall my own thought of the time that the whole Stevenson effort in 1956 suggested an almost obsessive resolve to fight again, in different

187

style, the contest of 1952. The final product thereby acquired the baffling impact of a filmstrip run backwards.

A perhaps definitive commentary on the 1956 Democratic campaign later was given me by its unhappy manager, James A. Finnegan. A fortnight after Election Day, we met by chance and spent a long evening in reminiscence on the obvious. His head shook sadly with the memory of his candidate's awesome fastidiousness with language, constantly causing his speech texts to be delayed beyond press-release time. "Sometimes" he recalled, "we'd have to keep our campaign plane in the air—with important local politicians waiting on the ground—while we circled and circled in the sky, as Adlai edited on and on." Such incidents, however, did not create the supreme problem. I asked what he thought this to have been. And he sighed:

"Very simple. We had two groups of people supposedly joined in running this campaign. There were the politicians—and the intellectuals. And for some reason, all the politicians were determined to try to make decisions as if they were intellectuals. And all the intellectuals insisted on trying to think and act like politicians. What the hell could you expect?"

The question had already been answered.

3

Back of all strategy and tactics, and beneath all the rhetoric of boast or lament, the campaign concealed a strange irony. This irony rose from the distortion—indeed, the inversion—of logic that dictated the areas of strength and of weakness of each party, in terms of domestic policy or foreign policy. A dispassionate assessment of the political record would have given a creditable enough score to the Republican Administration on domestic affairs: it could claim a moderate check on inflation, a sound anti-trust record, an extension of Social Security, an increase in labor's share of the national income—all within a reasonably healthy economy. A comparably fair appraisal would have raised most serious doubts on matters of national defense and foreign policy.

And the irony was this: each party recognized that its popular strength was plainly greater in the sphere where its public record was plainly weaker. Democrats feared popular distrust of their foreign policies as deeply as Republicans feared popular distrust of their domestic policies. Each was haunted by its own caricature —the Democrats as "the Party of War," the Republicans as "the Party of Depression."

Neither side could do very much to erase these images so grotesquely distorting the political scene, but both strove passionately to avoid any act or word tending to renew the credibility of the myths. On the Democratic side, there were all the rather gratuitous affirmations of anti-Communism, and the scathing renunciations of "appeasement"—to prove the absurdity of any notions that a Democratic regime would stumble into "foreign wars." On the Republican side, the air resounded with those ardent, quadrennial reaffirmations of concern for labor, social security, unemployment insurance, health, and education—to prove to the electorate that the supreme mark of Republicanism was not soundness of budget but greatness of heart.

To strike and to hold this benign posture—even for the duration of the campaign—was no easy task, however, for some departments of the Eisenhower administration. Thus, for example, in the third week of September, the northern part of Texas, suffering its worst drought in history, was urgently appealing to the Department of Agriculture for millions of dollars in immediate help. The department gave some assistance, then suddenly—with the gentle reflexes of a bank threatened by a run on its deposits—decided to reject all further claims, instantly and arbitrarily, to halt depletion of its emergency reserves. Only by chance did the White House learn in time of this proposed mid-campaign display of humanitarianism. Even then, vigorous argument was required to persuade the frugal department to continue its aid.

One other moment of political danger came at about this same time. It rather oddly and silently passed, for it could have been serious. By late September, the President had delivered his retorts to Stevenson's suggestions on curtailing the military draft. Suddenly, a rumor began circulating in official Washington that some vaults in the Pentagon were almost bulging with recommendations drawn by Admiral Radford ("the Radford plan") for dramatic economies to be achieved by still greater American reliance on the "nuclear deterrent" and still deeper cutback in ground forces. These rumors even reached West European allied governments, who privately expressed some alarm to the Department of State. For this strange spell in the campaign, therefore, it seemed altogether possible that Stevenson might challenge Radford to give rebuttal, in effect, to the President's insistence on the necessity of the military draft. The Democratic candidate never did so, however, and thereby the electorate was spared a possibly hilarious spectacle: a forensic alliance between Stevenson (deploring defense-dictated-by-budget) and Radford (designing defense-dictated-by-budget)—against a profligate Eisenhower wasting the citizens' money on superfluous conventional forces.

By the first week of October, all such bizarre perils seemed past, and the campaign appeared to have already taken its decisive turn toward an Eisenhower victory even surpassing 1952. The signs of this, as I noted them in my diary of these days, seemed wholly persuasive. Politically indicative, if not overwhelmingly important, was the news of Harry Truman flatly dissenting from Stevenson's view on nuclear testing. A much clearer omen came with an authoritative report from Stevenson's councils that his closest advisers had just completed a "strategic review" of the campaign and had concluded that the most hurtful issues confronting them were three: the draft, nuclear testing, and the confused charges about aid to Perón. Since all three issues had been brought into the campaign at Democratic initiative and insistence, this did not seem to speak well for their forward progress.

By October 9, I could write in the day's entry: "More and more one can foresee a *wide* margin of victory." On this day,

Eisenhower had moved into the Democratic stronghold of Pitts-burgh—to be hailed by nearly 150,000. And his highly successful speech of that evening—one half straight rebuttal, one half appeal for "sacrifice"—set a formula from which there was no deviation thereafter. "They," he charged his opposition, "have urged stout military defense with greater reliance on modern weapons—but have advised stopping our atomic tests. They have promised national security and a bold role in world affairs—while they urge us to start thinking about ending the military draft. Now I . . . as your President and Commander in Chief of the Armed Forces cannot and will not make proposals contrary to the national interest—nor offer you attractive prospects if they are unjustified by world realities. . . . Strong—we shall stay free. Weak, we shall have only our good intentions to be written as our epitaph."

There was much unspoken irony in these words. For they almost suggested the voice of Stevenson 1952 shouting the retorts to Stevenson 1956.

And the President continued thus through all his campaigning, East and West, to the end. . . . "We need our military draft—for the very safety of our nation. . . . Nor can we urge our allies to shoulder arms—while we throw ours to the ground. . . . I do not believe that any political campaign justifies the declaration of a moratorium on common sense. . . . As your President, I cannot and will not tell you that our quest for peace is simple, or its rewards swift. This quest may, in fact, cost us much—in time, in effort, and in sacrifice. . . . We cannot be very tolerant of the suggestion that the peace of the world can be bought . . . in a political bargain basement. . . . We shall seek escape from no toil—or any sacrifice—that freedom demands of us. For we know that a people that values its privileges above its principles soon loses both."*

As Eisenhower publicly strode so confidently toward re-elec-

* Speeches in Los Angeles, October 19, 1956, and in New York, October 25, 1956.

tion, he privately displayed—in small gatherings of his staff, in quiet conversations between us in early morning, or in still more relaxed chatter in his upstairs study at day's end—most of the political moods and attitudes, remarkably unchanged, that had marked the candidate of 1952. There was the same kind of emotional insurance he earlier had accorded himself, voiced again early in this September: "Hell, if the people were to decide not to re-elect me, I sure couldn't feel desperately unhappy about it." There persisted—even to the point of reluctance to retort on such major issues as the military draft—his old aversion: "I just hate hacking away at the other guy all the time." And again, a month later: "I hate this firing back at what the other fellow said. It's the old, old story: you're no bigger a man than the man who can get your goat—no bigger than the things that annoy you." In this curious way, the man who so shunned "personalities" in politics still tended, quite unconsciously, to personalize issues—by conceiving their aggressive public debate to be rather akin to vulgar remarks in a hushed drawing-room. While he deplored public discussion of nuclear testing for reasons of national security, his desire to avoid *any* response to Stevenson on the matter also bespoke his feeling that such argument itself was quite unseemly. "I just don't think it's worth getting into," he said a number of times. "The whole thing's a tempest in a teapot."

His responses to words themselves continued to reflect old disciplines and habits—and none of his apparent public disrespect for grammar. He was always capable of the sudden, critical remark of the editor, as with his smiling complaint about a speech draft one day: "I always knew you had a weakness for alliteration, but don't you think you've gone a little strong on the onomatopoeia here?" Again, doing a last-minute review of his final speech of the campaign, he spent an amused while, on the train from Washington to Philadelphia, correcting some half-dozen improper uses of "shall" and "will." And every speech felt the effect of his shyness toward rhetoric. "These last couple of paragraphs are fine and ringing," he would say, "but I can't get away from the feeling that they make me sound like St. Peter."

His emotional response to routine politics and politicians, too, remained consistent—in its curious ambivalence. His warm surge of pleasure, in great gatherings and before shouting rallies, was open and genuine: the excitement still deepened the ruddy glow of his cheeks and widened the famous smile. Yet—at any distance from such thronged scenes—he could speak of them with cold dispassion. "We need maybe a few more 'cheer lines' in this speech," he would say a little sardonically, " 'cause a mob like this doesn't want to think—they just want to yowl." And however animated and interested he would seem, in hotel-room conclaves thronged with local politicians, the first instant after their departure often would see him sigh with relief that the "bunch of clowns" had finally retired. And the GOP leadership on the highest national level did not receive, of course, any higher esteem than it deserved. As he glumly observed to me one morning early in October, with the Middle East tensions humming menacingly in the political background: "It's amazing how little some people can understand about the world we live in, even on the simplest level. Look at the Suez—with the British already furious with Dulles and me because we're trying to hold them back. And along comes Knowland to this office yesterday, to sit right down there and say seriously: 'Just one thing I ask you to assure me—that you won't let the British drag us into another one of their wars.' If that isn't the silliest damn kind of talk!"

There flickered through these days, however, some small but notable changes of temper from past years. For one thing, his capacity for anger was newly and markedly disciplined: not once in these months did there explode one of those outbursts of raging impatience so familiar in the past. Even more striking was a heightened sensitivity to serious criticism of his presidency. He always had suffered a slight tendency to confuse a critique of his methods with a questioning of his purposes: since

193

he viewed the latter as beyond challenge, the charge would seem demonstrably absurd. But now this self-consciousness was sharpened to a keener edge by the many abrasive Democratic accusations of weak or vacillating leadership. At moments, his agitated reaction reminded one less of a politician, being predictably taunted by his opponents, than of a soldier, being publicly charged with unfitness for command. One day in mid-campaign he responded, in fact, in just this spirit. He ordered from his secretary an assemblage of personal tributes received through the years from national leaders around the world, along with a careful scanning of Churchill's memoirs for all appreciative references to himself. And a few days later, as I sat alone with him in his office, he seemed still smarting from the latest slaps at his capacity for command, as he strode with his most martial air around the oval room, angrily snapping: "Hell, I don't have to *prove* I can fight. They *know* I commanded troops. And no officer ever got congratulations from me if I knew he let fifteen enemy soldiers get away that he might have taken." And at such times, the seemingly serene surface of his humility would suddenly appear to foam with little bursting bubbles of a hidden vanity.

All the while, he never lost his view of himself as standing apart from politics generally and from his own party in particular. Thus, one afternoon early in October, prompted by reading a warm personal tribute in a daily editorial, he spoke of *his* kind of leadership: "*This* is what I mean to people—sense and honesty and fairness and a decent amount of progress. I don't think the people *want* to be listening to a Roosevelt, sounding as if he were one of the Apostles, or the partisan yipping of a Truman. This business of rolling the drums to rally your own party troops has its place, but—damn it—everyone that comes into this office tells me that *I* am the only thing can pull this party through. So there's no use my making any compromises with the truth, supposedly for the party, because if I were caught in one falsehood, and what I stand for in people's eyes got tarnished, then not just me but the whole Republican gang would be finished."

Eisenhower's personal view of Stevenson, spontaneously voiced through all these days, suggested a rather volatile mixture of personal resentment and lofty disinterest. His most common adjectives of disparagement, upon hearing or reading Stevenson's latest forensic thrust, were "smart aleck" and "slick." (A bit ironically, the latter had been Stevenson's own repeatedly favored adjective of 1952, aimed at Eisenhower's campaign pledge to journey to Korea.) Much more heated were the President's reactions to Stevenson's abortive attack on Milton Eisenhower's nonexistent dealings with Perón and the "reckless" raising of the issue of nuclear testing. Yet he rarely read the full text of any Stevenson speech, dismissing any such suggestions coldly: "It's not going to do me any good to study what that monkey's saying, since I have no intention of answering him anyway." Nonetheless, a thinly veiled personal dislike for the man, whom he knew only most casually, gradually came to find some gruff manner of expression at almost any mention of Stevenson's name. And he simply exploded in anger, toward the end of the campaign, when both the Suez crisis and Stevenson's belated assault on Dulles' foreign policy came simultaneously. "I just cannot figure out," Eisenhower cried, "how that darn fool has the nerve to attack our foreign policy in this situation—with all the work and all the thought that have been put into it." The words expressed his honest conviction that Stevenson was crudely oversimplifying all the political complexities of the Middle East. Yet they were spoken with his characteristic air of disbelief that anyone should criticize the result of a political action when its underlying intent (or, as he would have said, *"instinct"*) was so indisputably decent.

A curious personal insight into the whole political encounter of Eisenhower and Stevenson emerged during an idle conversation between us one day in early October. This particular commentary on his Democratic opponent began with his admitting

195

quite candidly that his initial regard for Stevenson in 1952 had been such that he never would have entered politics if he had known who would be the Democratic nominee. He was stirred to the reminiscence by his memory of Stevenson's 1952 acceptance speech. "You know, I had great respect for the fellow, from a distance," he said. "Right after Taft and I fought it out, the Democrats went at it and came up with Stevenson, and at the time I was off in the mountains on a fishing trip with a couple of my friends. I *told* them if I'd known two months before that a guy as decent as Stevenson was going to be the nominee, they might never have gotten me to take a nomination. I even said to them, 'Let's hear his acceptance speech' and you know how *little* I like to listen to the *other* fellow. Then it *happened*. He got to that part in his speech about having debated with himself about accepting the nomination—and 'wishing that this cup might pass' from him. Right there, I snapped off the TV set and said: 'After hearing that, fellows, I think he's a *bigger* faker than all the rest of them.'" Implicit in the remembrance of the episode was one more revealing sign of the spirit in which Eisenhower had turned to the political scene in the first instance. He had, quite literally, imagined Washington to be a "mess" of "corruption," presided over by a slovenly Chief Executive. And for a fleeting political moment, the emergence of so fresh and different a Democratic figure as Stevenson had suddenly blurred the stark caricature.

The rarely broken posture of indifference toward "the enemy" would persist to the climactic moment of Election Night. Even then, when Stevenson appeared on television for his slightly delayed statement of concession, Eisenhower would walk past the screen, saying: "Nope—I went through the whole campaign without listening to him, and I'm not going to start now." And when someone called to him to pause and hear the words of concession, he gave the half-smiling but firm retort: "Listen, I never personally received anyone's sword in the war. I had the Germans surrender to someone else, and that's the way it's going to be now. *You* fellows watch. I appoint you to receive the surrender!"

Yet all this detachment and aloofness seemed, as the campaign neared its close, to become more and more offset by a livelier zest for combat than I had ever witnessed in him. In minor ways, he showed this in occasional readiness to strike back at opposition arguments, with an acid and scorn he would have shunned in his first campaign. On a much more serious level, just thirteen days before election—it was on the morning of October 24—he suddenly launched into a monologue to me that revealed a sharpened sense of the political realities behind the façade of the campaign. Looking up from a memorandum on his desk that set forth full details of his remaining schedule of speeches and engagements, he emitted a characteristic groan; and I not only murmured some commiseration but also suggested that too much last-minute activity might needlessly risk his overexertion, for an election already so safely won. But he had something else on his mind. "You're partly right," he said, "but, you see, the *size* of my majority seems to me terribly important. Next term, I'll be the first President to try to run things under the two-term limitation—with everybody knowing I'm politically on my way out. So the *size* of my majority will be the *most* important weapon I'll have for the next four years—especially with the Republicans. They have got to be made to understand what kind of principles and policies can win elections, and I'm going to need all the power I can show to get those monkeys to do the things I want for a change." By this point, he was pacing the quiet office quite excitedly. "So," he went on, "I want to do everything I possibly can to have this majority a *big* one. Frankly, if I were going to win by 50.1 percent, I just wouldn't want the job."

These words—and, on similar occasions, there were many more of kindred spirit—struck my ear as more than signs of political vitality, in a man whose mere physical capacity had stood in doubt only a few months earlier. They sounded, amid so much meaningless din of the campaign, like heartening whispers, at least, of the only hope that greatly mattered—the redeeming in the second term of the unfulfilled promises of the first.

Meanwhile, despite the President's vehemence of word, length of stride, and brightness of eye, the question of his unknowable physical resources haunted all weeks and most days. From the outset, this uncertainty had created a minor dilemma of campaign strategy. It was one reason for keeping his formal schedule brief and flexible, but this procedure carried the risk of creating the impression—as the schedule filled out through the weeks—of a campaign pace suddenly quickened by some political fear or anxiety. There was no alternative but to take the physical precaution and accept the psychological problems. So much did the whole issue trouble those closest to the President that Milton Eisenhower, by the middle of the campaign, was insisting to him: "It doesn't even matter what you *say*—just get out and around and show the people how healthy you really are."

While Eisenhower never volubly complained about any physical strain except "those killing motorcades"—which he endured with greater resilience than almost any of his staff—he was constantly and rationally alert to the physical problem and its political implications. As late as October 7, barely more than a week before he was to undertake his one campaign invasion of the West, he remarked to me: "I just can't afford to *look* tired, so I don't think I'll be taking any California trip." And he went on to explain: "I haven't had the slightest suggestion, you know, of any trouble whatsoever since the heart attack. But the doctors have warned me: If I feel the slightest bit weak and tired, I sit down —*right away*. Well, if I do that in the middle of a speech, we're *through*, that's all." But he made the western trip in mid-October, nonetheless, and he finished it without having to beg an hour's respite in his congested schedule. Only once on this trip, or in all the campaign, did I hear him betray any hint of personal sensitivity about his health. This came with an unguarded murmur in Los Angeles, on the last day of the western swing, as we were doing final editing on his speech for the rally in the Hollywood Bowl. And he frowned at a phrase and said: "That business of 'in these *last* three-and-one-half years'—let's change it to 'past.' I never like that word 'last'—it sounds as if this were *my* last year or something."*

As the President's stamina kept dismaying his ill-wishers into the final week, some of the disappointed chose to take matters in their own hands—with a sly whispering campaign. From places as remote from one another as Washington and Brooklyn and Los Angeles, there came reports of scores of phone calls to important local citizens from feminine voices claiming the identity of one or another of the secretaries of Leonard Hall. Spoken in warmly "reassuring" tones, their macabre message was: "I'm calling for Mr. Hall, who has been afraid you might have heard exaggerated rumors about the President's relapse. He wanted especially for *you* to know directly from him that the relapse has been very slight. Don't worry—because he's *sure* it won't be *too* serious." The effectiveness of this deceit did not prove any more serious.

To weigh against all rather bright signs of both physical and political vigor, the President did, from time to time, give signs of political habits and intellectual attitudes not quite so assuring. Some were trivial. Some were substantial. And all would cast their shadows on the remaining years of the Eisenhower presidency.

There were, on the less serious level, those little bursts of either enthusiasm or hostility that, periodically, seemed oddly to jar the man loose from deep convictions and basic discern-

* On this same trip and day, we heard the campaign's only amusing tale about Republican fund-raising. Producer Sam Goldwyn had been besieging one old friend who kept avoiding him with: "Sorry, I like Ike, but I'm a Democrat." A frustrated and suspicious Goldwyn thought this over, and decided to test his doubts by having someone else call his friend and solicit for the Democrats. "Sorry," came the reply, "but I'm a Republican." So Goldwyn called his friend directly: "Listen, you smart s.o.b. . . . ." and he shortly received a check for five thousand dollars.

ments. For all his essential temperance in foreign policy appraisals, he occasionally showed himself impelled to boast—in extemporaneous remarks more befitting a Midwestern Republican congressman—that "the shadows of Korean casualty lists have been lifted from the homes of America." For all his distaste for direct disparagement of an opponent, he could be provoked by some sudden resentment to contend—as he did with me on one occasion—that he ought to attack Stevenson for the "scandals" in his administration as Governor of Illinois. And for all his usual caution in judging individuals politically, he could sometimes be so stirred to sudden appreciation as to suggest, in a meeting of local political leaders in Seattle, that Arthur Larson, author of *A Republican Looks at His Party*, ranked as a promising possibility for the presidential nomination in 1960. Improbable as this seemed—along with far more frequent and ardent eulogies of Robert B. Anderson, who would succeed Humphrey as Secretary of the Treasury—all such remarks perhaps did convey one intended inference to his political listeners: Eisenhower did not regard the eventual succession of Nixon as a blessing either inevitable or irresistible.

All such questions of tactical judgment, however, were of little moment—so I believed—beside one matter of crucial political principle: the profoundly reticent view of Eisenhower toward the whole struggle for civil rights. The record of his Administration did not lack achievements in spheres directly and plainly within its competence, such as in federal employment, the armed services, and the District of Columbia. Beyond these limits, however, Eisenhower both thought and acted with most conservative caution. This circumspection was not, as so many critics apparently believed and harshly insisted, a product of presidential laxness or indifference. Quite like his constraint in policy toward the Congress, this determination *not* to act reflected positive *belief*. In civil rights, as in congressional relations, his political faith rested on the slow, gradual power of persuasion.

Our differences on this issue punctuated our reviews of almost every campaign address he made. For my own drastically different convictions forced me to question the political hope or the moral value of any "Republican philosophy"—be it called "modern," ancient, or eternal—that failed to reaffirm grave and binding commitment to the authentic spirit of the party at its very creation. Consequently, through all the preparatory process on almost all speeches, the text on civil rights signaled the playing of a kind of rhythmic game between us, accepted but unacknowledged—I toughening every reference, he softening it, I rephrasing upward, he rewording downward. The drift of political events, however, fortified his caution, for the campaign had not run half its course before all reports indicated a clear chance for Eisenhower to carry such states as Florida and Texas. So on Election Eve it was quite characteristic for the President—as we sat watching the elaborate telecast of rallies across the nation—to greet a Negro speaker's salute from a Detroit rally with the wry comment: "*That* will sure win us a lot of votes in Houston!"

His feelings on civil rights, however, struck roots deeper than such campaign superficialities. Before he had delivered even his first speech of the campaign, he voiced these feelings to me vehemently. "I am convinced," he insisted, "that the Supreme Court decision *set back* progress in the South *at least fifteen years*. . . . It's all very well to talk about school integration—if you remember you may be also talking about social *dis*integration. Feelings are deep on this, especially where children are involved. . . . You take the attitude of a fellow like Jimmy Byrnes. We used to be pretty good friends, and now I've not heard from him even once in the last eighteen months—all because of bitterness on this thing. . . . We can't demand *perfection* in these moral questions. All we can do is keep working toward a goal and keep it high. And the fellow who tries to tell me that you can do these things by *force* is just plain *nuts*." And there was so much vigor and certitude in these feelings that I could not help wishing, more than once, that they were excited by other matters and enlisted in other causes.

In a wholly different sphere, there appeared something else to give disquiet: the evolving nature of Eisenhower's relationship to his closest staff. This relationship had always had two characteristic marks: the deep personal affection he evoked from all, and the dominance of his own personality over all. By virtue of these, he could shake even so strong a man as Sherman Adams —sharply asserting a will, an impatience, or a caprice that (as I witnessed more than once) would spin Adams completely around to reverse a decision already fixed in his own mind. But now there appeared a new dimension to the old deference: an acutely conscious solicitude for the President's health of body and peace of mind. So fond a concern often seemed to threaten to insulate Eisenhower against the impact of critical or unwelcome facts. Thus, one morning, following a telecast of a question-and-answer "conference," the evening before, the President delightedly pointed out to me a stack of congratulatory telegrams on his desk. Happily, he exclaimed: "Not a single bad one!" The patent improbability of this provoked me to inquire of others on the staff, and I quickly discovered, of course, that all less-than-laudatory comments had been stopped at the door of his office.

And one final shadowing question appeared to reach beyond the President's relation to his own staff—to the far-from-new question of the precision and firmness of his mastery of the whole intricate machinery of the federal decision-making process. Thus at the outset of the campaign, for example, we had a slightly disconcerting little exchange about a key point in his first address. In this serious survey of world realities, he was to include a reaffirmation of the proposal, originally made in his foreign policy review in April of 1953, to commit the nation to giving a share of savings, achieved through any disarmament, to a world fund for aid and reconstruction of less-developed economies. Yet now, at one point, he confessed a kind of helpless pessimism about the renewed assertion, as he explained a little indifferently: "You know what the problem always is: it costs money. And lots of these fellows around here like nothing worse than talk about spending money." It was hard to detect, in such a remark, an inflection of militant resolve.

Still more disquieting was an incident much later in the campaign, in a conference devoted to more immediate matters. It was the day (October 23) of the release of one of the President's policy statements on nuclear testing, and the final substance and phrasing of the statement had been hammered out at a long afternoon meeting with the President, John Foster Dulles, and Lewis L. Strauss, Chairman of the Atomic Energy Commission. One highlight of the discussion came with another display of Eisenhower's pacifist fervor—and the World War II soldier's view of nuclear war as "unthinkable." Expanding on the horror of hydrogen bombs, the President went on: "My God, we have to simply figure a way out of this situation. There's just no point in talking about 'winning' a nuclear war." And waving a despairing arm vaguely in an easterly direction toward the Atlantic, he concluded: "You might just as well talk about going out and swimming that ocean." The emotional drift of his distress carried him to the question of what *could* be done to slacken the pace of the arms race and to deal with the Soviets on nuclear-weapons control. He then turned, with an aggressiveness near anger, to Strauss: "You know I've asked you and your office and everyone else to come up with some *new* proposals in this field. We've just got to get going here. And you haven't done much." This lament —at once sharp in tone and vague in content—forced Strauss to wince. And he answered in two parts. The first part was simply: "Sir, all we can do is to explore what is practical, and the real breakthrough has to be made on the *diplomatic* front—where *we* have no business." This was said with a quick, sidelong, and uncomfortable glance toward Dulles, whose impassive face suggested he had heard not a word. And the second part of the response was: "We are looking at a lot of ideas, you know—including this rotation business on testing, for instance, with one country by agreement testing one year, another country taking another year. Of course, there have been a whole lot of really impractical notions. But we are *working* on it all the time."

And that evening I wrote to myself: "One senses a kind of impasse." The word was inexact: it was another of those gray moments when a dialogue on the gravest issues finished in utterly hollow silence. A thread of conversation ended—neither in a conclusion nor even a snarl. It simply ended.

Meanwhile, at this particular moment, Dulles, as well as the entire Eisenhower administration, had more urgent matters to meet.

The crisis of the Middle East was exploding.

4

The slowly unfolding experience of one man trying, as best he can, to know and understand another is, in each instance, unique. No two such experiences could have been much more sharp in contrast than in the personal instances of Dwight David Eisenhower and John Foster Dulles. In the case of the President, the experience consisted of coming gradually to perceive that the seemingly simple structure of the man was, in fact, complex. In the case of the Secretary, almost the reverse seemed to occur: a personality initially suggesting great complexity grew to appear, with time, increasingly simple.

The essence of Dulles as Secretary of State—to oversimplify a little—was this: the man was a lawyer. As Secretary, he lived, acted, spoke, reacted, advanced, retreated, threatened, courted, summarized, analyzed, briefed, cross-examined, responded, appealed, objected, thrust, parried—like a lawyer. It is true that he displayed almost two distinct personalities: the public posture, rigid and categorical, righteous and doctrinaire; and the private demeanor, relaxed and communicative, supple and sophisticated. But the two contrasted like those of a lawyer—in and out of the courtroom.*

The analogy struck deeper. The Secretary of State saw himself as an advocate crucially and anxiously preoccupied with the daily progress of his litigation. As such, he was quickly excited by small gains, suddenly shaken by minor reverses, and ever prone to contemplating the drastic remedy of the massive retort. He was certain, too, that no case on the calendar of this court could match in importance the one that he was contesting. He responded, moreover, with the courtroom dramatist's sensitivity to the public beyond the railing. He was troubled by any signs of loss of their sympathy, especially if they were public figures, like congressmen or senators; and he glowed with reassurance whenever his words or gestures sent murmurs of admiration rippling through the audience. And all this endowed him with a rare and conscientious fervor, a great and inexhaustible energy, and a self-conscious sense of grave destiny. For he saw himself in no ordinary court: he stood before the bar of history.

So intense and so personal a sense of advocacy inspired much of the apparent righteousness with which he played the role of Secretary of State. He was, in effect, the prosecutor assigned to the historic labor of arraignment, condemnation, and punishment of the Soviet Union for crimes against freedom and peace. Serving this solemn commission, how could he be less than morally outraged and politically uncompromising in his appeal for "lib-

---

* The most curious example of Dulles' legalistic reflexes had occurred with a memorable blunder in a press conference in the first week of September 1953. On the eve of crucial national elections in West Germany, he had been carefully briefed to answer any question on the elections with a simple assertion of our respect for any free decision by a friendly people, and he proceeded—moments later—to stun his colleagues by flatly endorsing Adenauer before the world press. After the smoke of West German indignation had cleared, Bedell Smith explained to me a few days later: "It may seem incredible, but Foster cannot stop reacting like a lawyer. After the press conference, he knew without anyone telling him that he had made an absurd blunder. But *during* the press conference, he slipped back into the mentality of a lawyer facing questions of a *client*, and he answered as if he were in a private discussion in his own law office."

205

eration" of East European nations, for were not the facts of their enslavement the most documented and damning evidence to convict the Soviet Union? And how could one "negotiate" some mitigation of the basic indictment—with a defendant allowed to go unpunished for such offense? And did it not follow, like the logic of law, that nations confessing the "immoral" idea of "neutralism" disqualified themselves from taking part in the judgment of this historic court? For the issue was a capital offense, and these unallied nations admitted, in effect, their disbelief in capital punishment itself.

There was no anomaly in all the Eisenhower Years so remarkable in nature, and so historic in consequence, as the official kinship of this President and this Secretary of State. Their differences in personal temper and world outlook attained an almost unblemished study in contrasts. Where the one was expansive, the other was suspicious; where the one was occasionally vague, the other was fastidiously precise; where the one valued the thrust of "instinct," the other lived by the rule of logic; where the one would warmly hail the hope of a new act or initiative, the other would stoically press the warning of its peril or cost; where the one might risk credulity, the other risked cynicism. All this was equally apparent to American officials and to foreign diplomats acquainted with both men. Typically, at the height of Asian anxiety over the status of Quemoy and Matsu in 1955, an Indian representative of Nehru could almost despair of his several futile interviews with Dulles, could cross West Executive Avenue for one brief private meeting with Eisenhower, and could emerge glowing: "What a remarkable man! A real man of peace!"

Dulles, perhaps more acutely than Eisenhower, sensed the great gap between them, occasionally confessing privately his distress with the President's possible "naïveté." Accordingly, he practiced constant vigilance over all officials having or seeking direct access to the President. Similarly, it appeared to the Secretary a matter of both personal prudence and national policy to discourage the President's direct contact with either other chiefs of state or other officials of the State Department. Thus, again, Dulles saw himself as not simply the representative of the President in foreign affairs, but rather the legal advocate—the man of skill and steel retained to press the case of a client too malleable for his own best interest, unversed in the ways of litigation, and needful of strict professional counsel. And all this intensified still further the fiercely proprietary spirit with which Dulles approached his labor: essentially it was *his* case to argue, lose, or win.

Precisely this possessive fervor toward his labor tended to produce the most paradoxical result: it impelled the more coldly logical man to behave and to react as the more emotional and more impassioned of the two. While Eisenhower was far less austerely rational, the President's greater emotional detachment allowed him, in fact, to respond to the movement of world events in a more level and even way, less broken by sudden surges of hope or slumps toward despair. Thus, for example, as Eisenhower viewed Eastern Europe's occupation by Soviet forces, he would occasionally admit: "I have always thought Foster was a bit too optimistic about changes or upheavals there." And again, the President would show far less anxiety or alacrity than his Secretary in invoking military force to counter a Communist gain—as when, in the spring of 1954, he had overruled all recommendations, including the urgings of Admiral Radford, for an American air strike to support the beleaguered French in Indochina. In quite anomalous contrast to this cautious soldier-President, Dulles rather lived at intellectual ease with the conviction that, in his own historic litigation, he might have to appeal to force and war. As once he remarked to me, this particular September: "Standing away from my job, I guess I don't think the chances of war are more than one in four. But *in* my job, I've got to act as if they are fifty-fifty." From almost any other Secretary of State, these words would imply little more than sensible appreciation of the hazards of world life. From Dulles, however, they carried an inflection subtly suggestive of a disconcerting readiness to invoke martial power to prove a diplomatic point.

One long and candid private conversation that I had with Dulles, as the 1956 campaign was barely beginning, rather remarkably illuminated some of his mental ways—above all, his capacity to mingle the political and the personal, his sense of history and his sense of self. The two of us were scanning the world scene, as background to all presidential speeches during the campaign, and his general assessment reflected his thinking at its most broad and lucid. He spoke sensitively of America's dilemma of being "caught in the middle between the new nationalism and the old colonialism." He appraised clinically the historic impact of the Soviet Union's clear emergence as a mighty industrial power. He turned to Southeast Asia, with half of Vietnam now gone, and realistically concluded: "We have a clean base there now, without a taint of colonialism. Dienbienphu was a blessing in disguise." Reviewing diplomatic successes and failures of the last three years, he philosophized judiciously: "Sure, we have new problems all the time, but so long as they are not the *same* problems of a time past, we can think we are making progress." I recall, at this exact instant in his monologue, my immediate, self-accusing thought: he sounds far more measured and discerning than I have believed for the last year or so. Then the thought was suddenly shattered. The Secretary stood up, as if to acknowledge some unspoken compliment, and, most heartily, he said of himself: "Of course, of all the things *I* have done, *I* think *the most brilliant* of all has been to save Quemoy and Matsu." And I felt an almost physical reaction before the icy breath of his self-esteem.

Both sides of the Secretary's official character—the sophisticated and perceptive, and the self-concerned and shallow—continued to find voice, it seemed, throughout these months. Thus, a little while later in the campaign, he could talk to me privately of the world scene in these enlightened terms: "The concepts

208

and words that matter, in all we say, I think, are simply *peace* and *change*. We live in an age of deep change. You can't stop it. What you can do is to bend every effort to direct it—to see that it is evolutionary rather than revolutionary—and to retain, in the process, all that is good in the past. Most particularly, this is true of the whole Afro-Asian problem. What the Western world is moving toward is a new role with these peoples—a role of partnership rather than rule." Yet such signs of the Secretary's sense of balance—and sense of history—could seem harshly contradicted, not long after, when Vice President Nixon would greet the rupture between Britain and America over the Middle East as "a bold American declaration of independence." For, shortly after reading this partisan rationalization, I ascertained that it had been no impetuous outburst by an overwrought campaigner: the extravagant text had been authorized, prepared, and written for Nixon by Dulles himself. The Secretary, quite obviously, felt *personally* incensed by the inconsideration of others in frustrating his diplomacy in the Middle East.

For months preceding this late-October crisis, as one scanned the speeches and the schemes of statesmen from Moscow and New Delhi to Paris and London and Washington, one grew ever more anxiously aware that all roads were leading to Cairo. As far back as mid-1955, the Western capitals had glimpsed the first warnings of a Soviet-sponsored arms buildup throughout the Arab world, with special Soviet appreciation of the aggressive capabilities of Egypt's Gamal Abdel Nasser. The Egyptian president had responded with avidity and gratitude—stocking up on Czech weapons, recognizing the government of Communist China, and lashing the West's Baghdad Pact. Through the spring of 1956, the sands of the Arab world thus began to shift ominously, and Great Britain had appealed to the United States for joint policy and action to check Communist penetration of Egypt, astride the Suez Canal. Washington demurred, preferring to play for time. The crisis of Egypt in 1956 thus caught London and Washington in an exact reversal of their respective roles during the crisis of Indochina in 1954—when Great Britain had shied from any American suggestions of joint initiative.

Meanwhile Nasser, while turning East for arms and political texts, had turned West for economic help on a grand scale, to build the Aswan High Dam on the Nile. Eisenhower had reacted in a spirit true to his unwavering belief that wise statecraft should seek to extend economic influence, rather than impose economic isolation, on the politically doubtful. He accordingly favored answering the Egyptian call. So, less categorically, did Dulles—provided Cairo would pay the price of loosening its bonds with Moscow. But by the time a surly Nasser seemed receptive to such American help, the temper of Dulles was equally exasperated. On July 19, 1956, he publicly withdrew all offer of American help, issuing a castigation of Egypt whose tone bordered on the petulant. On July 26 Nasser seized the Suez Canal—barely a month after Great Britain, nudged by Washington's fervent anticolonialism, had withdrawn from the Suez region the last of its military forces. Rarely had the progress of British and American policies together paced off so disorderly an out-of-step march.*

The snarl of the Middle East, throughout the political campaign of 1956, made of Dulles a nettled Secretary—and a distraught lawyer. Zealous to press the crucial case against Soviet world policy, he deplored the whole Middle Eastern scene as a kind of irritating distraction—to be fought off as if it were imma-

* The New York *Herald Tribune*, not known for undue harshness toward the Eisenhower administration, ran a mid-campaign editorial (September 23, 1956), headed "Too Little and Too Late," tartly deploring the Administration policy toward the Middle East, thus: "American action . . . has been a series of improvisations and inconsistencies. . . . The State Department was well aware . . . before the summit meeting in Geneva that Nasser would seek arms and economic assistance where he could find it. . . . The United States merely dawdled. . . . The manner of the American reversal on Aswan was brusque, and there was obviously little preparation for a counter-stroke . . . The progressive thinning out of Western resistance to Nasser's action . . . [has inspired] naturally enough great bitterness in both Great Britain and France. . . . It is essential now that the United States should think through a policy on the Middle East."

terial and inadmissible evidence. Quite literally, he knew that any aggressive Anglo-French action against Egypt would only complicate his own case against Soviet aggrandizement. Thus, month after month—improvising proposals for the several hostile and enraged parties, assuaging and cajoling and procrastinating—he had appealed, with motion upon motion, for postponement of the dread hearing.

The diplomatic effort, always industrious and occasionally ingenious, was fated to fail.

In the last week of October the Central Intelligence Agency began gathering the bad news. Israel was mobilizing: more than one hundred thousand men were under arms, and armor and men were moving into positions along the Egyptian border. Paris and London were diplomatically quiet in a disturbing way—behaving suspiciously like people careful not to answer their phone till they were sure who was calling. Throughout the world of Western diplomacy, it was a humid, ominous moment of silence, before the sudden thunder of crisis.

The record of the next days in the White House, as I saw them in part, still tells a good deal of the men whose thoughts and acts and moods ruled the course of not only these turbulent days but also all the Eisenhower Years.

The record went like this. . . .

Sunday, October 28.

President returned from Walter Reed Hospital this afternoon, where he spent yesterday for his promised end-of-the-campaign physical checkup. He also sent off from there his appeals to halt Israeli mobilization (now speeded up overnight). Scheduled to fly south tomorrow for a fast series of "prop-stops" in Miami, Jacksonville, and Richmond, he calls me into his office in late afternoon to check tone and content of these, already drafted, and also to prepare short text to insert in them summarizing danger of Middle East situation. We talk for almost an hour on whole current scene. Annoyedly he recognizes political exigencies pressing him to make his southward campaign swing despite world situation: "If I did call off the southern trip, though I don't think it's necessary to do so, it would be misunderstood. There'd be political yapping all around that the doctors yesterday *really* found I was terribly sick and ready to keel over dead." Wryly, he refers to yesterday's work of preparing note to Ben-Gurion, between trips up and down hospital corridors for his tests and X-rays, and concludes: "Israel and barium make quite a combination."

The whole Middle Eastern scene obviously leaves him dismayed, baffled, and fearful of great stupidity about to assert itself. "I just can't figure out what the Israeli think they're up to. . . . Maybe they're thinking they just *can't* survive without more land. . . . But *I* don't see how they can survive without coming to some honorable and peaceful terms with the whole Arab world that surrounds them." . . . And pondering the reports of French complicity from Paris, his concern gets heated. "Damn it, the French, they're just egging the Israeli on—hoping somehow to get out of their *own* North African troubles. Damn it, they sat right there in those chairs three years ago, and we tried to tell them they would repeat Indochina all over again in North Africa. And they said, 'Oh, no! That's part of metropolitan France!'—and all that damn nonsense."

When I come back a little later with draft of a few innocuous sentences on the crisis for tomorrow's speeches, he says he already has word that State Department is ordering Americans out of Israel and Jordan and Egypt. In a few minutes, he gets report on Hungarian revolt: Budapest Radio claims great concessions to rebels. Bad news, though, is mounting suspicion that British are with French in encouraging Israel. His affectionate regard for the British makes him incredulous. "I just can't believe it," he keeps saying. "I can't believe they would be so stupid as to invite on *themselves* all the Arab hostility to Israel." And in terms of British relations with Washington: "Are they going to *dare* us—dare *us*—to defend the Tripartite declaration?"*

The pieces of the picture fit together fairly clearly, though, through all the fog of uncertain information. From the viewpoint of Israel, the timing looks superb: Russia is deep in satellite trouble, Britain and France are straining at the leash for a crack at Nasser, and the U.S. is in the middle of a national election. Thus the chance looks golden. . . . Finally, President breaks off, with a not very cheerful smile, heads for the doors to the terrace, and the slow walk to "the house," sighing a bit heavily: "Well, I better get out of here or—despite all those doctors—these things will have my blood pressure up to 490."

Monday, October 29.

Just about 3 P.M., the press office news-ticker clicks out the first reports of Israeli troops moving across the Egyptian border. Andy Goodpaster—almost overwhelmed these days, in maintaining White House liaison with Pentagon and CIA—tells me President's plane got the news just as he was taking off from Jacksonville, en route back via Richmond. With typical solicitude for crowds turning out to see him, President decides to touch down in Richmond despite events.

As we wait for President's return, there takes place in Adams' office one of the rare "strategy" meetings of the campaign, i.e., Leonard Hall, "Jerry" Persons, and two others of White House staff along with Adams and myself. It turns out that the timing could hardly be more incongruous, for purpose of meeting is to

---

* The Tripartite Agreement of 1950—the "basic document" for Western chancelleries in the Suez crisis—bound Great Britain, France, and the United States to take joint action, either within or without the United Nations, to use force if the borders specified in the 1950 armistice, between Israel and the Arab nations, were crossed or threatened.

hear Hall's plea that President's campaign windup speech in Philadelphia, scheduled for Thursday, include strong appeal for a GOP majority in Congress. Adams gives the standard White House retort: "Look, the *most* use and help the boss can be to all those fellows is to pile up his *own* majority as high as possible. Hell, with this war on our hands, he may not even get away from his desk to give *any* speech. If he does, it's fine with me if he talks to a political rally so seriously he doesn't get a single burst of applause." Amen. Hall further reports on last-minute whispering campaign about Eisenhower's "slight relapse." To guard against more of this, it's arranged to have President filmed as he votes early Election Morning—then rush films from Gettysburg to the television stations.

This evening (I fear) produced not much clarification of facts or policies. It was after dark—just around 7 P.M.—when President's car pulled up to rear entrance of White House and he rushed directly to residence. Waiting to confer with him there were Foster and Allen Dulles, Radford, Adams, and Persons. Earlier Dulles' office had told me Secretary felt sure there'd be no public statement tonight, but at 9 P.M. Hagerty reports to me brief text of statement being handed to the press. Its key sentences: "At the meeting the President recalled that the United States, under this and prior Administrations, had pledged itself to assist the victim of any aggression in the Middle East. We shall honor our pledge." A nice moralistic stand. But what does it mean? And how does one back it up? Literally read, it would seem to admit of two choices. One: We shall "assist" Egypt against Israel and against Britain and France if they move in. *Really?* Or two: We "pledge" flowers for the funeral of Nasser.

Tuesday, October 30.

A day to make one wonder—and worry. . . .

It begins at 8:40 with a quiet half-hour with President: his face drawn, eyes heavy with fatigue, worry, or both. Adams joins us, and it's agreed to cancel fast campaign trip to Texas scheduled for tomorrow. As Adams reports: "Foster would feel better if you're in town." Adams also startles me with suggestion of possible televised "report to the nation" tonight or tomorrow —with not a hint of its possible content. President deflects this with: "No, I'd rather avoid that. Under this damn FCC principle, the other fellows would right away be claiming equal time, and then we'd be in just the sort of public discussion we *least* need at this time."

Piecing together news and intelligence as the morning passes, I gather that (1) everyone at last night's council with President agreed that "we couldn't go back on our word" and had to reaffirm 1950 pledge; (2) we intend going to the UN despite Anglo-French opposition; (3) French in last days have been stepping up shipments of war matériel to Israel regardless of 1950 Tripartite Agreement; and (4) talk of a possible special session of the Congress fills White House corridors. Goodpaster, closely watching all Intelligence, pictures on-the-spot military situation as "more than retaliation, less than war." And finally morning ends with statement at noon by Eden to House of Commons—a 12-hour ultimatum to both Israeli and Egyptians to pull back 10 miles from Suez Canal, while reporting London has "asked" Egypt to admit Anglo-French forces to Suez zone.

Hagerty and I fall into a heated agrument at lunch on wisdom of precise wording of last night's "pledge." He reflects general White House optimism that statement itself will deter further action: "We've already slowed the British down, and it doesn't make much sense to expect them to prefer France to the U.S. as an ally." I argue that this seems both over-optimistic and oversimplified. Is it credible that a Britain that felt itself impelled to go this far in both political and military plans now will turn back because of President's statement? And *if* they do not, what does our reiteration of pledge *mean?* Again reflecting sanguine consensus of last night's meeting, Hagerty confidently suggests: "Let's wait and see if British don't pull back."

At 5 P.M. I spend 20 minutes with President reviewing fast-shifting situation. Find him torn between anxiety and, I fear, overoptimism. More calm (as usual) then either White House staff or State Department—all of whom are whipping themselves into an anti-British frenzy—he relates: "I've just finished writing an answer to an informative cable from Eden this morning, saying I understand and even sympathize with him on the problem he faces—but just hope he's figured out all the risks. . . . I'm not at all optimistic: I'm afraid the British'll come out of this with more loss of face. What are they going to do—fight the whole Moslem world?"

Without wanting to get into debate with him at such a juncture, I still have to ask how he interprets impact of our reaffirmed "pledge." Most hopefully, he says: "I think that problem will take care of itself if the Israeli stop fighting, and I'm pretty sure they will, with this ultimatum from the British. I'm quite confident that'll be over within 24 hours." And if not—will we be joining Nasser against our Western allies? "Hell, I don't know *where* we'll be at. . . . You see, London and Paris say now they regard the pledge as void because of Nasser taking arms from the Russians. But that doesn't go in *my* book. Nobody told *me* the pledge was void—and if it was, why didn't they say so before this?" This much seems clear in his mind, but he pauses in obvious dismay at the still-unanswered dilemma, finally adds helplessly: "Well, if the Israeli keep on fighting, we'll be in a hell of a fix. And I suppose if the other two powers, Britain and France, don't support the Tripartite Resolution, *we* would be

justified in taking that into account in not supporting it ourselves. . . . I don't know. . . . Maybe we'll just have to get off
the hook by talking about Russian arms going to Cairo." And
he winds up his unhappy soliloquy: "I've just never seen great
powers make such a complete *mess* and *botch* of things. . . . Of
course, there's just nobody, in a war, I'd rather have fighting
alongside me than the British. . . . But–*this* thing! My God!"

After 6 P.M.–a bleak little experience. Adams calls me to
his office to join a meeting already in progress with Hagerty
and Persons, and he explains: "We've been discussing the President maybe making a speech–it would be before the General
Assembly if it only were in session–laying out the whole problem . . . talking about our concern for the UN and its principles
. . . maybe saying the time has come for the UN to take stock
as to where the Western powers are dragging us all. . . . How's
that strike you?" Impatiently and sharply, I assail the notion: "In
the first place, I think public hand-wringing by the President–
and throwing off on our allies, with whatever provocation–is
not going to sound like effective leadership. In the second place,
as for our so-called moral position, it would appear on this basis
to amount simply to taking a stand on the same ground already
claimed by Bulganin–in his messages this afternoon denouncing
the whole Anglo-French-Israeli action as a barefaced plot to grab
the Canal from Nasser. So–politically *and* morally–I deplore
the whole idea of the President going to the people just to
curse the British and the French." And unkindly I find myself
adding: "The damn trouble is that we *don't* have a policy in
this crisis, and you *can't* try to use a *speech* as a substitute."
Adams nods reluctant agreement: "Well, let's kick it around
some more tomorrow . . . then try to decide something. . . ."

Depressed and angry, I phone Persons and Adams a half hour
later and suggest a breakfast meeting to talk rationally in the
morning. The need for the President to say *something* to the
nation is growing more obvious: he can't stay silent much
longer. But surely he must do something more than merely to

point an accusing finger at the British for all the trouble. . . .
An act of statesmanship—or an exercise in self-absolution? . . .
The U.S. is hardly unimplicated in all events leading up to this
crisis. It should have something civil and constructive to suggest
by way of leading us *out* of it.

Wednesday, October 31.

A wearying day, with some remarkable moments. . . .

The air at the 7:30 breakfast conference (Adams, Persons,
Hagerty, Goodpaster, Hauge, and I) seems thick and heavy
with the righteous wrath against Britain that is beginning to
suffocate the White House. And the righteousness even seems
petty—as if the *real* crime of London has been to contrive so
thoughtlessly to complicate President's re-election or at least
whittle down his majority. Indignation finally teeters on the kind
of frivolity that is frightening, as one of the staff, fatigued and
intemperate, blurts out this proposal: "I've been trying to think
of what we should *do*. Well, perhaps this is the time for a—let's
call it a '*Bomb for Peace.*' It's as simple as this: let's send one
of Curt LeMay's gang over the Middle East, carrying an atomic
bomb. And let's warn *everyone:* we'll drop it—if they *all* don't
cut this nonsense out." This suggestion was greeted with the
pained silence that was the most polite reply possible. But the
crude fantasy underscored (1) the capacity of some in this
Administration for little more than parochial, self-preoccupied
distress, and (2) bizarre results attainable from a White House
staff totally untouched by serious experience in foreign affairs.

As the meeting returns to immediate business at hand, I again
annoy almost all present with question whether anyone knows
what "honoring the pledge" of 1950 means in terms of national
policy. All insist "we're doing our best" to deter Anglo-French
aggression, and Goodpaster avows that merely making statement

proves "we're ready to play our blue chips on this—in the price we're paying in terms of our relations with our allies." All a little confusing. Meeting finally ends with agreement Adams will discuss with President phoning Dulles and getting Secretary to prepare draft for a possible "report to the nation"—*tonight!*

At 11:30 spend one hour with President—initially to review draft I wrote last night for (possible) Philadelphia speech tomorrow night. He generally approves—especially line of argument appealing to "law" in world community as condemning aggression "no matter who the attacker, no matter who the victim." ("We cannot subscribe to one law for the weak, another law for the strong; one law for those opposing us, another for those allied with us. There can be only one law—or there shall be no peace.") With not much enthusiasm, for I know it oversimplifies far too much, I had written out this approach to the crisis last night, for the sad reason that no other reasonable approach occurred to me, to validate U.S. position *without* vilifying our Allies. President, less tired than yesterday evening, still laments: "I just don't know what got into those people. It's the damndest business I ever saw supposedly intelligent governments get themselves into." And his passing remarks suggest that what really troubles him most is neither moral nor political—but *military*—judgment. He suspects British don't know *technically* what they're doing. This kind of demurral is refreshing contrast to White House staff's political righteousness prevailing just outside his office door.

Midafternoon brings total crisis in White House. British planes now bombing Cairo airfields—signaling end of massive "deterrent" effect of U.S. statement on "pledge" Monday night. Meanwhile, all now is geared to a 7 P.M. telecast to nation, but Dulles' promised draft fails to reach me till 3:15. Worse: his text is impossible. It recites and rambles, with no force of argument. To my surprise, Dulles, the lawyer, largely ignores the word "law"—and what other word or idea exists to appeal to? I rush to President, who's just finished reading his copy of Dulles' text, and I find him shaking his head sadly over it. He's in Cabinet room—since his own office is already overrun with TV men and cables for the speech just over three hours hence! We hastily agree (1) to junk Dulles' draft and start anew; (2) to divide speech equally between events in Hungary and in Egypt; (3) to tone down Dulles' references to "irresistible" forces of "liberation" unleashed in Eastern Europe; (4) to affirm American intent to appeal to UN on Middle East strife; and (5) to relate U.S. position to concept of "law" in international community.

By now time is 4:15. Next two hours fearfully tense. Two secretaries take dictation from me in relays, to speed typing. With time too short to send slow-forming text to Dulles at State, I have to phone him to come and join me in Cabinet room, to scan sheets as typed. Under strain and watching clock moving past 5:00, am drenched with perspiration. President has left us to relax through all this—hitting golf balls from the edge of lawn just beyond the Cabinet windows. Confession: it's the first time I've almost resented his ability to play golf, so incongruous does it seem in these mad minutes.

We go past 6:00 still dictating, typing, pencil-editing, with Dulles reviewing text as it comes back from typewriter. He is ashen gray, heavy-lidded, strained. His shoulders seem to sag as he murmurs: "I'm just sick about the bombings . . . the idea of planes over Cairo right now!" He suggests only most trivial word-changes—except for characteristically deleting a temperate phrase about hopes in Hungary ("There seems to appear the dawn of hope") to read confidently: "There *is* the dawning . . ." Rush to President's bedroom just after 6:15 so he can read text aloud once while he dresses. He has just one substantive enjoinder as he starts reading: "I want to be sure we show clearly in here how vital we think our alliances are. Those British—they're still my right arm!" He approves text with scarcely any change and I race back to Cabinet room to start underlining, for speech-emphasis, his large-type reading copy.

He enters at 6:45 and sits across from me, as I underscore text with grease pencil and unceremoniously push it across to him page by page. It's four minutes before seven as I hand him last page. He clutches them, jesting: "Boy, this is taking it right off the stove, isn't it?"

Speech comes out surprisingly coherent, summarizing first East European scene, secondly Middle East conflict. In both, keynote is moderation, sharply contrasting with extemporaneous vehemence around White House in last days. On Eastern Europe while hailing hopes for freedom in Poland and Hungary, President ends with direct remarks to Soviet Union disavowing any "ulterior purpose" of U.S. and avowing anxiety "to remove any false fears that we would look upon new governments . . . as potential military allies." On Middle East, temperate note is even more evident. He reviews military actions, notes that Washington "was not consulted in any way about any phase," acknowledges that "we believe these actions to have been taken in error"—but quickly adds: "To say this . . . is in no way to minimize our friendship with these nations, nor our determination to maintain those friendships. And we are fully aware of the grave anxieties of Israel, of Britain, and France. We know that they have been subjected to grave and repeated provocations." Nonetheless—he concludes—"the United Nations represents the soundest hope for peace in the world. . . . For this very reason, I believe that the processes of the United Nations need further to be developed and strengthened."

Scene for all these words was heavy with tension: President looking trim in gray, behind his desk and under glaring lights, seemed the most calm man in room. Press was edgy with expectancy, since no moment since Korea has seemed so charged with war peril. Even technicians around cameras were hushed and anxious. President's voice strong and assured, and he finishes at stroke of 7:14. As he passes me in doorway on his way back to "the house," he grins with relief and says: "I just said to George Allen over there, I had been thinking maybe I'd have to have you hidden under the desk to hand me page after page as I talked! Went fine, though."

Immediate press and telephone response most reassuring. The press (exposed to so much wild corridor-talk lately) appears almost astonished at cool presidential demeanor—and pleased by absence of any hysterics, ranting, or carping. . . . So maybe, in all this fantastic frenzy, we stumbled upon some way at least to articulate a United States position that has *some* perspective, and dignity. . . . As always—one can only hope.

One more scene from these days stays vivid in memory.

This took place Monday, November 5: an Election Eve darkly overcast by political tragedies in distant places. In Hungary, in the days immediately following the President's report to the nation, Soviet tanks and troops had suddenly swung around to slaughter the rebels in the squares of Budapest—summarily extinguishing "the dawn" envisioned by the Secretary of State a few hours before. In the Middle East, British and French land, sea and air forces seemed more committed than ever to full-scale invasion of Egypt. In the "neutral" nations, watching both arenas anxiously, there stirred a sardonic awareness of witnessing exhibitions, singularly naked and simultaneous, of both the "old" colonialism of Western Europe and the "new" colonialism of the Soviet Union. And to the White House, at about 4 P.M. of this particular afternoon, there had come the ominous message from the Soviet Union's Chairman of the Council of Ministers, Nikolai Bulganin—urging joint action by American and Soviet naval units in the Mediterranean to prevent Anglo-French "aggression."

The President summoned me at 5 P.M. to join a meeting in his office for preparation of a White House statement answering the Bulganin letter, which Moscow had already released to the public. With Dulles suddenly hospitalized by the cancer that forewarned the coming terminal phase of his illness, the State Department was represented by Under Secretary Herbert

Hoover, Jr., and Herman Phleger, the department's legal adviser. The President seemed poised and relaxed. But the lines and pallor of his face betrayed fatigue, under the lights just turned on in the fading afternoon.

The discussion was somber. We agreed on the adjective "unthinkable" to dismiss the Soviet suggestion of joint military action in the Middle East and characterized the Bulganin letter as "an obvious attempt to divert world attention from the Hungarian tragedy." But no stern and indignant rhetoric could make the moment less perilous, less precarious. For the obvious danger existed that Moscow might be irresistibly tempted toward aggressive action, on a massive scale, by *both* hope and fear—the hope that Egypt signified a deep division of the West, and the fear that Hungary threatened a kind of earthquake within the Soviet sphere. The combination looked explosive. And the President described it pithily: "Those boys are both furious and scared. Just as with Hitler, that makes for the most dangerous possible state of mind. And we better be damn sure that every Intelligence point and every outpost of our Armed Forces is absolutely right on their toes."

Nor was Eisenhower, at this moment, facing merely the imagined need of counterthrusts against skirmishes or local aggression. He was thinking, with cold realism and as Commander in Chief, of the menace that seemed to him implicit in the Bulganin message. "You know," he said tautly, "we may be dealing here with the opening gambit of an ultimatum. We have to be positive and clear in our every word, every step. And if those fellows start something, we may have to hit 'em—and, if necessary, with *everything* in the bucket."

Even in this atmosphere, the President's faculty for wry humor persisted in flickering. Both Hoover and Phleger related that the CIA had reports of growing fear around Nasser, and in Nasser himself, that his position, before a resolute Anglo-French action, might fast become hopeless. Dryly, Eisenhower com-

223

mented: "Tell Nasser we'll be glad to put him on St. Helena and give him a million dollars."

And so the dark and the light blended in this quiet scene in the President's office—as the political campaign of 1956, in the nation outside, came to its close. We were interrupted by a frantic message from Ambassador Bohlen in Moscow, counseling all effort to bring the fastest possible cease-fire in the Middle East, to cut the ground out from under the Soviet threat of broad-scale military action. Grimly, the President read the message and sighed: "There has to be some way out of this impasse." Prophetically, Phleger confessed his belief that the issue of victory or defeat in the Middle East had now become so tense and dramatic, and the worldwide stakes so high, that the crisis could end only in the flat terms of a choice between political and personal destinies: either Nasser must fall—or Eden must fall.

And the President brought discussion to a close with the tart commentary: "All I can say is—it's one hell of a way to conduct a *world* election."

5

Election Night . . .

This time the scene is the presidential suite in Washington's Sheraton Park, with all the drab little hotel rooms opening off a long corridor of the third floor. In the ballroom downstairs, the throng of press and campaigners and well-wishers mill around, watching returns posted, every moment or two, on cards hung against a huge curtain. They chatter, cheer, laugh, groan with each fragment of early news, but a sense of confident, almost gay expectancy fills the air, with even the correspondents murmuring boldly: "It's going to be a short evening." Upstairs, the loud battery of television sets are jabbering out the first returns from New England villages, border states, isolated big-city precincts—punctuated by the solemnly phrased exercises in verbal caution that, at an early hour, pass for political commentary and analysis. And before 9 P.M. many of those closest to the President are there to savor the expected taste of victory . . . Milton Eisenhower and Herbert Brownell, rivaling one another in buoyant anticipation and bursts of guffawing laughter . . . "Jerry" Persons grinning with relief, as he thinks back to the moment, just a little more than three months ago, when a gray and dispirited President murmured that he might not be able to go on . . . Sherman Adams squatting comfortably on the floor in a small room, quietly disdaining all the noisy gregariousness of the corridor and main suite, unsmilingly staring at the moving screen before him, as if commanding it to hurry and get its serious business done with. . . .

The President has already had a full day, starting with his early-morning visit to the polling booth in Gettysburg. He had flown back to the capital for a twelve-thirty meeting of the National Security Council. Then he had rested a couple of hours after lunch, as now was his fixed routine; a little later, he was checked over quickly by his White House doctor, the devoted Major General Howard McC. Snyder; and then he had taken another hour's rest, to prepare for the length and excitement of the evening. Thanks to Suez, he has given up all hope of an immediate post-election respite of golf, as his solicitous secretary confides: "He's as disappointed as a kid who had counted out all the days to Christmas." Now it is past 10 P.M. when he leaves the White House to come to the hotel, as we who are awaiting his arrival watch him on the hotel's television screens. Twenty minutes later, he is coming down the narrow corridor in a little triumphal march to the irregular rhythm of pattering applause from the doorways of each room. Trim and erect in his gray suit, he grins broadly in frank pleasure, and his cheeks hold a healthy flush of excitement.

Nor can the excitement of the moment be chilled by the cool presumption of victory. In a realistic sense, the high drama

225

of Election Night is always contrived: the great national act of decision is over before the witnessed drama begins, the polls (almost everywhere) have closed, the levers have been pulled, the verdict written beyond recall. All that is left is an exercise in arithmetic. Yet none of this dulls the tension of the long, slow process of piecing together all the fragments of the decision, scattered from ocean to ocean—on Texas plains and along Oregon shores, in the hills of West Virginia and the valleys of Southern California, along the flat, blank-looking plains of the wheatlands and in the jagged, congested canyons of the great cities. Piece by piece, the fragments are discovered, related, assembled—a little section here, a larger section there, slyly giving glimpses of the full picture-to-be. Then gradually one begins truly to *know*, not merely guess or believe or assert, the answer to the forever inscrutable question: what did *they* do—the watching, waving, shrieking, clutching, cursing, cheering millions? What did they really *do*—finally, quietly, alone—in that instant of solitude when they are utterly sovereign? In all the world, there is nothing to match or compete with this. No other free people, no other democratic system anywhere, audaciously leaves the final choice of its leader to this decision by direct, definitive vote of the millions. . . .

So there is no denying the intoxicating power of the fumes of these hours of decision. The air is stale with smoke from hundreds of cigarettes nervously puffed and snuffed out, with scores of whisky glasses half-gulped and left to stand and turn to water, with simple sweat from all the brows and bodies waiting, waiting, waiting. . . . Even when you fancy that you know the outcome—you *do*, don't you?—you cannot shake off the sense of exhilaration. For it really is not whisky you have been sipping, all these hours. It is wine—the strange vintage so elaborately mellowed in the hours and days, that have seemed years, of talking, traveling, writing, arguing, cheering, doubting, deciding, fretting, raging, hoping—through all the sleep-defying nights and nerve-twisting days. And when the wine, at sweet long last, bears the taste of full-bodied victory, it proves a heady brew. If only for the instant . . . with no dark thoughts of the morrow . . .

Upon this particular night, there occur a few special, odd or touching little moments for remembrance. They illuminate, here and there, little recesses of the man, Dwight David Eisenhower. For it is almost inevitably an occasion for him to be reflecting upon himself, even to be speaking of himself, as the rough surge of exciting news knocks down barriers of reticence and frees many a word for candid utterance.

Already early in the evening of watching and computing, his glee is as frank as his grin. Some of the returns carry pleasant surprises. And his gruff humor responds heartily to my telling him at one point, as he sits idly on a corridor bench, that he holds a fair lead even in Louisiana. He explodes: "Louisiana? That's as probable as leading in Ethiopia!" And he starts pacing around more animatedly, nudging and jesting with whomever he encounters.

Some while later, short of midnight, he slumps down beside me on the hard-benched seat in the bleak corridor. He sighs and begins murmuring aloud, as if half to himself: "Boy, I've got to sit down. I had my rest this afternoon, but, you know, the thing is for me to take it a bit easy so I *don't* have trouble. It's funny, you know. *Emotions* are the things you got to watch out for. So all the doctors say. The worst is anger. . . . You notice I don't get *angry* any more—like I used to? . . . Just don't *let* myself. Can't afford to. . . . And after anger, any great emotional strain or worry is bad. . . . Very curious. . . . But these *are* the things that do affect the heart. . . . Haven't had a twinge since the first one, but . . . just got to be careful, I guess. . . ."

Around us, the clatter of voices and glasses and television and laughter continues in rowdy chorus—alive and gay and unreckoning. For a moment, listening to Eisenhower so softly reflective, I feel as if the two of us are isolated behind an invisible shield, locked inside a little bubble of a life apart. The world—just a

227

few feet away—is counting votes. He is counting the beat of his pulse.

Suddenly, the bubble bursts. The high and triumphant voice of "Jerry" Persons proclaims, in rich Alabama accent, the glad tidings. "I want *all* of you to know," he cries, "that the cradle of the Confederacy—Montgomery, Alabama—has just voted for a Republican for the first time in its history!" Cheers spiral up with laughter. And a no longer pensive President throws back his head to roar appreciatively.

A little later, I find and hear the old soldier again beside me. The returns are piling up his massive victory. But he surveys the battlefield with clinical concern and a proud passion for victory. "There's Michigan and Minnesota still to see. You remember that story of Nelson—dying, he looked around and asked, 'Are there any of them still left?' I guess that's *me*. When I get in a battle, I just want to win the whole thing . . . six or seven states we can't help. But I don't want to lose any more. Don't want any of them 'left'—like Nelson. That's the way I feel."

Minutes—ten, twenty, forty—pass. And now the President gets visibly impatient for the concession from Stevenson. It is 1952 all over again: "What in the name of God is the monkey waiting for? Polishing his prose?" He starts assembling his family for the victorious appearance on television, and he avows he'll proceed without a formal concession from his opponent, if the meaningless delay continues. Then, when he hears that Stevenson is appearing on the TV screens in the main room of the suite, he stoically stalks through the room to the bar, explaining: "I'm just looking for a drink." And he passes back and out of the room, with his dry over-the-shoulder instruction to others to watch the defeated candidate and "to receive the surrender."*

* The "terms" of the "surrender," electorally speaking, came even closer to an "unconditional" triumph than 1952. Eisenhower's popular vote of 35,581,003 topped Stevenson's 25,738,765 by nearly 10 million—more than 50 percent greater than the margin by which he had won in 1952 (33,778,963 against 27,314,992). And the victory in the electoral vote went up from 442 vs. 89 in 1952, to 457 vs. 73—with Stevenson carrying nothing outside of seven southern states.

For a few minutes, then, he disappears into a quiet room, alone. When he returns, he has changed—with curious fastidiousness —to a blue suit. And he leads his family downstairs for their formal appearance before the nation watching their television screens. Winner—and still . . .

Suddenly he who has just left the room appears on our television screens. The famous grin seems nearly as wide as the outstretched arms raised in victory.

The words are spontaneous, unrehearsed, persuasive in their freshness and feeling.

This is a solemn moment . . . My most grateful thanks . . .

The only thing I can say to all the people . . . is our earnest prayer that nothing we can ever do—or shall ever do—will betray that trust. . . .

As we look ahead . . . let us remember that a political party deserves the approbation of America only as it represents the ideals, the aspirations, and the hopes of Americans. If it is anything less, it is merely a conspiracy to seize power. . . .

Modern Republicanism looks to the future. . . . As long as it remains true to the ideals and the aspirations of America, it will continue to increase in power and influence—for decades to come. . . .

My friends, I conclude with a pledge. With whatever talents the good God has given me, with whatever strength there is within me, I will continue . . . to do just one thing: to work for 168 million Americans here at home—and for peace in the world.

The commitment rang with truth and feeling.

One among many, I was moved. And I dared, again, to hope—a little.

CHAPTER SEVEN

The Faltering Force

We live in a land of plenty, but rarely has this earth known such peril as today. . . .

The air rings with the song of our industry—rolling mills and blast furnaces, dynamos, dams, and assembly lines—the chorus of America the Bountiful.

This is our home, yet this is not the whole of our world. For our world is where our full destiny lies—with men of all peoples and all nations who are or would be free. And for them—and so for us—this is no time to ease or rest. . . .

The building of . . . a peace is a bold and solemn purpose. To proclaim it is easy. To serve it will be hard. And to attain it, we must be aware of its full meaning—and ready to pay its full price . . . in toil patiently sustained, in help honorably given, in sacrifice calmly borne. . . .

One truth must rule all we think and all we do. No people can live to itself alone. . . . No nation can longer be a fortress, lone and strong and safe. And any people seeking such shelter for themselves can now build only their own prison. . . .

We honor the aspirations of those nations which, now captive, long for freedom. . . . We honor, no less in this divided world than in a less tormented time, the people of Russia. We do not dread, rather do we welcome, their progress in education and industry. We wish them success in their demands for more intellectual freedom, greater

*security before their own laws, fuller enjoyment of the rewards of
their own toil. For as such things may come to pass, the more certain
will be the coming of that day when our peoples may freely meet in
friendship.*

*And so we voice our hope and our belief that we can help to heal
this divided world. . . .*

*May the turbulence of our age yield to a true time of peace, when
men and nations shall share a life that honors the dignity of each, the
brotherhood of all.*

The Second Inaugural gave brief but true testimony to the
gravest purposes that would inspire the second term of Dwight
David Eisenhower. These purposes would seem at first to soar,
then swerve, nearly vanish, again startlingly reappear, and—finally
—spend themselves. As they rose and fell, they traced, with almost the precision of a finely computed graph, the ascending and
the waning force of the Eisenhower presidency through its last
four years. Initially, they attested to the momentum—the stir of
activity and the surge of emotion—with which the new term began. As they became halting and hesitant, through 1957 and 1958,
so, too, did the men and their policies—as the nation's Secretary
of State gradually weakened toward death and its President
seemed to stumble toward distraction. And then, in the closing
years of 1959 and 1960, these deep intents would dramatically
appear again, to rouse and impel the President, quite literally,
upon a journey of some one hundred thousand miles.

The President spent the better part of three days in patient
work with me on the Inaugural words and pledges to accompany
the second taking of his oath of office. These were, to me, lively
and encouraging days: he had seemed never more quick and
explicit or more deeply committed to vigorous action. And he
happily related, the morning after the Inaugural ceremonies, a
distinguished friend's response the day before: "Sam Rayburn,
my gosh, he almost embarrassed me yesterday," he reported. "He
was so full of praise after the speech. He came up to me and
said so seriously, 'I'd never say this publicly, and I'd never admit

it to another Republican, but that was just the finest speech I've heard in forty-six years in this town.'" When I remarked that the Address's clear forewarning of broader—and costlier—action on the foreign front would exasperate or enrage Republican ultra-conservatives, Eisenhower merely gave a wide grin and a deep growl: "I don't give a damn about them. What I try to keep getting across, all the time, is that they don't really speak for the party, so it doesn't matter to me what noises they make." Nor was he the least perturbed by the fact of Democratic control of the Congress. "I think it's pretty obvious," he said, with no visible sorrow, "that when it comes to domestic affairs, the people would rather have the Democrats running things."

The one dilemma troubling him politically—in these earliest hours of his second term—was the elusive riddle of future Republican leadership. He recalled again his regret that he had failed to persuade Nixon to shift to a Cabinet post the previous year, but he acknowledged with cool realism: "The thing Dick may have figured was that 1960 didn't matter too much, and in the event of my—er—disablement, he'd take over and at least have the presidency for *that* long." But the question of political succession seemed almost to haunt him. "This whole problem of building up men capable of leadership," he lamented, "we've never seemed to meet it the way the British succeed in doing. When their Conservatives look around for a leader, they always seem to have two or three men all ready to go."

He went on to affirm, however, one more immediate concern. He voiced anew his resolve to compel more creative action by the Congress in the coming session, including heavy appropriations for mutual security and foreign aid. And he reverted to our last long talk before these days—the November past, when I had said farewell the day after Election Day—and he recalled his intent, so sharply stated then, to demand more fresh and concrete programs from the State Department, especially for the Middle East. The guns were silent there now, with the Anglo-French-Israeli suspension of military operations in the days following his election. But Eisenhower was still insisting: "I've ordered real programs to be drawn up for every country in that area, because the problems that hit us last November had roots going back long before then. And we'll have something to help those peoples, just so long as they stay away from the Russians. We'll have something—or I'll damn we'll know why not."

The words and the moment—close to noon, on January 21, 1957—would long stay alive in my memory. The second term was barely twenty-four hours old, and the President was pacing the oval office briskly: his figure trim in a favorite gray suit, his color high, his eyes blue-bright, his voice as resonant as ever I had heard it. Not a trace of fatigue, by word or gesture, gave sign that yesterday's long Inaugural festivities had strained or tired him. And the moment would stay so explicitly vivid in afterthought for the sorrowful reason that this, indeed, was the last instant when I could imagine that what lay ahead might yet revive and redeem the lost hopes behind us.

One faint, final echo of this moment would come four months later, almost to the day: May 21, 1957. By this date, the President was locked in difficult battle with the Congress, and the urgent issue was his call for $3.86 billion to support mutual security arrangements with forty-two other nations.* To meet the crisis, he decided to appeal directly to the people. Upon the sudden request of a distressed Sherman Adams, I rushed to Washington to work with the President for two days to draft his address for nationwide television. And the exhortation of the Inaugural was repeated almost monotonously:

* In the battle of the preceding year on funds for mutual security in fiscal 1957, the President had fared poorly—with a full $1 billion cut from his $4.86 billion request. This dismal result had been in considerable degree due to the flat hostility—through argument after argument with the President—of Senator Knowland, deploring particularly all financial aid to India or Yugoslavia.

233

Defense against Communist conspiracy and encirclement cannot be with guns alone. . . . You cannot satisfy hunger with deadly ammunition. . . . The cost of peace is high. Yet the price of war is higher and is paid in different coin. . . .

To try to save money at the risk of such damage is neither conservative nor constructive. It is reckless. It could mean the loss of peace. It could mean the loss of freedom. It could mean the loss of both.

I know that you would not wish your government to take such a reckless gamble.

I do not intend that your government take that gamble.

In the world of Washington long trained and alert to sensing those moments of decision that elude the crisp headlines of the daily press, this political instant seemed to register with as much force—and perhaps hopeful omen—as the private moment I had known, alone with the President, four months earlier. And the implications were shrewdly weighed by the New York *Times,* in a Washington dispatch from James Reston:

President Eisenhower has shown in the last two days what can be done when he mobilizes Presidential power and personal influence. . . . In what have probably been the two most effective days of his second Administration, he has regained the initiative over the opposition in his own and the Democratic Party. . . . The surprising thing . . . is that it has taken the White House so long to turn around. The storm warnings have been up ever since the collapse of the Administration's Middle East policy last winter. . . .

Can he now maintain the initiative? The feeling here is that he can if he will. . . .

The record in Washington is full of evidence on how to organize Administration support in the Congress. What General Eisenhower said last night about his so-called foreign aid bill is precisely what Franklin Roosevelt was saying about the Lend-Lease Bill sixteen years ago. . . . The difference is that President Roosevelt organized his supporters in the Congress during the Lend-Lease debate. . . . Thus the debate was kept in balance under conditions that were much more adverse to the Administration than those that pertain today. . . .

The point, therefore, is not whether the initiative can be maintained, but whether it will be maintained. And that is largely up to the President himself.*

The year of 1957 delivered, as retort to this question, a historic negative.

The full answer came in three parts—with three unhappily memorable events of the year. Each of these events appeared wholly distinct in nature and cause, yet all carried a single and clear portent: the faltering of power in the presidency. And as if three separate acts were conspiring to create a tidy drama for the full calendar, each would play itself out with a different season of the year.

Spring would witness the battle of Fiscal 1958—and the President's hapless retreat from a budget vital to his entire program.

Summer would make Little Rock, Arkansas, a city of dark fame across the earth.

And autumn would see the sky streaked—and all free nations startled—by *Sputnik*.

2

The tortuous ordeal through which any Administration's budget generally suffers does not often contain the essential ingredients of great tragedy or low comedy. This struggle of Fiscal 1958 suggested both. For it revealed an unsteady hand—and an unresolved will—in the office of the President. And, as befitted an Administration of paradox and ambivalence, it told a tale of profound and personal irony.

The simple plot was outlined on a single day: January 16, 1957. The budget submitted by Eisenhower to the Congress on this day faithfully reflected the spirit of both his spontaneous

* New York *Times*, May 23, 1957.

phrases on Election Night and the deliberated commitments of his Inaugural Address. The proposed expenditure of seventy-two billion dollars, deferring not at all to the Republican conservatives, called for sufficient increases in foreign aid and national defense, along with relatively substantial sums for resource development and welfare programs, including school construction. All this seemed a long way, indeed, from the visions of tax reduction, so tantalizingly depicted to the 1953 Eisenhower Cabinet by George Humphrey. But, on this same day, Secretary of the Treasury Humphrey released to the press a memorandum of lament upon his President's budget. At the very hour of the arrival of the President's Budget Message on Capitol Hill, Humphrey declared: "There are a lot of places in this budget that can be cut." Warming to his subject, he warned the nation that the "terrific" tax burden must be eased—or "I will predict that you will have a depression that will curl your hair."*

The spectacle of the Secretary of the Treasury publicly rebuking his President for his program was remarkable enough, but the stunning harm was yet to be done. And this was contrived by Eisenhower himself—at a press conference, only three days after his Inauguration. Meeting the obvious question as to his and Humphrey's conflict on the budget, the President replied: "Well, in my own instructions to the Cabinet and heads of all offices, I have told them that every place that there is a chance to save a dollar out of the money that we have budgeted . . . everybody that is examining the many details . . . ought to find some place where they might save another dollar. . . . I think if Congress can—its committees—it is their duty to do it." As for the basic memorandum that Humphrey had read to his own press conference, Eisenhower assured his listeners: "That written memorandum—I not only went over every word of it, I edited it, and it expresses my convictions very thoroughly."†

* Ibid., January 17, 1957.
† Ibid., January 24, 1957.

Thus, in the space of a very few minutes, the President of the United States assumed not one but two astounding postures: as the Chief Executive, he invited the Congress to attack his own requests, and he commended the alacrity of his own Secretary of the Treasury in publicly encouraging such attack.

With this, the political barometer seemed set for a season of vacillation, as the office of the President itself seemed blown about, now by sudden breezes of boldness, now by warning puffs of caution. Through the months of February and March, Budget Director Percival F. Brundage went through appropriate motions to give proof of the President's sincerity about saving money. Members of the national business community—with a sensitivity to presidential hesitation considerably superior to their sense of humor—propagated the slogan that "Brundage wants the shirt off your back" and, by parcel post, filled the unhappy Budget Director's mail with all kinds of shirts. Farce sped on—with the President occasionally (as in a March 27 press conference) showing sudden spurts of confidence about his own budget and denouncing cuts in foreign aid as "the poorest kind of economy we can find." This particular declaration came, however, the day after Republicans in the House had passed a unanimous resolution demanding deep cuts in the budget, so that Speaker of the House Sam Rayburn could mock the presidential words as "a pretty good answer to what his own folks did up here yesterday."* By April, the more "modern" Republicans, who initially had been eager to support the President's original budget, felt demoralized by the strong suspicion that he was no longer acknowledging its authorship.

The middle of May brought the dispiriting climax. On the night of May 14, the President addressed a "fireside chat" to the people. His defense of his budget was so vague and unpersuasive that Press Secretary Hagerty, the following day, refused even to comment on the response by mail. And on this same day, im-

* New York *Times*, March 28, 1957.

mediately after his appeal to the people, the President addressed his press conference in a manner calculated to destroy any doubt as to the abiding ambiguity of his position. . . .

I don't think it is the function of a President of the United States to punish anybody for voting what he believes. . . . I don't see how it is possible for any President to work with the Republican group in Congress . . . except through their elected leadership. . . . When these large sums are involved, there comes a chance right along for both the Executive and the Congress to do a squeezing process. . . . There is some squeezing possible, and I have never kicked about that.*

It was at this moment that I received in New York the appeal from Sherman Adams to lend assistance on a second telecast to argue the President's case for mutual security. I could not refuse: the issue was too critical. But I returned to Washington—for those forty-eight hours—with a reluctance edged with anger. In a personal sense, the weight of intellectual baggage perhaps balanced out: I was heavier with dismay than ever, but notably lighter in burden of illusions. Even a victory on mutual security could not redeem a lost campaign on the wide front of the whole presidential program. In part—but only in part—I could sense the almost certain causes for the disastrous display of irresolution. The President's own earnest sense of frugality and the personal authority of the voice of George Humphrey could all too readily render Eisenhower a man divided against himself, in a battle for so awesome a sum as $72 billion. And how could I fail to think back to the dreary day in 1953 when almost equally elaborate uncertainty had threatened, even then, to blur Eisenhower's first request for funds for mutual security?

I sought in the White House for any more precise explanation from those closest to Eisenhower. There was little they could say but the obvious. As one of the President's staff explained lamely: "Well, you know how the boss is when someone talks economy—especially when 'someone' is George. He just

* New York *Times,* May 16, 1957.

cannot bring himself to wage war against someone waving that banner. And he found himself saying to himself, 'Well, if anyone *can* find water to squeeze out of this budget, I'm sure not going to denounce him, am I?'" And such commentary was voiced with a dispiritedness that seemed rather new in many on the White House staff. They recognized the political weakness and naïveté responsible for the Administration's plight. They knew the consequent confusion, in public and party alike. Yet there more than ever seemed to prevail the kindly but paralyzing consensus—to avoid "upsetting the old man" with any too realistic reports of the disarray in his own ranks. Solicitously, but destructively, the President's aides were adjusting themselves to the quietly accepted task of laboring for a man whose *physical* welfare must be their first concern. And the shadow of such concern seemed almost visibly to warn of the settling, upon all the White House, of a time of twilight—a twilight of softened speech, muted feeling, hesitant motion.*

The prospect seemed profoundly sad. In this kind of half-light, there could be no serious practice of the *art* of politics. For the essence of this *art* was, and forever is, the subtle and sensitive attuning and disciplining of all words and deeds—not to mend the petty conflict of the moment, nor to close some tiny gap in the discourse of the day—but to define and to advance designs and policies for a thousand tomorrows. A President can practice this art only in the noonday light of clear fact, constant conviction, lucid execution. Instead, this President, so it seemed, would be left, by conscientious counselors, to labor with a poor counterfeit of the true art . . . to accept a sudden strategem in lieu of grand strategy . . . and—on all the myriad occasions for such choice and preference by any President—to murmur prose when the moment called for poetry. . . . All

---

* The final cost of this lost battle of fiscal 1958 amounted to: $4 billion cut from the over-all budget, including a cutback in mutual security from the requested $3.86 billion to an appropriation of only $2.8 billion. As Sherman Adams subsequently wrote: "It was a serious and disturbing personal defeat for him." (*First-hand Report,* p. 380.)

these—now it seemed inevitable—would be the melancholy mementos of such a political time of twilight.

There followed, not long after, two minor but noteworthy postscripts to the inglorious story of fiscal 1958. The first came in July of 1957. By this date, a rallying of senators had restored most House cuts in the military appropriations originally requested by Eisenhower and Defense Secretary Wilson. Precisely as the Senate conferees were battling with their House colleagues, they were confounded by the very leadership that they were striving to support. A sudden letter from Wilson promised a one-hundred-thousand-man reduction in the armed services, a reaffirmation of January's conservative estimate of needs, and an effective renunciation of the funds for which the senators had fought so strenuously. The Executive Branch, obviously, was still waging war upon itself.

The second postscript came another six months later, and the scene was a subcommittee hearing in the House. The witness was a representative of the Bureau of the Budget, giving testimony on a pending bill. He sought to clinch his argument by concluding that favorable House action was essential to *"the program of the President"* [italics mine]. And with this splendidly intended peroration, the witness threw all committee members, of both political parties, into immediate and uncontrollable laughter. Only fifteen months after the triumph of Eisenhower's re-election, a solemn allusion to "the President's program" thus provoked the hilarity befitting a sarcastic jest.

The essential irony in the tragicomedy, however, involved the personal relationship between the two men in its central roles. George Humphrey, still full of charm of person and force of conviction, departed from the official scene in July of 1957 (to be replaced by Robert Anderson, a man matching Humphrey in both personal conservatism and presidential esteem). Over the period of his four years in Washington, no man had grown closer to the President than Humphrey; no man so signally shared with Dulles a power to influence presidential action and policy; and no man more rightfully viewed himself as a devoted servant of the President. And such are the painful paradoxes of politics: these final months of service assured to George Humphrey the unwanted distinction of inflicting deep and irreparable damage upon the political repute and power of his friend, the President of the United States.

The ultimate irony lay in the fact that neither man could conceive this to be the truth.

3

The year's other great wounds to the Eisenhower administration were, in one respect, less painful. They were not self-inflicted—at least, not entirely.

The summer of 1957 brought Little Rock the fame that brought shame to the nation. The clumsy duel between federal and state authority was fought out in remarkably few thrusts, parries and counterthrusts. In 1956, a Federal District Court, pursuant to the 1954 Supreme Court ruling, had approved the plan for integration prepared by the school authorities of Little Rock. On September 2, 1957, Arkansas Governor Orval E. Faubus ordered the state's National Guard to take up its stations around Little Rock's Central High School, thus assuring "order" by preventing the entry of Negro students. A federal judge promptly ordered integration to proceed. When Faubus's troops stayed defiantly at their stations, a petition to enjoin the governor was put before the federal court, on September 10, with Attorney General Brownell one of the petitioners. The following day Faubus requested—and on September 14 was granted—a conference with the President, vacationing at Newport, Rhode Island. Nothing issued from the conference. And the climactic events swiftly came: a federal enjoining of the governor, his withdrawal of the National Guard, the unleashing of the mobs to drive the Negro children from school, and finally—on September 24—Eisenhower's Executive Order that led to bringing the Arkansas Guard into national service and dispatching five hundred soldiers of the 101st Airborne Division to Little Rock, there to remain on vigil for the school year.

A good deal of personal history lay behind Eisenhower's conduct through this particular ordeal. For irony—again—there was the memory of his first campaign visit to Little Rock, as far back as September 3, 1952. On that occasion, he had been wildly cheered for his attack upon a Truman attempt to order federal control of the strike-beset steel industry—an attempt turned back by a Supreme Court ruling. And Eisenhower had elated the Little Rock throngs with the cry: "Thank goodness for a Supreme Court!" It was precisely five years later, almost to the day, when Faubus ordered Arkansas troops to defy the application of the Supreme Court's decision on desegregation.

More meaningful than such bizarre memories, however, was Eisenhower's own private, abiding dissent from the Supreme Court action. This basic insensitivity—or stubborn resolve—on the whole issue of civil rights had colored all presidential actions before, as well as during, this time of crisis. Thus his limp direction of the struggle in Congress for the Civil Rights Act of 1957 had served almost as a pathetic and inviting prologue to Little Rock. Although this proposed bill, drafted by Brownell's Department of Justice, was a key part of "the President's program," Eisenhower met initial press conference questioning on its details with the deliberately tepid retort: "I was reading part of that bill this morning, and I—there were certain phrases I didn't completely understand. . . . I would want to talk to the Attorney General. . . . Naturally, I am not a lawyer."* Thus disheartening those fighting most ardently for the bill in House and Senate, the President proceeded two weeks later to rebuff further questioning with such aphorisms of caution as: "If you try to go too far too fast . . . you are making a mistake." As dis-

* New York *Times*, July 4, 1957.

242

order ran through Administration ranks on the Hill during the next two weeks, the President at last decided to argue clearly for one key provision of the bill—the conferring of authority on the federal courts to use a contempt action to support an order against interference with the right to vote. The effective sabotage of this provision was being sought by opponents of the bill through an amendment requiring a jury trial in any such contempt action, thereby blunting the court's authority. It was July 31 when Eisenhower finally declared opposition to this amendment. So belated was this action that the Senate promptly —the following day—adopted the amendment by a vote of 51 to 42. When the President met with his Cabinet the next morning, he confessed a lament strangely incongruous in view of the ambiguous struggle he had waged—for he mourned the Senate vote as "one of the most serious political defeats" that he had suffered in all his term of office.*

Such a presidential posture on civil rights could scarcely have filled Faubus with fear as he weighed his possible retorts to federal action. Nor were the President's personal views on integration a secret scrupulously guarded from all southern legislators. Almost as if to invite the worst, the President had bluntly told a July press conference: "I can't imagine any set of circumstances that would ever induce me to send federal troops . . . into any area to enforce the orders of a federal court, because I believe that the common sense of America will never require it. . . . I would never believe that it would be a wise thing to do."†

---

* *First-hand Report*, pp. 342–43. The bill passed by the Senate was so emasculated that, for the month of August, it seemed likely the President would find himself in the awkward political position of having to veto even its timid provisions. In Senate-House conference, however, the proviso for jury trial was amended to apply only in cases entailing civil rights and only when the judge himself so directed. Thus modified and signed, the Act did become the first such legislation in eighty-two years.

† New York *Times*, July 18, 1957.

The Arkansas governor, pleasantly encouraged by all such recent history, went to his Newport conference in mid-September with the understandably confident air of a man more firm in his purposes than the President. The confrontation itself was frowned upon by Brownell: the Attorney General could hardly applaud a meeting between his President and an official under summons from a federal court to explain his defiance of the law. As a political operation, the meeting amounted merely to a confused exercise in juggling papers by the two sides. They groped awkwardly for some joint statement, bland enough in language to suggest accord. And they ended with separate statements acknowledging the futility of it all.

Yet it was Faubus who, finally, miscalculated. The President, so slow to take firm federal action in support of civil rights, could and would respond with dispatch to a public challenge to presidential and constitutional authority. He could never view the first matter as anything but a dubious interpretation of law by the Supreme Court, trespassing close to a defiance of human nature. But the second question stood in no doubt: it was an issue of the dignity of the nation and its sacred founding documents. And the crisis ended to the sound of marching paratroopers in the streets of Little Rock, signaling, as Sherman Adams later observed, the performance by the President of "a constitutional duty which was the most repugnant to him of all his acts in his eight years at the White House."*

For the presidency, then, the drama of Little Rock was not quite what it seemed—a display of chronic indecision. It was something significantly different. It amounted to a complex testimony to particular personal beliefs of Dwight D. Eisenhower —beliefs that he embraced, in fact, quite *decisively*. Only the manner in which he rendered his testimony—all the belated acts, suggestive of unsureness, and all the hollow words, empty of affirmation—made the presidential performance seem hazy and

* *First-hand Report*, p. 355.

confused. But beneath the confusion there lay a definite and explicit resolve to try one's patient best—to leave things undone.

For the nation, on the larger stage of the world, all of this sadly signified something more. The tale carried faster than drum signals across black Africa. It summoned cold gleams of recognition to the eyes of Asians, quick to see the signs, in the heartland of America, of the racial enmities that had helped to make colonialism, through the generations, so odious to them. More than a few West Europeans—long since weary of the moralistic exhortations or pious injunctions of American policy—could smirk complacently at the crude practice of racism in the self-styled sanctuary of freedom: the preacher now was being taunted and ridiculed by his own congregation. And to all peoples of all lands, the trained and instructed voice of Soviet propaganda could relay, in almost affectionately fastidious detail, the news of Little Rock—breathing scorn as it spoke.

There came—at almost this very moment—something else, something new, to which the Soviet Union could dramatically point. The spirit of this gesture was wholly different. For its object was of Soviet making. . . .

Around the globe, the year, already, had not been a bleak one for Kremlin leadership. At home, Khrushchev had consolidated his own political control by following Beria's execution with summary demotion of all contenders to power—Malenkov, Molotov, Kaganovich, Shepilov, Zhukov. Abroad, the Middle East was proving hospitable to new Communist venture. The frustration of the Anglo-French-Israeli attack on the Suez had left a vacuum of power. Washington had tried to paper this over with proclamation of the "doctrine" that American aid would go to any Middle Eastern country wanting help to rebuff Communist threats. Since the plain peril in the Middle East was not overt international aggression but internal subversion, the relevance of the "doctrine" seemed unclear. Nasser's Egypt disdainfully ignored it. And Syria staged its own domestic coup, assuring effective Communist control.

245

Above—and around—the globe, there now suddenly appeared a dramatic sign of new Soviet power. On October 4, the first man-made satellite went streaking through the skies. The Soviet Union called it *sputnik;* it weighed 184.3 pounds; and it sped around the earth at about eighteen thousand miles per hour. There was something incongruous in the soft whisper of the signal—the faint beep-beep—that it flashed to listening ears on earth. It seemed too quiet and well modulated a voice for the Soviet Union to use—to inform the United States that the frontier of the Age of Space had been crossed and that America, the proud pioneer, must pursue this new and awesome exploration by trying to glimpse and to follow the traces left by giant Soviet strides.

The American responses to the historic moment varied sharply.

The Eisenhower administration tried to comport itself in the manner of a busy man reluctantly looking up from his evening newspaper, glancing around with an expression of studied disinterest, and finally shrugging his shoulders as he returned to more absorbing matter. The President assured his press conference that Soviet and American space programs had never been "considered as a race," and even though *sputnik* intimated "a very powerful thrust in their rocketry," nonetheless, "the satellite itself . . . does not raise my apprehensions, not one iota."* Secretary of Defense Charles E. Wilson, just retired from office, looked back hurriedly and imperturbably to acknowledge "a nice technical trick."† And Sherman Adams, in a rare display of shallow partisanship, disparaged all public concern with "an outer-space basketball game."‡ All this seemed to pitch the response of the Administration at no more serious a level than the wry humor of a worried public, soon confronting the news of a second Soviet satellite, this one carrying a dog through the

* New York *Times*, October 10, 1957.
† *Time* Magazine, October 21, 1957.
‡ New York *Times*, October 15, 1957.

skies. The next such event—so the jest went—would see the Soviets hurling cows into space, and this would signify, indeed, the herd shot 'round the world.

A graver view came from Democratic Senate Majority Leader Lyndon Johnson. The voice he gave to his distress was as edged with partisanship as the words of Sherman Adams. But the substance responsibly related to the facts:

"The Roman Empire controlled the world because it could build roads. Later—when men moved to the sea—the British Empire was dominant because it had ships.

"Now the Communists have established a foothold in outer space. It is not very reassuring to be told that next year we will put a 'better' satellite into the air. Perhaps it will even have chrome trim —and automatic windshield wipers."*

The world at large, but especially the politically restless and uncommitted nations of Africa and Asia, reacted with unabashed wonder and excitement. These peoples—already afire with desire to vault miraculously into the modern industrial age, to achieve swiftly an evolution that the greatest Western nations had needed several generations to accomplish—were eager to hail the spectacle of sudden Soviet technical triumph as practical proof of the rationality of their most gaudy fantasies. Surveying these aroused areas of the world, the London *Economist* concluded that they were all reading, with avid attentiveness, one message: "We Russians, a backward people ourselves less than a lifetime ago, can now do even more spectacular things than the rich and pompous West—thanks to Communism."†

For these African and Asian peoples, so sharply repelled only a few weeks earlier by the spectacle of Little Rock, the portents of America's future now appeared doubly clear. The West's great land of the free was displaying more than a want of virtue. The same mighty land of the machine was betraying, no less plainly, a lag in power.

* *Time* Magazine, October 28, 1957.
† The *Economist,* October 12, 1957.

Thus, as 1957 neared its close, the stock of the United States, computed in the stern measures of sheer might or quoted by the gentler degrees of simple respect, sharply slumped on the greatest of all markets of the world—the universal arena where men and nations meet to weigh words, exchange esteem, assign trusts, and seal bonds.

4

I returned to Washington for a visit on the last weekend in October. I spent an hour with the President, in the familiar oval office. It was exactly three weeks since the morning when the nation had wakened to learn of *sputnik*.

The President seemed in hearty enough spirit, on this particular Saturday morning. The hour was early, and his energy yet fresh and untapped by the day ahead. His light brown suit reminded me of the legend of earlier years that this color forewarned of a dark mood. He did not display one. Yet I thought I detected—and it was the first such occasion I could recall—a new deepening of lines in the strong face, a slightly lower bent to the shoulders. Whatever the visible evidence, there was somehow in the office a troubling sense of—age.

Within minutes of conversation, however, Eisenhower was snapping out opinions, curt and tart as ever. He sputtered indignation at the Democrats: "The idea of *them* charging *me* with not being interested in *defense!* Damn it, I've spent my whole life being concerned with defense of our country." And wheeling around, as always, to fire at the other flank: "These Republican right-wingers are no damn better! Take this Simpson [Representative Richard M. Simpson of Pennsylvania] in the House, always plugging for higher tariffs. He's spending forty-five thousand dollars a month in charge of congressional campaigns, and he hasn't gotten a damn Republican elected yet. But he's found time to make three speeches attacking me and my policies." And as for Knowland: "You know, he's a good leader in many ways, but he gets the most cockeyed notions about world affairs. He comes in here, sits over there, and wrings his hands about neutral nations getting our money. So I say to him: 'What do you want? You want to drive them *closer* to the Russians?' Right now, he's keeping quiet on foreign affairs, so that's good. But I've told him plainly: 'I'll support you for governor—but not a damn thing higher than that.'"

Only the previous week Great Britain's Queen Elizabeth and Prince Philip had visited with the President, and the remembrance touched off his comments on *sputnik*. The words were self-exonerating, in tone and substance. "You know, when the Queen and Philip were here, they were amazed," he reported, "at our press reaction to *sputnik*. Each one, independently, told me so. They said that people in London just gave it one day of excitement, then went on about their business." I demurred that popular concern in the United States could only help to stimulate support for necessary counteraction. Quickly—almost too quickly, I felt—he agreed: "Oh, absolutely. Anything that will get us out of complacency—and make this next Congress realize how serious things are—that's all to the good." A year earlier, I thought, I would have heard such a remark with pleasure and would have said so. This year I no longer knew what the words meant, where any affirmations were aimed. And I said nothing.

He was eager, however, to launch into spirited defense of the Administration record in the space and missile sphere. Again deploring Democratic critics, he summoned his secretary to bring his "book" on Defense, and he opened it to a chart of government expenditures on ballistic missiles. Angrily jabbing at it with his finger, he went on: "*Look* at these lines. Up to 1954, there's almost nothing—at the highest, nine million dollars in one year. Now look at *our* line—so damn high it goes right off

249

the chart finally—$1,390,000,000." He knew that he had some facts on his side here, for the slackness of the missile program in the last Truman years was well remembered in Washington. Soon, however, he reverted to his basic argument, in purely economic terms. "Sure, we had a huge satellite program and could have pushed it. But first these science boys come to me and want twenty-two million dollars—and I say, 'Sure.' After a while, they want sixty-odd million more, and I say, 'Fine.' So they pack some trickier instruments into the thing—and want eighty million or so more. And I say, 'Okay.' But—finally—when they say they need another 150 million dollars, I *have* to say: 'Just a minute, fellows. Where does all this *end?*'" From this, he veered to his deeper concern lest military strength alone be regarded as sufficient, without regard to "the economic strain over the long pull." And he ended his argument with his favorite projection of warning: "If we let defense spending run wild, you get inflation . . . then controls . . . then a garrison state . . . and *then* we've lost the very values we were trying to defend."

Our talk swung back to domestic politics, and he unqualifiedly stated his personal choice for Republican presidential nominee in 1960—his new Secretary of the Treasury, Robert Anderson. He began by bracketing Anderson with "some good new young fellows," of whom he only identified the new Attorney General, William Rogers, and with Sherman Adams—"although he'll be sixty-one in 1960, and that's pretty old for this job." Only at the end of his mental list did there come the words, ". . . and Dick Nixon, too." But after a moment's silence and thought, as if he were making some definite and irrevocable decision, he concluded: "Of all these fellows, the one who has the broadest gauge—best in experience and sense and the right age—it's that Bob Anderson. Boy, I'd like to fight for him in 1960!"

Through all the talk of 1960, he punctuated his comments with a touching little parenthesis. As if shying from the presumption of looking so many months ahead, he would murmur the reservation: ". . . if I live that long." The condition was cautiously appended three times in the space of a few minutes.

I finally turned our discussion toward foreign policy and the Secretary of State, offering the simple assertion that I feared neither one commanded great confidence, either at home or abroad. And this precipitated the longest rambling soliloquy I ever heard Eisenhower speak upon Dulles. With the omission of most of my dissenting interjections, it went thus. . . .

"I know you're right to this extent—people just don't like that personality of Foster's, while they do like me. The fact remains that he just knows more about foreign affairs than anybody I know. In fact, I'll be immodest and say that there's only one man I know who has seen *more* of the world and talked with more people and *knows* more than he does—and that's *me.* And I can't take his job and move over there. . . .

"All right, I know what they say about Foster—dull, duller, Dulles—and all that. But the Democrats love to hit him rather than me, even though not one of these critics of our foreign policy has a *constructive* thought to offer. And you take this Harold Macmillan—and I think he's the best Premier Britain has had in I don't know how long—and *he* thinks Foster is just about the ablest man around. . . .

"Look, I know—I admit—you're right in a lot of what you say, but . . . look at things today—against some years ago. It isn't *all* black. We had a mess in Iran—and cleaned it up. We were told nobody could save Vietnam and Diem was no good —but now look! Austria was divided. Trieste was a thorn in everyone's side. And the Communists working effectively in Central America were stopped cold! . . . No, it's not all black."

Then, quite abruptly, there came a curious digression—and admission. . . .

"I've *thought* about who *could* take Foster's place. But who is there? Maybe Al Gruenther—he's got what it takes. But a soldier in that job—with me here? . . . All right, I suppose it could be done—we have, in a way, the precedent of George Marshall. . . . But, well, I shouldn't get talking about how much I admire Gruenther. If he were *not* a soldier and a Catholic . . . though I think the Republicans could get away with running a Catholic when the Democrats couldn't . . . I'd be for *him* taking over *this* spot right here in 1960. . . . How I'd like to roll up my sleeves and go to work for *him!*"

Then the speculations on a successor to Dulles ended as suddenly as they had begun, as if their mere murmuring had done thoughtless hurt to a friend. His final affirmation of loyalty was more intense than ever. . . .

"It's just like the case of Benson—with people writing or coming in and telling me all the time I have to get rid of *him*. Same thing with Dulles—not one in ten who write me have a good thing to say for him. But *I* would be a scoundrel—and it wouldn't, for that matter, even be good politics—if I let Benson go when he's trying to do the right thing and I know it. And I feel the same way about Dulles."

As our talk drifted toward its end, he strolled slowly toward the tall windows facing the southern White House lawn. For a full minute, he stood there, silently, looking out. His glance wandered upward inquiringly, toward the sky. It was as if—so the thought teased my mind—he were scanning the horizon for some new Soviet satellite. And he might well have been—for, as he turned back, he said in his curiously soft but firm tone of resolution:

"Boy, there's just one thing I really *know*. You *can't* decide things in *panic*. Any decision you make when you are panicked, you can be sure of only one thing. It will be a bad one."

The burden of the office, I felt more than ever, was growing heavy upon him. I knew, now, that I had not merely imagined that the shoulders of the soldier were lower, hunching a little forward. And as I left, I found myself wondering if his last words, of conscious and confessed strain, really referred, not to some unseen menace in the distant sky, but to this much nearer weight.

It was late in the afternoon of the same day when I left the White House to walk, slowly and thoughtfully, to the State Department.

Here, too, it was a time of twilight—literally. In the spacious office of the Under Secretary, Christian A. Herter, a couple of lamps feebly fought the shadows. And the scene and the dialogue—different though they were from the morning's conversation with the President—brought no more cheer.

Herter was a striking figure. He had come into the department only a few months earlier, at the urging of the White House, particularly Sherman Adams. His enjoyment of good favor in the White House, however, alone sufficed to impel Dulles to view him with some anxiety and distress.* But Herter nourished no ambitions that could trouble any sensible superior. A veteran of public life and a serious student of foreign affairs, he was stirred by only one urgent concern—a sense of his nation slipping toward grave peril. A handsome man of strong countenance, austere spirit, and steady mind, I found him, too, hunched forward —much more than the President. He was moving on metal crutches, under the pain of arthritis.

The burdens of which he talked, however, were not physical but political.

He spoke—with candor but without rancor—his fears for both the state of national defenses and the conduct of foreign policy. As for the first, he confessed: "I am more worried than I have ever been. We—in the State Department—are only now learning serious things we never knew before about the limits of our military capacities." As for daily diplomacy, he reviewed in rueful detail some recent clumsy clandestine American attempts to

---

* The White House had pressed Herter to accept an appointment as Under Secretary of State, but in his first meeting with Dulles to discuss the post, Dulles had confused both the man and the issue by suggesting he take the conspicuously lesser post of Assistant Secretary for European Affairs. Only Adams' intervention had redressed matters.

253

spur Turkish forces to do some vague kind of battle with Syria, currently under increasing Communist influence. But he lamented more gravely—for this affected all the conduct of foreign affairs—the dispirited morale of the Department of State, over which Dulles reigned in almost monarchic seclusion from the views of most subordinates. Sadly, Herter acknowledged: "It is hard to know what use I am around here, you know. I have been given no authority, and no area of work is specifically my task. Everyone finds it difficult to know what Foster is either doing or thinking. So . . . I just keep trotting around after events, trying to piece together the true shape of them, so that I can at least be conversant with affairs when Foster is away from Washington."

Not bitterly, almost gently, the Under Secretary came to his own final, somewhat agonized appraisal. "It is discouraging," he concluded. "I have left this office, many nights, thinking quite clearly that I should do only one thing. And that was—to go home and pack up my bags."

By the time I left the State Department, there was chill in the autumn air and darkness in the quiet streets.

And within me, I felt a little of both.

5

One month later, the President suffered his third illness in twenty-six months. On the afternoon of November 25, in his office just before 4 P.M., he suddenly had to break off dictation to his secretary. He felt a chill, and departed for "the house." Not long after, as he talked to Dr. Snyder from his bed, the doctor's ear caught the ominous warning sound of slurred speech. The word "international" emerged as "internatt-nl." And, a few hours later, diagnosis confirmed the signs of a cerebral spasm.

Although the following weeks again gave proof of the

President's gallant recuperative powers—as he rebounded from this third illness more swiftly than from the previous two—the nation itself, at the end of 1957, could not be completely confident of enjoying such resilience. And there was more to cause worry than the facts of rising unemployment at home and declining repute abroad.

The year as a whole had seemed almost to shout a warning. The admonition pointed directly to the danger that the second term of Eisenhower would echo with those sounds from the first term that had been, from the beginning, most discordant and most disconcerting. Indeed, each one of this year's three signal events, in the political life of Eisenhower, carried precisely such a mark and such an omen.

Thus: the sudden menace of Soviet missile power could trace its origin, in some measure, to the clamor, in the first of the Eisenhower Years, for "a brand new model" of American defense —the kind that would come with guaranteed tax deductions.

Thus: the lamentable Executive performance on Fiscal 1958 had elaborately re-enacted, for public view and disbelief, the more private and limited disorder attending the mutual security program as early as 1953.

Thus: the shadow of McCarthy in 1953 had now been matched by the shadow of Little Rock in 1957. Both shadows— on the national scene—had been allowed to grow larger and darker by an Executive policy of buying time against the unwanted issues. Both—on the world scene—had brought comparable damage to the dignity of the nation as a whole.

Such nearly exact analogies, between times and policies four years apart, bespoke more than chance or coincidence.

They suggested—appropriately to the newborn age of missiles—laws of motion and direction as rigorous in politics as in science. They hinted at a kind of trajectory, secretly spanning years and events, unswervingly bearing men and their decisions on predetermined course. The political impulses so deep in the

255

first moments of the Eisenhower Years, all those initial thrusts of political action, had firmly fixed, so it now appeared, the historic course—its distance, speed, arc, rise, and fall.

The end of the trajectory appeared, at last, too clear.

CHAPTER EIGHT

The Last Resolve

The divided and ambiguous political nature of the year 1958 found true portent in two roles that Eisenhower played, during the turn-of-the-year fortnight. Both scenes were brief. And both were enacted before huge audiences.

The setting for the first scene was Paris. Here, before December had ended, throngs of Parisians cheered their admiration for the almost miraculously resilient President. Only a few weeks earlier, the death of Eisenhower—and the imperilment of all American leadership—had been forecast in the black headlines of the French press: *L'Amérique décapitée.* Suddenly, here he was before them, waving and bowing and beaming, as he rode for seven miles in a motorcade along the route followed thirteen years before by General Leclerc's liberation troops, under the Eisenhower command. In the stately chamber of the Palais de Chaillot, he joined the representatives of the fourteen other NATO powers to agree upon wider dispersal among their lands of American missile power, while still pressing the Soviet Union toward disarmament negotiation. And here, too, the assembled heads of state felt some of the affectionate wonder of the crowds in the street, at beholding the hidden strength of the man whose nation's strength made him their leader.

The second scene, in the first days of the new year, was projected across the United States on the television screens of an anxiously watching nation. The President—averse as ever to solitary appearances requiring his people "just to look at my face"—appeared with Secretary Dulles, to report the modest results of his NATO conference. For the greater part of their report, the President sat in wan profile, idly turning his eyeglasses in his hand and self-consciously fixing his face in a pose of grave attention, while the Secretary spun forth a languid résumé of recent events. Uninspiringly, Dulles concluded by assuring the nation that the NATO decisions amounted to "quite a lot, assuming, of course, that they are carried out with vigor." The very demeanor of the two men sufficed to discourage any optimism on this last point. The cheers in France were echoed by groans at home. In the East, *Time* magazine lamented that the solemn report "showed neither vigor nor urgency." In the West, the Republican *Oregonian* of Portland bitterly derided "the spectacle of two tired, aging men talking about the gravely compromised half-measures which bind and separate America from its European allies." And former President Harry S. Truman seemed to sum up the national consensus by gladly acknowledging that he had found himself "just about as thoroughly bored with Mr. Dulles as the President was."*

It seemed baffling and hardly believable that the same man and the same politics could so swiftly devise two scenes so confusing and so severe in contrast.

Yet the same distracting capacity was promptly repeated—in written form. This time the incongruity was achieved by Eisenhower's two crucial January messages to the Congress—the messages upon which all labor of the political year would be based. The first, the State of the Union address, seemed forceful and

* *Time* Magazine, January 6, 1958.

incisive in content, spirited and vigorous in delivery. It ranked as one of the finest speeches of Eisenhower's presidency, and Speaker Rayburn saluted it as the "strongest" the President had ever made before the Congress.* And yet, a mere four days later, the Congress read with near-astonishment a budget message for fiscal 1959 that seemed either to ignore or to refute the earlier message. Calling for total expenditures of $73.9 billion, it set forth almost minimal requirements in the spheres of defense and space. On the domestic front, its conservative orthodoxy suggested the invisible initials of George Humphrey beside almost every section, as it urged a ban on all new starts for power, flood control, and reclamation; narrowed the legal limits on programs for hospital construction, urban development, and welfare; and abdicated all effort to win aid for school construction. Assessing the total effect, the Washington Bureau of the New York *Times* summed it up as "an effort to return to the spirit of a traditional Republicanism never before seen in the current White House."† And the two carefully deliberated documents, in short, stood beside one another in contrast as astonishing as the earlier scenes enacted by the President in Paris and in Washington.

And this was largely the way all the year of 1958 was to be. Such political successes as the year would produce seemed to come never whole but in fragments, generally random and always uneven. They were apt creations of a presidential behavior that itself seemed, ever more unpredictably, to lunge ahead, then stumble back. And from press conference to press conference, from one presidential appearance to the next, the watching eyes of journalists and congressmen, foreign diplomats, and domestic politicians, came to suggest the half-veiled glances of physicians, secretly and shrewdly scanning a patient's face, feeling his pulse,

* New York *Times,* January 10, 1958.
† Ibid., January 19, 1958.

tapping his reflexes—for the symptoms of the sudden quickening, or abrupt faltering, of energy.

The course of congressional relations and legislative action throughout 1958 faithfully recorded the chart of this leadership —in a line as jagged as an electrocardiogram. Two issues of the greatest concern to the President, foreign trade and reorganization of the Department of Defense, zigzagged toward half-accomplishment in almost identical fashion. On foreign trade, Eisenhower drove even Dulles to lament privately the contradiction between proclaimed intent and practical action; and the President finally summoned his first Budget Director, Joseph Dodge, to return to Washington to "co-ordinate" foreign economic policy. But when the battle at last had been waveringly fought, all that the President could sign into law in August was a bill allowing no significant changes in national policy but merely extending for four more years the existing policy on reciprocal trade agreements. . . .

As for reorganization of the defense establishment, this initially so stirred presidential interest that he drafted most of the wording of the proposed legislation himself—an exceedingly rare procedure, calculated to emphasize to the Congress the intensity of his resolve. Yet this show of force had been preceded, in press conferences of earlier weeks, with such self-denying pronouncements as: "My personal convictions, no matter how strong, cannot be the final answer."* Then, following his personally phrased plea to the Congress, there occurred another one of those too familiar breaks in communication between the President and a Cabinet officer—in this instance Neil H. McElroy, the successor to Charles E. Wilson. The President had acknowledged to McElroy that he did not regard the precise language of his bill as wholly untouchable. Thereupon, in testimony before the House Armed Services Committee, the new Secretary of Defense conveyed, in his own words, the presi-

* Ibid., January 16, 1958.

dential suggestion that the words of the President need not, after all, be taken too literally. A vast amount of presidential energy was expended, throughout the spring of 1958, in fighting for this cause so close to the President's personal desires and experience. His essential object was to strengthen the authority of the Secretary of Defense against harassment or evasion by individual Secretaries of the several services or by members of the Joint Chiefs of Staff. Three amendments in the House countered and limited this objective. And the bill that the President finally signed, when the Congress's work was done, included all three unwanted provisions.

In the wholly different sphere of civil rights, there stirred far greater moral passion in the people—and the dignity of the nation itself, in world eyes, stood far more at issue—than in these matters that the President pressed with the Congress. Here, however, the behavior of the President continued to be one of discreet drift. Under persistent questioning, Eisenhower kept affirming his resolve to maintain respect for the law, in Little Rock or anywhere else in the federal union. But he refused, with equal tenacity, even to hint that he personally respected the *worth* of the law. When one press conference in August confronted him again with the invitation to state, in some explicit way, his own conviction on school integration, he replied that it was "just not good business to do so." He confessed, in fact, to believing that it might "weaken public opinion" if the Executive were to comment on actions of the Judiciary "where I might agree or disagree."* This cool detachment, on a matter that so considerable a part of the people held to be a vital issue, was now appearing, more and more incongruous—in an Administration so prone to voice its opinions on far more prosaic affairs, in highly moralistic accents.

Yet there came other occasions in the year's national business when the same impassive and imperturbable qualities, the same

* New York *Times,* August 21, 1958.

stoic spirit of determination, seemed to bear better fruit. Observing these instances, I thought back to Eisenhower's last words to me in his office the preceding autumn, when he had voiced his abhorrence of "panic"—almost the *fear* of its power to corrupt true judgment. For he managed this year to prove again that, toward this emotion, he stayed a proud and stubborn stranger.

One such demonstration was provoked by the politics of the Middle East, still smoldering since Suez. The dangers of conflict and chaos had grown since February, when Nasser had welded the anti-Western sovereignties of Egypt and Syria into the United Arab Republic. Week upon week, thereafter, the Egyptian dictator had sought to buttress his position as a leader of the Arab world by quickening both his program of inflammatory propaganda and his buildup of arms. The rewards for his strenuous labors upon Arab opinion were considerable but ambivalent: even as he made Arab hearts pound excitedly with his lusty threats to great Western powers, so did he make other Arab rulers shiver in anxiety with his republican disdain for traditional authority. Through spring and into summer, Iraq seethed silently within, while Lebanon was wracked by civil and religious disorders, most cheering to the Communists. And on the morning of July 14, 1958, two urgent overseas messages reached the White House almost simultaneously. A completely unexpected military revolt in Iraq had thrown the nation into turmoil with the assassination of King Faisal II, Crown Prince Abdul Illah, and Premier Nuri as-Said, just as the king and prince were preparing to fly to Istanbul for a meeting of Moslem members of the Western-sponsored Baghdad Pact. And from Lebanon, President Camille Chamoun desperately appealed for immediate American military assistance to restore order in the streets of his capital city of Beirut.

The day—a Monday, the air heavy with Washington heat, a dismal drizzle of rain beading and clouding the long windowpanes of the President's office and the nearby Cabinet room—proved that, on critical occasion, the men indoors could defy the elements by assuming for themselves an air of clean and crisp decision. Nor was the issue simple or easy. Military doubts matched political hazards. The Air Force regarded the Middle East as so vulnerable to Soviet airpower that it had preferred to keep its strategic bombers at the safer distance of Spanish and Moroccan bases. The Army viewed the whole Mediterranean with the somber knowledge that a half million French troops, even while occupying all strategic centers, had been unable to maintain firm control of Algeria. The Navy, even with its Sixth Fleet cruising the Mediterranean on leisurely exercises, sensed painfully the difficulties of supply over a line thirty-eight hundred miles from Atlantic bases.

But Eisenhower's decision—to act—vaulted over all such concerns. He was impelled by awareness that the whole Western position in the Middle East, so perilously poised since Suez, now could crumble. And this day he moved as fast as the clock. At nine forty-five, he reported and reviewed with the National Security Council his decision to deploy on the eastern shore of the Mediterranean the largest peacetime concentration of American military power ever assembled. It would include more than nine thousand marines and paratroopers, seventy warships, more than four hundred Navy and Air Force planes. At 2:30 P.M., he met with twenty-two ranking Republicans and Democrats from the Congress. With both Dulles brothers strongly supporting him, he argued the need for action within a matter of hours. Although Knowland and Bridges offered the understandable but unhelpful comment that there probably would be no such crisis now if the Administration had taken a different view of the Anglo-French-Israeli attempt to dispose of Nasser, the cautious and unenthused consensus was not to argue with the President in his assertion of authority. A little past 4:30 P.M., seated in the red leather chair behind his desk, at last alone with the Chairman of the Joint Chiefs of Staff, General Nathan F. Twining, the President solemnly nodded to go ahead and "send 'em in." And when the tense day was past, one who had watched his every move commented on Eisenhower thus: "It was good to see him so relaxed. There was no hurling of thunderbolts. . . . I realized as never before why a President is so important—to be able to give to others, at such a time, an impression of unruffled assurance and confidence."*

The show of presidential initiative, while it could hardly claim to have lanced the malignant danger of war in the area, carried important political impact. It reminded the lesser powers around the world, as they nervously eyed Communist threats from within or without, that the United States, when it so decided, could act with speed and effect in their defense. Nor could Moscow fail to be impressed with such deployment of American military power, defiant of risk only a few hundred miles from Soviet borders. And the military execution of the maneuver, swift and flawless in detail, quite dramatically contrasted with the clumsy and sluggish Anglo-French operation against the Suez. To critics of the past political wisdom of the President's foreign policy, leading up to the Suez fiasco in 1956, the Commander in Chief now had at least a soldier's retort: if the earlier operation, once launched, had been as skillfully executed as this, the issue might have been happily resolved.

The man who so despised panic showed notable steadiness of political behavior on another front in 1958—with decisions far less dramatic, yet even more demanding of strong resistance to contrary political pressures. This front was the nation's domestic economy. And it suffered, from late 1957 through 1958, the third and deepest recession since World War II. Business investment in new plant and equipment fell back sharply. By April of 1958,

---

* *Time*, July 28, 1958. Spirited as was the presidential action, the attempt by the Administration to credit the checking of danger in the Middle East to "the Eisenhower doctrine" was an exaggeration reaching toward a half-truth. In the first place, the military action would have been quite as valid and prudent without any such "doctrine." In the second place, the form of the threat was never overtly international (to which menace the "doctrine" addressed itself) but subversive and domestic.

manufacturing production had tumbled nearly 14 percent from its peak in the previous year. By June, unemployment had climbed to 5,437,000—an unwanted pinnacle, unmatched since days before World War II.

The Eisenhower who faced this near-crisis had to spend the greater part of the year fighting off surges of temptation and pressure to yield to expediency. A stampede toward a tax cut, urged by many Republicans, threatened constantly to break loose. A plunge into emergency spending on government projects, urged by many Democrats, tempted with the promise of more votes in the coming congressional elections. Uncompromisingly, Eisenhower rebuffed all such attacks—from both sides—against his basic economic belief in the need to check threatened inflation and to hold his government's budget near balance.

The whole performance reflected Eisenhower's constant, consoling faith in "the long view." Essentially, this was the same faith that had endowed him with such forbearance in confronting a McCarthy, such moderation in projecting future national defense plans and costs, such muting of tone in asserting leadership toward the Congress, such willful slowness in supporting the struggle for civil rights. In this instance, he defiantly insisted upon looking over, past, and beyond all the grim warnings of possible depression—to discern, farther ahead, the more distant and (to him) more ominous dangers of inflation. Whether or not his economic sense was ultimately sound and precise, or whether immeasurable forces within the national economy contrived their own obscure methods of correction, the fact was apparent, by the end of the year, that the worst had passed. Manufacturing production recovered some 75 percent of its lost ground. And the ranks of the unemployed dwindled by almost 30 percent.

Aside from all economic consequences and arguments, the political conduct of the President bespoke, again, one abiding quality of the man: the reserve of tenacity—so akin, in a sense, to his physical resilience—that lay deep beneath all surface signs of irresolution . . . even while it defied, so often and so stubbornly, the most urgent efforts to reach it and to tap it in other causes.

2

True to the temper of the time and the man, the better and the bolder strokes continued to be countered and contradicted—as the summer of 1958 passed—by the painful half-acts or the ill-chosen words. Already, long since, these had cost him much in the wide and open political arena. Now, the price for them would become personal and intimate, to be paid within the small circle of this official family. For they conspired to cause him to lose the man closest to him—the dour and faithful Sherman Adams.

The ambiguous White House handling of the dilemma of Sherman Adams made the man's own original imprudence appear petty by comparison. As the House Subcommittee on Legislative Oversight had delightedly discovered, the Assistant to the President had intervened on several occasions with both the Federal Trade Commission and the Securities and Exchange Commission to elicit information of interest to a friend of his, the New England textile manufacturer, Bernard Goldfine. On the basis of a friendship more than fifteen years old, Adams had occasionally received gifts of clothing and frequently accepted payment of hotel bills for himself and his family. To counter the public chastisement by Democrats—and the yet more intense private glee of the most conservative Republicans—Adams voluntarily appeared on June 17 before the subcommittee. He there acknowledged that he might have acted with "a little more prudence"—the only lapse, in essence, of which he stood accused or to which he could confess. The following day, Eisenhower met with some of the White House staff and reaffirmed his resolve to defend and retain Adams. The President thereupon proceeded to his press conference to read a prepared statement. And its key affirmations were: "I personally like Governor Adams. I admire his abilities. I respect him because of his personal and official integrity. *I need him. . . .*"*

I watched with much sorrow the personal drama that now unfolded, for it betrayed an aspect of the Administration's collective character that could only be described, with the maximum of charity, as intellectual and moral confusion. One central source of this confusion—as I ascertained from friends on the White House staff—was the remarkable political naïveté of the President, for he had confidently believed that his press conference statement, as Adams subsequently wrote, ". . . would end, once and for all, the speculation about whether I would remain . . . in the White House."† Equally apparent was Eisenhower's unawareness that the baleful words "I *need* him" would only be heard as a confession of presidential weakness, rather than an assertion of Executive purpose. The blame for such an utterance, moreover, had to be partly shared by a White House staff flawed by something worse than poor judgment. As one of the staff later sadly admitted to me: "Several of us had spent a night pondering what the President should say to help Adams in his press conference. And when we went in to the boss the next morning, he surprised us by reading what he himself had prepared. Not one of us caught the hollow ring of the words 'I *need* him.' And we all just sat there—and said it sounded swell." And so each passing month, it seemed, was deepening the disposition of the staff to dull its own faculties of criticism, to leave the President at peace in a world of gleaming and consoling assents.

The political encirclement of Adams implacably continued. Its avid and determined leadership came from Republican conservatives eager to smash the symbol of the "liberalism" they fancied as haunting the halls of the White House. By September, some of the larger contributors to Republican party

* *First-hand Report,* p. 446.
† New York *Times,* June 19, 1958.

funds were flatly demanding removal of "the political embarrassment" of Adams. The besieged presidential assistant was summoned back from a brief vacation to Washington—to find that Eisenhower had left to Richard Nixon and to the Chairman of the Republican National Committee (now Meade Alcorn) the task of confronting him with the Administration's distress. As Adams later generously wrote: "The President did not ask me to resign."* But neither did the President even suggest that he stay. The first direct encounter between the two men in these days of decision did not come until Adams took a plane to the President's vacation spot at Newport—to hand to him the text of a prepared television statement announcing and explaining his resignation. In the ever-restrained phrases of Adams: "When Eisenhower finished looking at my statement and gave it an emphatic nod of approval, he picked up a letter which he said that he and Hagerty had been going over . . . 'Dear Sherman: I deeply deplore the circumstances that have decided you to resign. . . .' . . . The President looked up at me with a smile that seemed to reflect our years of friendship . . . and said, 'Will this be all right?' I thanked him. There was nothing else that I could say."†

Nor was there much that Adams could do but politely decline —when advised by the White House social secretary, shortly after his resignation, that Eisenhower wished to commemorate his departure with a testimonial dinner in the White House to be followed by square dancing in the East Room. It hardly seemed the moment for a square dance. For, through all of three months spent in mishandling the matter, the President could claim credit by no criterion of judgment: neither had he asserted a moral condemnation in his own name, nor had he practiced a political loyalty contemptuous of partisan charges. When the crisis, at its onset, might have been sternly construed by a righteous President to be a matter of principle, Eisenhower had defended Adams. When the issue became a crude matter of

* Ibid., p. 447.
† Ibid., pp. 448–49.

vengeful insurrection by the most wealthy and vocal of the extreme Republican right, Eisenhower had left Adams alone—to write his own resignation.

I chanced to be in Washington the day before Adams' final departure from the White House. I called upon him to chat for a few moments, as he quietly, methodically cleaned off his desk in the large office of the West Wing. And I could not refrain from bitterly remarking: "Well, the vultures of the Grand Old Party finally descended." He only smiled tightly and shrugged: "That's the great game of politics."

The next day, Adams was gone. In his luggage, he carried his newest possession: a silver punch bowl. It was duly inscribed with tribute to his "tireless service" and "brilliant performance." And these were certified and attested—so the silver said—by "his devoted friend, Dwight D. Eisenhower."

3

The dismal episode of the departure of Sherman Adams did more than display the presidential will at its most slack and unsure. The moving currents of Republican politics ran deep here. As some of these currents found their source in the past, some freshly sped toward the near future.

For one thing, the President personally and the Administration generally, had found themselves still somewhat snared by the righteousness of their own rhetoric. They had proclaimed 1952 the "crusade" to sweep the "mess" from Washington. Just as its own extravagance of language had compelled the Administration five years earlier to perform the elaborate and empty ritual of purging the diplomatic record of "secret agreements," so now it had to "honor" its proclamations of civic purity. This had finally required the offering, in political form, of some human sacrifice. Thus, again, did the latest events in this second term keep signaling their lineage—back to the earliest hours, the first words, of the Eisenhower Years.

But more was at work than this self-afflicting heritage. The ouster of Adams by enemies within his own party warned of Eisenhower's greater heeding of the political thunder on the Right. His fight on the domestic economic front against "the spenders," month after month, had carried him closer and closer to preachment of the gospel favored by the most conservative in his party. On the diplomatic and foreign front, at precisely the same time, his general failure to carry through any initiatives or to score any successes affected Eisenhower just as seriously, for it deprived him of the sense of any accomplishment—or the sight of any trophies—in the sphere where he might have hoped for acclaim from more liberal Republicans. Thus currents of both determination and frustration tended to converge—to carry him toward a role in the November congressional campaign that would be one of his most uncharacteristic and humiliating political performances.

With a seeming passion for anachronism, the Republicans, actively led by Eisenhower and Nixon, fought the 1958 campaign with rhetorical axes and bludgeons whose dullness and uselessness had been abundantly proven in repeated assaults on Franklin Roosevelt and the New Deal more than twenty years earlier. Their charges of "socialism" and "left-wing extremists" exploded harmlessly and meaninglessly in the political air. When Nixon raged against "the Acheson foreign policy [that] resulted in war," charged the Democrats with "retreat and appeasement," and unsmilingly saluted the "military strength and diplomatic firmness" of the Republican Administration,* there came a moment when Eisenhower winced and deplored to his press conference "this kind of thing"—only to be spun quickly around by Republican dismay into publicly reassuring Nixon: "No one can do this more effectively than you."† In no less than six key

---

* New York *Times*, Oct. 14, 1958.
† Ibid., Oct. 16 and Oct. 17, 1958.

states, meanwhile, the Republicans raced toward disaster by insistent advocacy of so-called "right-to-work" laws—most passionately urged by William Knowland, now running for Governor of California. Embarking on a campaign swing of almost six thousand miles, Eisenhower gave most devoted attention to California and to the candidacy of the Senate leader whose defiance of the White House had thwarted so many hopes of his own presidency. In the most harsh and graceless partisan speeches of his political life, Eisenhower exclaimed that "there will be no appeasing Communist aggression while I am President." He exulted that "the so-called missile gap is being rapidly filled." He singled out for strident excoriation, among his opponents, the "political radicals . . . self-styled liberals . . . [with] the irresistible impulse . . . to squander money—your money."* With all this, the standing of Eisenhower, in the sober judgment of Knowland, soared to new heights.

By the judgment of the nation, however, the Republican party slumped to a political low for the decade. The Democrats swept the political field from coast to coast. Even stoically Republican Vermont made a gentle nod to the times, sending to Congress its first Democratic representative in 106 years. On the distant coast, Knowland disappeared from all political view, under an avalanche of Democratic ballots.

And the results in two other states seemed to be edged with special meaning. In New York, Nelson A. Rockefeller, had turned to elective politics to run for the governorship—and to give voice to the kind of Republican policy for which he had vainly hoped and worked in Washington. The stunning exception of his victory by more than a half million votes seemed to flash to the rest of the GOP a dramatic message of what-might-have-been. In all the nation, only Ohio could match this surprise—in a different way. For it reported the totally unexpected defeat of Senator John Bricker.

* New York *Times,* Oct. 21, 23 and 28, 1958.

An Eisenhower who had spent almost as much energy in the 1958 campaign as he had in the 1953 struggle to fight off the harassing Bricker Amendment must have borne at least this part of the general disaster without undue melancholy.

4

Whatever the year brought in the way of political adversity at home was to be surpassed by the final sum of misfortune overseas.

These reverses in world diplomacy most often lacked either the drama or the simplicity to command banner headlines. There even appeared some occasional signs that the national policy might be succeeding in "containment" of Communist aggressions. The three boldest Communist threats of the year, in any event, were blunted by American resistance: in the Middle East, the action in Lebanon spared further grave deterioration of an already unstable situation; in the Far East, renewed Chinese Communist threats against the islands of Quemoy and Matsu took the leisurely form of artillery barrages rather than amphibious invasion; and in Europe, while Khrushchev vehemently challenged Western rights in Berlin, he actually fired no ammunition more lethal than invective. On a still more encouraging note, this was the first year of life for Europe's new Common Market, with all its implied hopes of future continental unity; and American policy could justly take some credit for having tirelessly pushed the nations of Western Europe in this direction. In general, the Western world seemed to be feeling more reconciled and relaxed than a year ago—in those dark months immediately after *sputnik*—as it confronted the reality of Soviet economic and scientific power. The free peoples passed the year, at least, without the sense of earthquake beneath them.

Yet erosion and attrition are not much smaller perils than earthquake—certainly not in the eyes of those who took a view of "the long pull," as Eisenhower constantly counseled. And the progress of these sufficiently deadly processes advanced apace across the globe. The basic policies of the United States stood, in critical cases, on soft and shifting ground. Thus, a full decade after the memorable blockade of Berlin in 1948, broken by the magnificent improvisation of the airlift, Washington faced the threat of a renewed blockade without any precise plan or method ready for countering it. The Administration that had deplored in 1953 the total absence of prior planning for political conditions following the death of Stalin had somehow managed to let five years pass without pondering seriously the means to defend its most exposed position in all of Europe.*

Dangerous laxness in one area seemed matched by dangerous rigidity in another. The Secretary of State's obsessive fear of direct diplomatic encounter with the Soviet Union still kept American diplomacy in a posture so frozen as often to invite ridicule. Thus, for example, the American landings in Lebanon had provoked shrill Moscow cries against the American threat to "peace," and Washington had retorted with the sensible suggestion that Khrushchev should meet any such imagined threat, not by warning the world of the destructive power of Soviet missiles, but by soberly stating his grievance to the United Nations. But no sooner did Moscow indicate that this notion might have some merit than Washington recoiled before the distasteful notion of the Soviet Premier even touching American soil. As a diplomatic spectacle, all this lacked either logic or dignity.

The most grim news, however, came from the place on earth most close to home and most presumed to be politically secure—Latin America. As far back as May, Vice President Nixon, tour-

---

* In the halls of the Department of State at this time, the irony of one fact was not overlooked. More than a year before the 1958 threat to Berlin, one voice had loudly and publicly warned: "There is a stubborn tendency . . . to forget about the Berlin situation so long as it gives us no trouble. . . . The Western position in Berlin is by no means a sound or safe one . . . a sure portent of trouble." The warning voice belonged to the veteran diplomat whom Dulles has so discourteously dismissed in 1953—George Kennan. (Quotation from *Russia, the Atom and the West*, p. 40.)

273

ing Peru and Venezuela, had been the victim of anti-American passions that were variously expressed by stones and spit, shouted jeers and shaking fists. If a British dignitary a few years earlier had been subjected to so savage a reception in India, it would have been acknowledged sorrowfully in Washington as proof of British insensitivity to the outrageousness of their own colonialism. If a Soviet dignitary had suffered such public humiliation, it would have been hailed exuberantly as proof of Communist blindness to the hatred stirred by their own tyranny. But when the American Vice President (with poise and patience) endured such indignities, the Administration vaguely suggested that the event merely gave proof of the gross public manners of Communist agitators. Privately, however, the White House did not so foolishly deceive itself. As Sherman Adams subsequently wrote: "June, 1958, was a disturbing and unhappy time for Eisenhower and all of us. . . . Why were the Vice President of the United States and his wife publicly abused and ridiculed in these countries where our prestige had once been so high? If the wild demonstrations against the Nixons had been aroused by Communist agitators, as it was reported, why were the Reds so successful in stirring up such an open and defiant anti-American resentment?"*

In June of 1958, these were candid and cogent questions to be asked in Washington.

The next six months of reflection, however, seemed to inspire no comparably cogent answers. On the last day of 1958, the tattered armies of Fidel Castro lustily broke into the streets of Havana, as President Fulgencio Batista fled to foreign sanctuary. And there began the slow and painful birth of the first Communist regime to rise in the Americas and to proclaim its defiant alliance with Soviet Communism.

It was little more than a year since I had heard the President—stating his apologia for the progress of American policy, as he

* *First-hand Report,* p. 381.

274

restlessly paced his White House office—emphasize the achievement of erasing the Communist threat to the south.

It was little more than two years since the day, just a month after Eisenhower's re-election, when an almost unknown Cuban exile by the name of Fidel Castro had secretly landed on the southern shore of his native island commanding an "invasion" force of eighty-one men—now to proclaim rule over a population of almost six and a half million.

As the clock of New Year's Eve turned to signal 1959, the most pathetic spectacle in Cuba was the sight of hundreds of families searching through police cellars, damp ditches, and unmarked graves for the bodies of their rebel sons. And in Washington, there were officials of the Government of the United States who began to spend hours and days looking through thick files of diplomatic dispatches—to discover how all this had come to pass.

Here, of course, there was no scouring of unmarked graves. For no one yet was utterly certain—or ready to admit—that anything was dead.

5

As 1958 neared its end, I visited the White House and the President once again. In the dwindling dialogue between us, this was to be our last long encounter. And from it I learned how Eisenhower would spend the waning months of his presidency.

Our meeting this time had been brought about by a gracious, yet curious letter from the President late in November. Reading between its lines and through its phrases, one sensed his clearly knowing, without explicitly acknowledging, that there was something chronically wrong with the deepest impulses of national conduct, the ruling directions of foreign policy, and the *élan* of free peoples everywhere. Yet all that he affirmed, in this unexpected letter, was that he had long been pondering the need

275

to assert American purposes, before all the world, in terms more proud, and in measures less mean, than sheer material might.

The President's words and phrases bespoke a restlessness—a kind of healthy dissatisfaction and spirited discontent—with most of the martial clichés of the struggle against Communism. Quite explicitly, he confessed his fatigue with the familiar, resounding definitions of American strength in terms of military power or simple anti-Soviet truculence. He groped, as he said, for a way to give practical testimony to the higher kind of power—and the "spiritual values"—that inspired all civilizations based upon a religious faith. No, he acknowledged freely, he did not know himself quite how to translate mere profession of faith into the proving deeds of politics. Perhaps, he ventured, the heads of state of all free countries should be asked to answer the troubling question: how do we bear witness to our *positive* beliefs? All that seemed clear was his pained conviction: sometime, somewhere, by someone, an effort must be made.

All the halting, anxious phrases could not fail to touch, to move, and to trouble one. I promptly wrote to thank him for his thoughtfulness and arrange to come to talk with him as he had invited. Yet I had to include in my reply the confession: "I should mention one feeling I think we share. The value of the word, divorced from the act, is at best debatable. It can even be self-defeating: a good way to damage a principle or ideal is to affirm it passionately, then fail to give it true testimony in deed."

By the time we met this December day in his office, however, he had already decided the dramatic kind of testimony that he was going to give. . . .

We spoke, first, of the recent Republican disaster in the November elections. To my suggestion that perhaps he lately wished that he had stayed more aloof from the campaign, he gave a brisk dissent. He hurled familiar rage at party management: "Imagine the head of the Congressional Campaign Committee going around—and after getting four hundred thousand dollars from the National Committee—and advising Republican

candidates to choose carefully what *parts* of the President's program they should support!" But he seemed rather undismayed
by the general results of his labors. "I'm glad I did what I did,"
he avowed. "I've been told it definitely helped three senators to
get in—from Maryland, Pennsylvania, and New York. And it
allowed me to get around to renew a lot of acquaintances and
privately get my ideas across. I'm not sure it turned out so badly.
Maybe now the heads of these party leaders can get knocked together, and they can be made to start thinking about how to pull
together to win an election." He implied, however, no particular
action to encourage this exercise in self-examination. Nor did he
suggest any fear lest his own growing identification with the least
progressive Republicans might, in itself, be helping to blur the
party's political profile.

He went on, now, to a more personal allusion to a political
event more remote in time—an event that plainly still stung in
memory. His remembrance of some recent, acid political comment from Harry Truman triggered an explosive exclamation.
"God, this man goes around," he cried, "saying that I let
George Marshall be called a traitor in my presence and I never
said a word. Why, I was never on any political platform where
any such thing took place in my presence. George Marshall is
really one of the few men I've ever known whom I'd call 'great'!"
Thus do footnotes to history get garbled even in the minds of
men who made the event: the recollection of compromise in
1952 was still a little too bitter to taste truly.

Then came the brisk transition: "Well, let's talk about other
and more important things." And the actual drama-to-be of the
coming months was verbally rehearsed in the quiet, oval
room. . . .

Only the night before he had received from Press Secretary
Hagerty a long memorandum summarizing a number of their
recent conversations. These had dwelt upon the problem of
"the image" that the Eisenhower administration should strive to
construct as its last months, as the popular verdict of 1960 ap-

277

proached. Their thoughts had dwelt, too, on the fact that the Secretary of State, who these many years had so personally prescribed the American "image" in the world, now almost certainly faced a fatal recurrence of cancer. And through these conversations of theirs, too, there had been a half-spoken acknowledgment that the rigid American diplomatic posture, so forbidding to direct political encounter with the Soviet Union, had become, at last, too stiff and awkward to hold. The Press Secretary's memorandum then had posed the question: how should the Administration "dramatize" its character so persuasively as to ensure that the election of 1960 be a sweeping act of ratification—and national thanksgiving—for the achievements of the Eisenhower Years?

The answer was crisply set forth in the memorandum.

The President should assume the role of "the Man of Peace." He should play this role on the widest possible stage—the world itself. More specifically, he should embark on three kinds of action. He should appear at the United Nations more frequently to fill its halls with a newly strong voice of American policy. He should travel to a ring of nations girdling the globe, beginning with India. And he should welcome rather than shun both summit conferences and direct meetings with Soviet Premier Khrushchev. All these displays of initiative, the memorandum stressed, would be enhanced by the fact of Eisenhower being a "lame duck" Chief Executive unable to seek re-election: his obvious lack of self-interest would place such dramatic conduct on a level of indisputable and impersonal national service, high above all political suspicion or attack. Thus he would emerge, through all his words and actions and travels, truly as "a Tribune for the People."

I instantly felt the force and portent of this memorandum. There was a curious and unmistakable incongruity in its almost coldly candid confusion of national need and partisan gain—along with the vivid anachronism that draped the stately, flowing robes of ancient Rome around the shoulders of this leader of the most powerful democracy of the twentieth century. More important, however, was the fact that the moment, so full of implications far beyond deciphering, plainly marked a sudden turn in the nation's destiny, with signal as clear as the loud chime of a clock, forever dispensing with one hour and summoning the next. For all the proposed actions were wholly alien to the world of diplomacy as conceived, from the Administration's first hours, by the now afflicted Dulles. The striking of a historic hour, indeed. But—on the right day? . . . Or altogether too late in a whole season of history? . . .

Meanwhile, I listened to the President. And he sent out his own thoughts and words, in hesitant but hopeful reconnaissance, to catch glimpses of the untrespassed terrain ahead. . . .

"This is what I've been thinking. There are two schools of thought about what we—especially *me*—ought to be saying and doing. One school thinks it's enough to keep denouncing the enemy and warning the world of all that is wrong with him. I belong to the other school. My own sense tells me that is *not* enough. For when you're all finished and done with excoriating the other fellow—*then* what?"

Suddenly I felt a strange sensation. We were not looking forward but backward in time. These were not words I heard, but echoes. This was not December: it was March, and the year was five years dead. And we were talking about the President's *first* speech on world affairs, in the spring of the first year of his Administration—as he paced this same room, raised this same voice, spoke these very thoughts. The hands on my imagined clock were spinning crazily. . . .

Some kindred, self-conscious thought must have crossed his mind, for next I heard him say . . .

"This is the kind of problem I've been wrestling with for five years now. It began with the First Inaugural that you and I spent so much time and sweat on. Now we look around, and well —we don't seem to have accomplished much.

279

"So the next question is: what can be done in the months left to me?

"I agree: a speech or two isn't going to do it. We have *said* a lot of things. But what we really need is a program of action to talk for us. We have to plant a kind of tree. We have to really affirm what we believe—not at all abstractly but in the most earthy way possible. And I think if we begin to do this, we can get a lot of others—fellows like Macmillan and Fanfani and Diefenbaker—truly to join us. As for me personally, I guess I still have some reputation in the world to put to use here."

Suddenly, as if made uneasy by such self-mention, he seemed impelled to digress an instant—to give retort to some unspoken thought of his own. . . .

"I know a lot of people have been saying all along that I should have been out front more. I'm supposed to have left too much to Dulles. Well, there never has been any man more loyal to his superior than Dulles—and he has never done a *thing* that I did not approve beforehand."

With this most sincere of bows to the past, he turned and looked again ahead. . . .

"If we get anything like this started, we have to follow through. What I would *finally* like us to be able to do would be to come up with some kind of positive offers to Khrushchev and his boys. I'd like to lay before them things that would make clear to all the world our good intentions—things with no strings attached—things positive—things no one could suspect or attack. We should be—generous without surrendering. . . .

"Maybe it's in the area of armaments. . . . Now take these ground forces of ours in Europe. They bother the devil out of me—ground forces that *we* supply while Germany enjoys the great bonanza of not paying for its own defenses and France wastes all its forces trying to settle Algeria. . . . Airbases ought to be enough, with our nuclear power, to defend these places—and *not* ground troops. . . .

"And there are other kinds of things we could be doing. You

know, I had an idea I thought was pretty good, but a bunch of the boys thought up too many objections to my going with it to the Hill. It was an offer to bring over here for one year, say, maybe ten thousand Russian students of college age who could handle some English—and let us put them through school here for a year. No reciprocity, no strings—just offer to do it.

"Well, I'm sure there are a lot more important things we can do, but everything counts to get across the idea—this idea of being *generous without surrendering*. . . ."

While I murmured approval of these warm generalities, I felt constrained to suggest as tactfully as possible that the spirit of the President's approach could hardly be said to be animating the Secretary of State's department of the government. Briefly, he acknoweldged the fact—in part: "Well, it's true that there's no department so jealous of its prerogatives as State. And even Foster's hackles rise when he thinks someone is butting in. Why, when Nelson Rockefeller was on the White House staff here, producing ideas in this area, he got Foster so fuming that I just had to do something about it. . . ."*

And after this almost shy and unwanted glance toward the distance separating him and Dulles, in basic temper and outlook, the President seemed to falter a little in his fervor. And the lofty arc of his conversation gradually came down—from affirmations suddenly seeming too astral, back through little gray clouds of speculation, slowly drifting down into the better known atmosphere of the tentative, the prudent, the immediate. . . .

* Significantly, Sherman Adams, the man closest to Eisenhower's daily work through most of the years of his presidency, in his most temperate and restrained reminiscences, wrote this appraisal: "Granted that Dulles was a man of great moral force and conviction, he was not endowed with the creative genius that produces bold, new ideas to gain hitherto unattainable policy goals. Giving Dulles the *responsibility for initiating foreign policy*" [italics mine]—a phrase that Eisenhower would have deplored and denied—"brought positive results in our taking firm stands for certain alliances, for certain treaties and understandings and for new attitudes toward heads of various governments and plans of strategy. But just as often his view was strongly negative." (*First-hand Report*, p. 110.)

"Maybe I should go abroad someplace to make a major speech . . . or a conference of free nations in the Mediterranean area . . . or perhaps the Caribbean—in a place like Puerto Rico? . . . Or I might have a meeting with this new President of Mexico. . . . Maybe go as far as Monterey.

"I guess I better stay out of the mountains and Mexico City. . . . It wouldn't bother me, in the least, I'm sure . . . but I know the doctors—they wouldn't like the idea . . ."

Finally, the words trailed off . . .

"Well, let's think some more. I'll do some thinking. And I— I'll be talking to Foster as soon as he gets out of the hospital.

"Yes, that's what I'll do. And then . . . well, we'll see where we go next."

Soon all the world would see. For he would go to many, many places.

CHAPTER NINE

The Setting Sun

The grandest designs of political life can turn, notoriously and sadly, upon the cruelest details of personal life. In the last months of 1955, the story of the Eisenhower Years had anxiously awaited upon the effects of injections of heparin to keep clots out of the arteries running to the heart of Dwight David Eisenhower. In the first months of 1959, the ending to the full story of these years depended, no less fatefully, upon the effect of injections of radioactive gold, and the impact of a million-volt X-ray, upon the cancer-stricken body of John Foster Dulles.

For Eisenhower, through these weeks of waiting and sorrow now upon him, the central path he trod, in fact and in thought, was the two miles between the White House and Washington's Walter Reed Hospital, where the Secretary of State he now viewed as "a brother" bravely fought back death. The wide world of politics bustled with longer journeys and more historic itineraries. In Cuba, the rebel armies of Fidel Castro swept victoriously through the last cities and vales and mountains awaiting "liberation." In Moscow, Nikita Khrushchev dispatched his Deputy Premier, Anastas I. Mikoyan, to tour the United States—after gaily jesting at the Kremlin's New Year's ball: "If he doesn't come back, he has to promise that he won't work against us there."* A second object, almost simultaneously dispatched by Moscow on a vastly longer journey, found its mark without having to come back—a rocket fired past the moon and into solar orbit. Across the boundaries of divided Europe, meanwhile, Great Britain's Prime Minister flew to Moscow, there to impress upon the Soviet Premier the readiness of his nation for negotiation at the diplomatic summit, notwithstanding the notorious reticence of the American Department of State. Far away, across the highest mountain ranges of Asia, Tibet's Dalai Lama fled southward to India before the ruthless aggression of Communist China. But for the President of the United States, for an unhappy period of three months, none of these journeys could match—in meaning or in pain—his constant trips to sit by the bedside of the man whose friendship and counsel he so deeply cherished.

I found strange memories stirring, as the daily press carried its frequent photographs of the two men, conferring intimately in a hospital room. Thoughts went back to my first sight of them together more than six years ago. The conference room of the cruiser *Helena* seemed, in memory, almost as antiseptically spare and cold as the room where now they met. Then, however, the President-elect had leaned forward neither with interest nor solicitude: he had simply leaned back in boredom, whenever the other man had spoken.

I could not pretend to comprehend well the singular evolution in their relationship, so defiant of the personal and political temper of each. Only a few elements seemed clear. During their first years together, the rude task of learning about the highest level of government—as both men started from an almost common lack of experience—had created some real sense of mutual dependence. No doubt, too, each had come to sense in the other a kind of strength he perhaps suspected might be lacking in himself.

* *Time*, January 12, 1959.

Like the famous gladness and the famous glumness in the countenance of each—so the two men evidently came to believe—the rigor of one's logic and the thrust of the other's "instinct" together could contrive a rare blend and balance in the nation's diplomacy. And as the first years slipped by, and the political repute of the Secretary fell almost dangerously, a harsh event contrived to seal their closeness—the onset of Dulles' cancer in November of 1956. Striking at the political moment when the Suez crisis found both men embattled in a dark and precarious cause, the personal tragedy carried a heightened personal impact: from that moment onward, they were two men sharing a far more intimate common struggle—against sheer physical defeat. Finally, in any event, there were the revealing words with which the President first spoke publicly of his grief, in February, when the Secretary's last illness began: "America *needs* him. And I think each one of us *needs* him."* The verb was significantly the same as the one he had applied, only the previous summer, to Sherman Adams.

The presidential visits to the hospital finally ended in the fourth week of May: early on the morning of May 24, 1959, John Foster Dulles died of cancer and pneumonia quietly in his sleep. He was seventy-one years of age. He had attended his first memorable international meeting fifty-two years earlier: a college student, he was taken to the Second Hague Peace Conference in 1907 by his grandfather, John Watson Foster, who had been Secretary of State under President Benjamin Harrison. At the age of thirty-one, he had gone to the Versailles peacemaking of 1919 as a presidential adviser on reparations—this time accompanied by his uncle, President Woodrow Wilson's Secretary of State, Robert Lansing. As Secretary of State to Dwight D. Eisenhower, he had clocked 559,988 miles in his tireless diplomatic travels. This jet-age phenomenon was more than twice the distance traversed by a Soviet rocket to the moon.

* New York *Times,* February 11, 1959.

To his critics, whom he successfully fought off till his death, the enduring political worth of all the journeys of the man might have been far surpassed by the impact of the single flight of the missile. But critics and foes, philosophic or partisan, had to extend to the man something more than sympathy for his pain or admiration for his stamina. They had to see—and to respect—in him a rare ruggedness of will and a deep capacity for commitment of heart and mind to his beliefs. Nor could they deny that this commitment sometimes seemed to surpass, in vigor and in constancy, the more mercurial will of the President whom he served with such energy.

2

Dwight David Eisenhower, now, in this spring of 1959, took the command and turned the direction of American foreign policy with an abruptness that dazed a fair portion of the diplomatic world. And the relative swiftness of change was rendered the more remarkable for remaining forever unacknowledged, officially or privately. Indeed, few political assertions of any kind so infuriated Eisenhower as any suggestion—almost invariably appreciative—that his views and impulses, now freely at work, differed notably from those of his late Secretary of State. But the pattern of six years of disciplined diplomacy was utterly broken. The familiar postures were abandoned, the old strictures ignored, the technical procedures bypassed. What ensued was not merely a new chapter in the diplomacy of the Eisenhower Years. This was an entirely new volume, distinct in content and independent in authorship. And the essential *styles* of the old diplomatic ways and the new contrasted as sharply as the sounds of the slow scratching of a quill pen—followed by the racing chatter of an electric typewriter.

The pace of the new diplomacy, from the first, seemed breathless. Two months—to the day—after John Foster Dulles died in his sleep, Richard Nixon was in Moscow to open the American National Exhibition. There, in a bizarre scene, the Vice President and Nikita Khrushchev dueled with jabbing fingers before the Exhibit's display of an American kitchen, more model than their "debate"; and the most malicious mockery could hardly have contrived a spectacle more disdainful of the late Secretary's preoccupation with agenda and protocol. Within days thereafter, the Vice President was exploring a Siberian copper mine, speaking on Moscow television, and, finally—in a courageous political gamble—appearing in a motorcade in Warsaw to catch bouquets of flowers from cheering thousands. By the first week in August, Eisenhower was announcing that Khrushchev had accepted an invitation to visit the United States.*

In the pragmatic terms of domestic politics, as set forth in the Hagerty-Eisenhower memorandum of December 1958, the rehearsal for political triumph in 1960—with only an understudy, the Vice President, winning such accolades—was already surpassing all hopes. A performance that did so superbly well "on the road" could hardly fail to win ovations on Election Night, one year hence.

In a serious historical sense, of course, all this political pageantry had deeper cause and reason than the tragedy of one man's death. Ever since the Geneva Conference of 1955 had witnessed West and East signing—in discreetly invisible ink—their mutual recognition of a nuclear stalemate, the Iron Curtain had been swaying before the gusts of many unseen pressures. It is doubtful if any man—even one gifted with the honest intransigence of a Dulles—could much longer have held it firm, as

* Again suggestive of the ambiguity of relations between Eisenhower and Nixon was the peripheral role left to the Vice President in the handling of this invitation to Khrushchev. Eisenhower prepared the personal invitation on July 11. It was transmitted through State Department channels to Soviet First Deputy Premier Frol R. Kozlov, one of 1959's visiting Soviet officials, on the eve of his return to Moscow. Not only was Nixon not enlisted to carry the invitation: he was not consulted on it, and he was informed of its existence only on the day before his own departure for Moscow—more than ten days after Eisenhower had acted.

either barrier or shield. Even in the rather innocuous and apolitical guise of cultural exchange, the passage was being made by thousands of scientists and tourists, students and politicians, athletes and engineers and entertainers. In the sterner dialogue between foreign offices of the Western world, the urgings—especially from London—to reach out toward Moscow, in some manner of direct contact, could not tolerate much more deafness in Washington. The essential fact was that a haughty American diplomatic posture, trying to dictate political quarantine, had become as obsolete and irrelevant as a military posture brandishing the threat of "massive retaliation." If anything were needed in Washington to underscore the prudence of the Geneva Conference's tacit acceptance of mutual vulnerability, this want was amply supplied by the statistics on Soviet rocket-thrust. And all this hinted, perhaps, that the death of a man in May of 1959 might have been secretly merciful for the statesman—who could have lived a little longer only to watch his idea of the world die.

The President personally assumed the leading public role in the new diplomacy exactly ninety days after his Secretary of State had been buried and little more than thirty days after the lavish publicity attending the Nixon-Khrushchev "debate" in Moscow. To reassure Adenauer and De Gaulle and Macmillan that the Soviet Premier's imminent visit to the United States implied no drift toward unilateral American diplomacy, the President paid flying visits to their West European capitals. And there he left behind, for history, the first of the numberless dramatic vignettes to commemorate the tens of thousands of miles he would travel in these months ahead. . . .

There, at the airport outside the West German capital of Bonn, as the two men faced and greeted one another, one glimpsed the strong and striking profiles of the sixty-eight-year-old Eisenhower and the eighty-three-year-old Adenauer. They seemed two silhouettes in stone. And this moment of stillness was quickly shattered by the cheers of more than two hundred thousand voices for the presidential motorcade, passing beneath banners proclaiming, "Ike, We Trust You"—as Germans hailed the commander of their conquest less than fifteen years before. . . . There he stood again, outside the gray granite walls of Balmoral Castle, fifty miles from Scotland's Aberdeen, in discreet half-bow before the Queen of England, with the modest murmur: "How nice of you to let me come!" . . . Suddenly, there he appeared on all the television screens of England, in unprecedented public dialogue with Harold Macmillan, staged from 10 Downing Street, London. Trim in dinner jacket, as relaxed as a visiting Kansas manufacturer comfortably chatting with a wealthy London client after a satisfying meal, he assured the listening nation: "Well, Harold, let me tell you right away and tell to all those good people out there . . . we are mighty glad to be back visiting again this lovely country." . . . And there he stood, in the twilight in the hushed heart of Paris, beneath the Arc de Triomphe, erect and soldierly and motionless beside the tall, khaki-clad figure of De Gaulle—first receiving in firm grasp a gleaming ceremonial sword, then rekindling the flame beneath the monument, as a bugle tremulously broke the silence. . . .

The political meaning of it all? More than extending a necessary diplomatic courtesy to allies, Eisenhower undoubtedly touched and affected the throngs in London, as easily as he stirred them in Los Angeles or Louisville; and the force of his physical presence excited a sense of comradeship, warmed by the admiring memory of the World War II commander. Nonetheless, the political capitals could not suppress or conceal, so it seemed, a vague, uneasy feeling that the witnessed drama was a thing of more scenery than substance. Even without awareness of the special role of Press Secretary Hagerty in the very conception of the drama, the London press sensed the fervor of Hagerty's concern with publicity, and the *Observer* made a cool appraisal: "He is no analyst. . . . His philosophy of practical politics is 'they slap us; we slap them.' He is uneasy in foreign affairs and devotes himself to selling the President's performance. . . . He has brought the cultivation of the relation-

ship between the President and the mass media to a fine Mach-
iavellian art. Whether such an art is wholly desirable is quite
another question." And when the Manchester *Guardian* had
scanned the full social schedule of the American President's visit
to Great Britian, it concluded tartly: "Mr. Eisenhower and
Mr. Macmillan in the Chequers weekend have practised golf
shots, they have eaten grouse sent specially by the Queen from
Balmoral, they have attended matins in the local church, they
have paid a lightning visit to Oxford (while the rest of the company played croquet on the lawn), and they have talked over
the future of mankind."*

To the President, however, these were petty quibbles over
details in the necessary prelude to his meeting with Khrushchev. To any critics questioning the wisdom of this meeting,
Eisenhower already had given his retort on the eve of making
these West European rounds. He had been reminded at a press
conference of the charge by Harry Truman that the proposed
Soviet-American exchange of heads of state visits might damage
the prestige of the presidency. Bridling—and with no apparent
awareness that he might equally well be responding to a posthumous complaint from John Foster Dulles—Eisenhower had
flatly explained: "What we are talking about now is finding some
little bridge, some little avenue yet unexplored, through which
we can possibly move toward a better situation."†

Swiftly, as 1959 waned, the little bridges would appear to
grow into giant spans, the little avenues widen into long boule-
vards. As prelude, however, there first came the September visit
of Nikita Khrushchev. From the moment of his reception by a
twenty-one-gun salute at a Maryland Air Force base—on to his
climactic secret talks, twelve days later, at the not too distant
presidential retreat of Camp David on Maryland's Catoctin
Mountain—the Soviet Premier entertained, jarred, angered, and
amused the American public with a transcontinental display of

* Merriman Smith, *A President's Odyssey*, pp. 40–41, p. 58.
† New York *Times*, August 26, 1959.

political showmanship. Born in a hut of mud and reeds, a boy shepherd and a child laborer in Russian coal mines, and a youth barely literate until his mid-twenties, Khrushchev showed himself a volatile but sophisticated merchant of Marxist doctrine spiced with wit and drollery. His official escort, Henry Cabot Lodge, initially offered, on all public occasions permitting such oratory, the accompaniment of little homilies on the "economic humanism" of American capitalism. These were intended to sound assertive but succeeded only in sounding apologetic, and Khrushchev soon discouraged the rhetoric by puncturing it with such steely, anticapitalist thrusts as, "Only the grave can correct a hunchback!" In the Midwest, he jested with Adlai Stevenson for daring to talk with him: "You will now be investigated by the Bureau of Un-American Affairs." On the West Coast, barred in Los Angeles (by lack of sufficient security provisions) from a visit to Disneyland, he expostulated in mocking rage: "Why not? Do you have rocket-launching pads there?"* As a senator from Minnesota appraised the astonishing visitor: "He's a little like a candidate in the late stages of the campaign. He has heard all the questions many times, and his answers are sharp as hell." His serious diplomatic posture—assumed with rude disdain for his Chinese Communist allies—was plainly spoken: "There are only two nations which are powerful—the Soviet Union and the U.S."† In terms of American domestic politics, the scene was notable for one curious fact: while the Soviet Premier and the Republican Administration seemed to communicate with some candor and even cordiality, Khrushchev suffered his one defeat in "debate" in heated controversy with leaders of the AFL-CIO. Only a little befuddled by that encounter, he proceeded on to his final three-day rendezvous with Eisenhower at Camp David. From these days—lightened by such diversions as watching a Western movie and an inspection of the President's Black Angus cattle at Gettysburg—there emerged only one clear agreement:

* New York *Times*, September 18, 20, and 24, 1959.
† *Time*, October 5, 1959.

the Soviet Premier erased, as facilely as he had originally proclaimed, his ultimatum of a deadline for renegotiation of the
status of Berlin. Departing and leaving behind a public still somewhat breathless and gaping, he waved farewell: "Thank you, as
we say in Russia, for your bread and salt."*

The President of the United States thereupon swiftly completed his plans to toss his bread upon the waters of the wide
world.

The spectacular winter journey by Eisenhower across the
globe began with a jet flight to Rome on the third day of December. It would end two days before Christmas with the President
back on the south lawn of the White House to light the traditional tree and tell his people where he had been. Between those
dates, he visited eleven nations on three continents: Italy, Turkey, Pakistan, Afghanistan, India, Iran, Greece, Tunisia, France,
Spain, and Morocco. He flew high and fast above the ancient
paths of historic conquerors—Darius and Alexander, Genghis
Khan and Tamerlane. In less than three weeks, he spanned a
distance beyond their wildest imagining—more than twenty-two
thousand miles.

The progress of this twentieth century hero was marked and
honored in ways befitting each place and occasion. He was presented with an elephant in India and two gazelles in Tunisia,
jeweled sabers in Morocco and jeweled shotguns in Spain—
along with a varied assortment of rare wines, sugared fruits,
illuminated manuscripts, Persian rugs, and filigree fans. And he
reciprocated by reaching into baggage more prosaic but similarly varied: engraved vases and crystal bowls, frames of silver around autographed pictures of himself, ball-point pen desk
sets, transistor radios, and Polaroid cameras. But most important of all to distribute was his stock of hundreds of gold medallions. On one side, they bore the simple inscription: "In
Appreciation, D.D.E." And, the other side, they carried the
official motto for the pilgrimage—the refrain repeated again and

* *Time,* October 5, 1959.

again, in parliaments and public squares, in private conference and before vast throngs: "Peace and Friendship in Freedom."

And on this most audacious venture in personal diplomacy ever pursued by an American President, the true memorabilia again were the bright-hued vignettes, lived along the way. . . . There were the gaily turbaned Indians roaring the Urdu welcome, "*Hind Eisenhower, ki jai!* (Hail Eisenhower!)" and deluging their visitor with flowers, as his twelve-mile motorcade rolled along Kitchener Road into New Delhi, where new crowds cried out: "Long live the King of America!" And soon the spreading word of the honored presence brought villagers from the south into the capital city—to catch a glimpse of the imagined reincarnation of Vishnu, their most powerful protector. . . . There was the wild welcome in Ankara, as all of the half million citizens of the Turkish capital seemed to flee their homes to line Ataturk Boulevard—while the famed general rode beneath red, white, and blue arches, their legends exclaiming: "Take Our Love Back, Ike." . . . There was the ride into Casablanca beside King Mohammed V of Morocco, as thousands of Berber tribesmen swarmed down from the foothills of the Atlas mountains to line the passage and enthusiastically fire their ancient muzzle-loading rifles into the brilliant Moroccan sky. . . . There were the Roman throngs, huddled beneath umbrellas in the rain before the balcony of the Palazzo Venezia, once made famous by the bellicose orations of Benito Mussolini, now occupied by the smiling American who waved back thanks for the cries of, "*Viva* Eek–ay!" And not long after, he was walking solemnly across the wet stones of St. Peter's Square and past the steel pikes of the Swiss Guards, both agleam in the morning sun, to pay respects to Pope John XXIII. This was a gesture whose only precedent had been the visit in 1919 to Benedict XV by Woodrow Wilson, who had also been looking for "peace and friendship in freedom"—albeit unarmed with medallions.

While the ceremonial side of the journey could be acclaimed a sensational personal tribute, a verdict on its diplomatic substance

293

hinged on the evidence from Western Europe, primarily from Paris. Here, in the French capital's Elysée Palace, Eisenhower spent the better part of a weekend in conference with De Gaulle and Macmillan and Adenauer, to offer a common—and conciliatory—front to the Soviet Union. The meeting ended with agreement by all participants to invite Khrushchev to "a series of Summits," a prospect particularly pleasing to Macmillan, and this series was to commence with a rendezvous in Paris in early spring. The accord contained not a word requesting prior Soviet agreement on an agenda for the meeting—another flat reversal of one of the late American Secretary of State's most stubbornly argued axioms. In direct dialogue with De Gaulle, however, Eisenhower failed, as completely as in earlier pleas, to modify the French President's refusal to make more serious military contribution to the NATO command. And this disappointment offered a little reminder that all the fresh bouquets and recent receptions in Ankara or Kabul were not readily convertible into true political or diplomatic power.

This supposedly historic Summit Conference of the Western powers, moreover, seemed oddly marred by a few of the kind of minor incidents that almost escape the glance of an eye, yet tease the edge of memory. They were chance and trifling matters. Yet they left the casual witness vaguely uneasy, slightly disconcerted. . . .

There was the instance of the President's colloquial little sermon to the staff of the American Embassy in Paris, assuring them that the most different and distant peoples and nations could achieve some manner of union or harmony. And the words tumbled forth . . . "Where differences occur . . . one way I think we can keep them from becoming more noticeable . . . is when we don't help to make them worse. The criticisms we have of another people because they are different, in their background, their traditions, and their prejudices, than we are—all right, let's ignore them and have a good laugh on it and drink a Coca-Cola."[*]

* *A President's Odyssey,* pp. 133–34.

The headline of one Parisian newspaper—*Ike's Answer to Cold War: Drink Coke*—was unduly harsh. Yet such rambling presidential discourse again stirred Western Europe's politically alert observers to a little wondering upon the clarity of focus, or the precision of purpose, of this new kind of American diplomacy.

There was, too, the sad, almost touching scene of Eisenhower's arrival at the Elysée Palace for the first morning of the great conference. Newsmen and television cameras had been poised in expectation of a crowd of perhaps thousands, eager to glimpse the American President. As his bubble-car slowly turned into the Elysée, a mere two or three score Parisians watched in idle curiosity. And when Eisenhower alighted, there followed behind him no solemn retinue of diplomatic aides with significantly bulging attaché cases. Instead, there was only his aging friend and physician, the White House's General Howard Snyder—carrying his black doctor's bag.

There was—finally—something significant and ironic in the terse agenda that confronted these men meeting at the Summit. Exactly a decade earlier, in 1949, the heads of the three Western powers had conferred in this same city with representatives of the Soviet Union, to arrange ways for lifting of the Berlin Blockade. Then the simple agenda had read: "1: Germany, including Berlin. 2: Peace and Disarmament. 3: East-West Relations." Now —in 1959—the words of the agenda were precisely the same, except only for deletion of the word "peace" from the second point. Somehow this itself seemed a wry commentary upon all the strivings of the Eisenhower Years. It almost made a decade sound a little like a void. . . .

I found myself standing a long way from this scene, of course —watching and worried. And I may have reacted even less acutely and personally to it than to the eccentric political postscript that followed quickly upon the conclusion of the Paris meeting. For the solemn deliberations were no sooner finished than the President's "Air Force One" was aloft and winging southward—for a leisurely visit with Spain's Generalissimo Francisco Franco.

I felt no surprise on reading press dispatches reporting that the people of Madrid seemed notably unstirred by the synthetic exhortations of their controlled press and the official distribution of some two hundred thousand flags. They greeted the triumphant procession of the American President and the Spanish dictator with such a tepid and perfunctory display of feeling as Eisenhower had nowhere met on his long journey. The people of Madrid knew well, of course, the value that Washington attached to its air and naval bases in Spain, along with a total American economic investment in Spain of some two billion dollars. Yet they found it remarkable that the American President felt obliged to accord such tribute to their dictator.

And as I read of the President's agreeable visit to Franco's residence at the Prado—strolling between the stately rows of pines and cedars, breakfasting with Franco under the rich tapestries of the huge dining room—I was jarred into seeking out, and reading again, some phrases of the President's last long letter to me. And his words seemed suddenly sharp with irony—the appeal to *spiritual values*, the contempt for the merely expedient, the disdain for purely military power, and the stress upon the moral solidarity of all free peoples. The words had been written, in fact, just at the very time when he first was pondering and planning this historic journey, now about to end. And it did seem that there must have been some better way to bring to a close so dramatic a practice of so decent a preachment.

Forty-eight hours later, the President had left far behind the cedars of the Prado.

Now he stood beside the gaily lighted Christmas tree, towering over the long southern slope of the White House lawn. Around and overhead, too, were the stark lights of the television crews. And he reported to the nation—with unblemished assurance . . .

"I talked with Kings and Presidents, Prime Ministers and

humble men in cottages and in mud huts. Their common denominator was their faith that America will help lead the way toward a just peace."*

3

The New Year of 1960 brought to the White House the good tidings of a plebiscite without precedent. The American people, speaking through the latest Gallup popularity poll, had voted their President to be "the world's most admired man." The new summit of popular esteem towered over all previous peaks—immediately after his first election in 1952, after the signing of the Korean armistice in 1953, and after the Geneva Conference of 1955. Significantly, each higher-than-ever rise had followed upon some new seeming augury of peace.

The season in Washington appeared to overflow, in fact, with an abundance of political gifts, as President Eisenhower and Vice President Nixon looked out upon an appreciative nation and an agreeable world. The moment seemed one of those rare occasions, splendid to savor, when both international affairs and domestic politics, at one and the same time, were allowing respite and promising reward. From Moscow, Nikita Khrushchev had proven punctual with his Christmas gift: he had marked the day by assuring Washington that he would join the diplomatic celebration of the coming of spring to Paris, the Summit Conference—to be followed by Eisenhower's summer visit to the Soviet Union. From New York, the very next day, Governor Nelson Rockefeller had publicly given assurance that the presidential nomination of Richard Nixon would proceed uncontested.* As for the Democrats, they seemed wretchedly awed by the popularity of Eisenhower, intellectually frustrated in their attempts to define their doubt about the nation's foreign policy, disconcertingly confronted by general prosperity on the domestic front, and politically leaderless since Stevenson's two grievous defeats.

* New York *Times*, Dec. 24, 1959.

Moreover, they stood poised for one of their celebrated interne-
cine scuffles for power. Already—by the second day of the new
year—two of their most vocal senators had declared their formal
intent to fight through primary after primary, across the nation,
battling for the presidential nomination. One of these men
bringing momentary comfort to the White House and the Republican party was the forty-two-year-old junior senator from
Massachusetts, John Fitzgerald Kennedy.

Thus did almost all visible signs artfully and persuasively invite the Administration to raise its eyes and behold a political
vista sweeping, as serenely as the White House lawn, toward the
future.

The plausibility of the mirage was treacherous.

To disturb it, there appeared, at first, only casual warnings.
These emerged on the President's next journey overseas—his fortnight's trip beginning in late February through Latin America.
As he swung on this fifteen-thousand-mile arc to the southernmost
part of the Hemisphere—passing through Brazil, Argentina,
Chile, and Uruguay—he was spared any such indignities as his
Vice President had earlier known; and the crowds, though generally smaller than the hopes of the White House staff, were sufficiently large in number and loud in voice. But other omens
could not be measured in decibels. The journey's first stop-
over, in Brazil, was marred by enough mishaps to alert the superstitious: under driving rains from sullen skies, official arrangements were repeatedly mishandled, and the climax of the stay
brought the tragic air crash over Rio de Janeiro killing the members of the U. S. Navy Band arriving to play at the final state
dinner of Eisenhower's visit. Nor could all the ingenious resources of hospitality keep concealed the ferment of anti-American feeling throughout the continent. In Buenos Aires, an outbreak of *Perónista* bombings and demonstrations forced the
President to vault by helicopter from his airport landing to the
American Embassy. In Montevideo, the Uruguayan police had to
use tear gas to break up one cluster of students in riotous pro-

test against Eisenhower's arrival. In Santiago, the President had been reminded of the ruder facts of Latin American opinion by the Senate President who, even as he introduced the distinguished visitor to the Chilean National Congress, suggested that his own nation still awaited clear signs from Washington of "preferring your nearest neighbors, your truest allies."* These neighboring capitals of the Western Hemisphere, in short, proved sensitive, even in Eisenhower's presence, to the fact that he had scheduled his calls upon them only after journeying halfway around the globe—as if Pakistan and Afghanistan had clearly caught his eye before Brazil or Chile.

Nor were the politically sophisticated much impressed by Eisenhower's one vague formulation of a "doctrine" on the Communist threat to the whole hemisphere. He issued this with his statement before the Brazilian Congress: "We would consider it intervention in the internal affairs of an American state if any power, whether by invasion, coercion or subversion, succeeded in denying freedom of choice to the people of any of our sister Republics."† It seemed exceedingly difficult to grasp the relevance or application of this thesis to American policy toward either a Trujillo in the Dominican Republic or a Castro in Cuba. Undescriptive of past policy and unsuggestive of future policy, such a pronouncement invited, by way of response, little more than a puzzled look.

A mere eight weeks after the President's return from this journey all the world was looking toward Washington. And slight puzzlement suddenly gave way to great astonishment.

On May 1—only fourteen days before the scheduled Summit Conference in Paris—there appeared in the skies over Sverdlovsk, a big industrial complex in the Ural Mountains more than twelve hundred miles inside the Soviet Union, a long, black plane with a high tail and wide wings, a one-man cockpit and a single turbojet engine. The plane was equipped with sensitive infrared cameras and other delicate instruments capable of measuring the

* New York *Times*, March 2, 1960. † Ibid., Feb. 25, 1960.

effectiveness of Soviet radar, as well as sampling the air for radio-activity that would betray secret nuclear tests. Manufactured in the United States by the Lockheed Aircraft Company, the plane bore the official designation of U-2. Such a plane had made like journeys at frequent intervals for almost four years, flying along the spine of the Urals at the level of the lofty sanctuary of eighty thousand feet above earthbound antiaircraft batteries. This partic-ular flight had originated four days earlier at an American Air Force base in Turkey, had stopped over in Pakistan to await hospitable weather, and had set its course for a base in Norway —thereby linking three more nations to its fate. Now over Sverd-lovsk, the plane came into range of the eagerly awaiting anti-aircraft below and was shot down. Its pilot parachuted safely to earth—complete with his Social Security card, a half-used pack-age of filter cigarettes, and a wholly unused suicide needle. When premier Khrushchev introduced the captured pilot to the world, along with pertinent pieces of the plane's wreckage, he reported the prisoner also to have carried a bizarre assortment of French francs, Italian lire, Russian rubles, two gold watches, and seven gold rings. All of this provoked Khrushchev's sardonic remark: "Maybe the pilot was to have flown still higher to Mars and was going to lead astray Martian ladies."*

The way in which the Administration in Washington pro-ceeded to answer this and graver questions entailed a display of bad judgment and incoherent action so humiliating as to deny pleasure even to the most partisan foe or the most acid caricaturist. By successive stumbles, the government contrived, step by step, to worsen the bad and to blur the confused. First—confronting only an initial Moscow announcement of the shooting down of an unidentified American plane—the Administration tried (May 5) the tempting expedient of a lie, asserting that any such plane could only have been on an innocuous flight of weather research; and the State Department solemnly avowed that *no* American plane had *ever* been deliberately dispatched across Soviet borders. Next—confronting the Soviet proof of the American lie—the Ad-

* New York *Times*, May 8, 1960.

ministration acknowledged the incontrovertible, but the State Department (May 7) further explained that "there was no authorization for any such flights" from "authorities" in Washington. Third, the White House—suddenly aghast at the prospect of predictable Democratic charges of outrageous negligence allowing such "unauthorized" flights—sought to turn and fight this threat on the domestic front by allowing the President (May 11) to assume responsibility for the flights, while both he and the Secretary of State termed them "a distasteful but vital necessity," to penetrate Soviet military secrecy. And across the globe, Khrushchev, who four days earlier had been at pains to "fully admit that the President did not know" of the flight, now had to reverse himself swiftly: "The Russian people would say I was mad to welcome a man who sends spy planes over here."*

The Administration had needed only six days to amend its appraisal of the event so extravagantly as to transform an unthinkable falsehood into a sovereign right. And as the now shadowed Summit Conference drew near, only a couple of more days remained to complete the chaos. The time was not wasted. On the eve of the President's departure for Paris, Press Secretary Hagerty sharply denied published reports that the U-2 flights had been suspended. Three days later in Paris, the President, trying to check the flood of anger and invective from Khrushchev, sharply denied his Press Secretary's denial. "These flights were suspended after the recent incident and are not to be resumed," he assured Khrushchev. "Accordingly, this cannot be the issue." And thus did the wheel wildly spin full circle once again—with the "vital necessity" of only a week ago falling into sudden but total obsolescence.

In the mirror of domestic politics, the reflections of all these events danced darkly. The Republican retort was delivered with an audacity born of anguish. As the benign vision of global peace-making vanished, there seemed nothing to do but reverse course completely—and revive the grim vision of Communist menace. So the question was boldly hurled at all critics: are you

* New York *Times*, May 12, 1960.

"against" your nation acquiring "intelligence"? (The question referred, of course, to military and technical intelligence.) The inquiry was hardly relevant, however, to either the prudence of this particular U-2 flight or the lack of any political preparation against the chance of its failure. In like spirit, the GOP spokesmen asked the skeptic: would you have "apologized" to Khrushchev? This, too, was a question without content—once the President in Paris had earnestly assured the Soviet Premier that the "vital necessity" of aerial espionage was, after all, unnecessary and dispensable. . . . On the Democratic side, the issue was approached with the nervousness to be expected of politicians dazzled by the President's personal popularity and painfully sensitive to charges of "appeasement." After an uncertain spell, a few voices rose to answer the loud sounds of the Republicans. Adlai Stevenson summarized the breakup of the Paris conference accurately: "We handed Khrushchev the crowbar and the sledgehammer to wreck this meeting." And John Kennedy made a reasonable lament: "Sympathy, not respect, is the reluctant sentiment we elicit from our allies. . . . The maintenance of peace . . . should not hang on the constant possibility of engine failure."*

As these remarks most gently hinted, there had been flaws in the decision-making process within the Administration, long before its fevered efforts, after the event, to pick up the pieces of the U-2. The nation came to know these lapses, as the Congress investigated them. For one thing, the question of taking the precaution, on the eve of the Summit Conference, of temporarily suspending the U-2 flights had never even been raised, much less examined, at White House or Cabinet level. Secondly, there was the testimony of the Air Force Chief of Staff, General Thomas D. White, to refute all sly hints that this particular flight held promise of rewards peculiarly vital to national security: the General described the gamble as needless, and he said he would

* *Time*, May 30, 1960.

have counseled suspension of the flights. Finally, there had been ample warning of the risks being run in the fate of some earlier U-2 flights. Only the previous September, a U-2 had crash-landed near Tokyo, and an alert Japanese editor had examined the plane and reported extensively on its characteristics and purposes in his Tokyo magazine. These few facts sufficed to suggest a remarkably lax and permissive policy toward the flights—on the eve of the most important meeting of West and East in all the Eisenhower Years.

An apologia more plausible than most Republican campaign rhetoric asserted that Khrushchev had merely seized the incident to sabotage the Summit Conference. On behalf of this thesis, it was argued that (1) the Soviets had known of the flights for some time, without registering complaint and (2) the tone of recent Khrushchev speeches betrayed sharpened hostility toward the West even before the U-2 incident. Unfortunately, these seemingly reasonable arguments ignored other considerations equally meaningful in Soviet policy. In the first place, the silence of the Soviets in the past hardly proved toleration: they could not fire mere words at U-2 flights without confessing to the world their inability to reach the planes with more deadly ammunition. Secondly: a more belligerent tone in public speeches was both understandable and predictable Soviet preparation for its bargaining position at any international conference. Thirdly: even if Soviet policy had suffered one of its subterranean digressions, veering toward sudden toughness, this fact hardly made it more desirable for the United States Government to provide the diplomatic excuse for such a shift. Finally: it was an accepted belief of American diplomatic observers that Khrushchev was fighting an almost uninterrupted struggle against "Stalinist" critics charging him with "appeasement" of capitalist America and "naïveté" toward Eisenhower as a champion of peace. The crash —and hence the publicity—of the U-2 instantly rearmed all such critics of the Soviet Premier's "coexistence" policy. In this context, the anxiety of Khrushchev to exonerate the American Presi-

303

dent, by asserting that he "did not know," could much more logically be understood as an attempt to protect himself against hostile criticism in Kremlin councils, than as a device to trick the President into falsely professing innocence. To discredit Eisenhower meant—in Soviet domestic politics—to damage and endanger himself. In any event, the President's determined and explicit assumption of personal responsibility automatically disqualified him as a statesman with whom Khrushchev could negotiate, whether or not he wished to do so. The irrevocability of the fact is simply indicated by an imagined reversal of the roles of the two men: could an Eisenhower have led a divided government into serious negotiation with a Khrushchev who had publicly insisted, only days before, upon accepting personal responsibility for a Soviet spy plane shot down over Detroit? The American performance, in short, could find no excuse—no exoneration—on the basis of *any* speculative interpretation of devious Soviet policy. If Khrushchev had previously wished to evade negotiation at Paris, the conduct of America merely had made his wish easy. If he had still entertained hope for some negotiation, the conduct of America had made this impossible.

The inevitable diplomatic scenes at Paris' Elysée Palace imposed a grim ordeal on Dwight Eisenhower. He sat stoically, the deep sources of temper tightly controlled, as Khrushchev flung excoriation at him, in the august assembly of the heads of state. Coldly, the Soviet Premier exclaimed, before the three leaders of the West, that there was no point in conferring with them—until Dwight Eisenhower was no longer one of them. Painfully, Eisenhower edged close to an implied apology to his antagonist, assuring Khrushchev not only of the suspension of the U-2 flights but also of his own readiness to meet alone with the Soviet leader—to keep the American action from being the provocation to shatter the meeting of all four. Privately, the President confessed of the tension of the moment: "For the first time since I gave up smoking, I wanted a cigarette just to give myself something to do." But Khrushchev was ready and eager to lash the American President before the press of the world as "a thief caught red-handed in his theft." He had left Moscow with a position firmly fixed beyond the pathetic reach of all of Eisenhower's belated appeasing gestures. The projected visit of the American President to the Soviet Union next month, Khrushchev concluded, "should now be postponed"—forever. Out from the Elysée Palace he stalked, leaving behind the wreckage of Eisenhower's last hopes of world conciliation. And he pitilessly jested as he went: "Only my face is ruddy. Eisenhower's is white. And Macmillan's has no color."*

Once again, for Eisenhower, there was a postscript to Paris, as there had been last December.

This time, it was calm and sad.

The President flew homeward from the abbreviated conference via Lisbon. In this capital city of a tiny country on the edge of Europe, all of whose peoples he had hoped to help and to lead toward new unity and peace, Eisenhower conferred quietly with the seventy-one-year-old dictator of Portugal, Premier Antonio de Oliveira Salazar. The visit was designed to assuage Salazar's sense of slight when so much presidential courtesy had been extended, a few months earlier, to Spain's Francisco Franco. At least here, amends could be made.

For his overnight stay, the President stopped at the handsome and historic Queloz Palace, whose marble halls and formal gardens had housed and enchanted Portuguese royalty throughout the eighteenth and nineteenth centuries. Late in the afternoon, the President went walking slowly through the gardens, occasionally turning to chat with one of his staff. On his stroll, he came upon an American correspondent, traveling in the presidential party, who stood before one of the elaborate fountains, glintingly reminiscent of Versailles.

The correspondent was amusing himself by idly tossing into

* *Time*, May 30, 1960.

the water some French coins that—like so much else—were of no further immediate use.

"That how you're keeping busy?" the President asked, a wry half-grin cutting across the lines of fatigue in his face.

"No, sir, this is just for luck."

"Then you'd better throw some in for us all."*

And he walked slowly away toward the castle, his head slightly lowered, his hands clasped behind his back.

So ended the last journey of hope to Europe for the man who had commanded the allied armies, a decade and a half ago, to let the Continent be free again.

4

A scanner of omens might have rather nervously noted that, while all this was taking place in the Western world of diplomacy, there were three more U-2s based in the Far East. They were in Japan. And this Japan was to be the next—and the climactic —destination of the President on the long political pilgrimage that had begun the summer before.

Three weeks intervened between the President's return from the tragedy of Paris and his June 12 departure for the Pacific. Originally his visit to the Far East had been scheduled to follow directly upon his tour of the Soviet Union—with all its prepared calls on the nation's five major cities, a journey deep into Siberia, full-scale press conferences, and radio and television speeches from Moscow, Kiev, and Leningrad. Now he had nine days free for further investment in the Asian journey.

There was doubt, and there was debate, in Washington, during these days following fast upon the return from Europe, as to the wisdom of any grand venture eastward at this juncture. Harsh critics exclaimed: Paris was enough, let us not add to it the whole Pacific. More serious was the fact that Tokyo had

* *A President's Odyssey*, p. 203.

now been wracked by a full month of anti-American violence. The government of Premier Nobusuke Kishi had finally, on May 20, won ratification from the Japanese Diet of a new mutual security pact with the United States—after 107 days of turbulent debate and violent Socialist opposition. The President was supposed to arrive in Tokyo June 19, to celebrate the effective date of this fiercely fought treaty. When Press Secretary Hagerty flew to Tokyo early in June to make anticipatory arrangements, he had to be rescued by helicopter from a mob of several thousand Japanese angrily besieging him at Tokyo's International Airport. Their show of hostility not only conveyed opposition to the defense treaty; they had also been inflamed by Soviet warnings to countries affording bases to U-2 operations. Could the President reasonably embark on a trip with such an ultimate destination—without risking both personal safety and public humiliation?

The White House elected to gamble on the rewards of success in defiance of the odds. Indeed, the perils did hold possible promise of political advantage. A President daringly exposing himself to Tokyo mobs, partly under Communist inspiration, conveyed an even more exciting political image than a President suffering, with tight-lipped forbearance, the indignities of Khrushchev at a diplomatic conference in Paris. All damage incurred in Paris might even be erased. The serious hopes of world peace-making were dead. But the glittering partisan hopes of the Hagerty-Eisenhower memorandum of 1958 might yet—incredibly —be redeemed.

Accordingly the President took to his travels again, on June 12, 1960, this time via Alaska, for the farther shores of the Pacific. From Anchorage, he flew toward the Philippines via Wake Island. He was intersecting the course of the homeward arc of his first famed journey as President-elect—the 1952 trip to Korea. Here, at Wake Island, he had boarded the U.S.S. *Helena*—to frown, for the first time, upon John Foster Dulles as the Secretary-designate began to speak of a "new" and "positive" and "dynamic" foreign policy.

When the President reached the rim of Asia, there came an odd interlude in the sweltering heat of Manila. It was an interlude whose contrast between public triumph and private travail seemed one of the more harshly contrived scenes in all this drama, so sharp with irony. Philippine President Carlos P. Garcia and more than one million citizens of Manila crushed the American President in their embrace, surpassing even the popular spectacles witnessed in New Delhi a few months before. Yet, even as the Philippine throngs were cheering, the President's Secret Service was quietly and tensely measuring—and fearing—the hazards of a venture to Tokyo. On the climactic day of the visit, Eisenhower and Garcia stood side by side on the reviewing stand of the Luneta park, respectfully watching the parade of troops before them in the hot afternoon sun. Even while the bands blared, and the two Presidents stood at attention, Eisenhower's aides huddled beside the platform, communicating directly with Tokyo—to learn that the Japanese Cabinet, in emergency session, had decided to ask the President to delay his trip, for his own safety. And while a male chorus sang out a tribute especially composed for the great ceremony, "The Eisenhower March," one aide whispered the news to him, as he stared solemnly ahead. Thus did diplomatic defeat in the East come to the accompaniment of sounds far more agreeable than those heard a few weeks earlier in the West.

Under light rain squalls the same evening, the President boarded the cruiser U.S.S. *St. Paul* to head northward—with, again, a hastily revised itinerary. On board, it was decided to extend overnight the planned visit to Korea, along with a quick stop in Okinawa, and to proceed as scheduled to the island of Formosa that was Nationalist China. An armada of 125 warships, with some 500 aircraft, escorted the President. The vessels were of the Seventh Fleet, which—by solemn order of the State of the Union message of 1953—were no longer obstructing Nationalist Chinese military operations.

The ships moved along at speeds of higher than thirty knots, not because there was any destination to rush toward, but as a precaution against hostile submarines. Over on the Chinese mainland, Radio Peiping greeted the nearby presidential passage with broadcasts flailing Eisenhower as a "god of plague." As the armada moved through the Formosa Strait, the Communist artillery, barely one hundred miles away, gave its salute—the heaviest shelling in years of the offshore island of Quemoy, whose defense had constituted, for John Foster Dulles, "the most brilliant thing I have done." And American newsmen accompanying their President dryly quipped: "Ike's the only chief of state who ever got an eighty-thousand-gun salute."

Two days later, the President stood on Nationalist Chinese soil. There he was saluted by seventy-two-year-old Generalissimo Chiang Kai-shek. The encounter was as warm as the meeting, on a like moment but a distant continent, with the aging Salazar.

Three days later he was in Hawaii. This was the same place of pause as on his homeward journey seven and a half years before—on his return from Korea. And he halted there, now, for six days to rest, to golf, and to prepare his report to the nation.

In Washington, meanwhile, Secretary of State Christian Herter found himself forced, even before Eisenhower's return, to appear and testify before critical congressional committees. He could only acknowledge the obvious. There had been, indeed, some mistakes in judgment in evaluating the Japanese situation.

In New York—unhappily reading of the President's homeward journey—I could not help wondering if his memory, as mine, was drawn back to those days, just before his presidency began, when he had made the same halt in Hawaii. Did his thoughts retreat—reflectively—to the earnest, stale dogmatisms of Radford, remarking on the prevalence of anticolonial feeling in Asia . . . the crisp injunctions of Humphrey, deploring the

menaces of unbalanced budgets and unbridled inflation . . . the
soft but portentous sound of the voice of Dulles, insisting that
the nation, quickly and bravely, build a *new* foreign policy—
inspired with proud "initiative," disdainful of the petty purposes
of "containment," and zealous to "roll back the enemy"? . . .

By the time of the President's return to Washington, for his report to the nation on the night of June 27, he had clocked, in his
travels at home and abroad, close to 320,000 presidential miles.
If he had thought back, of late, to those earlier days in Hawaii, he
gave no troubled sign of it, as he talked to the people, at the end
of his last journey in quest of "Peace and Friendship in
Freedom."

He simply said . . .

The great value resulting from these journeys to twenty-seven nations has been obvious here and abroad. . . . They have resulted in
the creation of a more friendly atmosphere and mutual confidence
between peoples. They have proved effective in bringing closer together nations that respect human dignity and are dedicated to freedom. . . . One clear proof of the value to us of these visits is the
intensity of the opposition the Communists have developed against
them. . . . These disorders were not occasioned by America. We in
the United States must not fall into the error of blaming ourselves for
what the Communists do.*

All these assurances were meant, of course, to be soothing to
all stings, healing to all wounds, borne by national or personal
ego. And the assuaging ritual called forth, at last, the supreme
confession of a self-absolving helplessness. "After all," he concluded, "Communists will act like Communists."

The President's sad sigh of resignation was, in fact, an apt and
realistic enough response to the political reality confronting him.
There remained, quite literally, nothing further of moment for
him to do, in pursuit of the splendid dream of helping the world
to make peace with itself.

In the West, he had been stripped—by a cruel combination of

* New York *Times*, June 28, 1960.

bad luck and bad judgment—of any diplomatic power to deal with the leadership of the Soviet Union.

In the East, the fast-running currents rippling out from his initial misfortune had carried across the Pacific—bearing on its waters an American President politically adrift, unable even to disembark upon the soil of his country's most powerful and important ally in all of Asia.

All the gleam of political promise in his fantastic global journeys now was gone beyond recapturing. He had given unstintingly of his energy and his personality. He had been repaid in popular coin—the voices of millions yelling lusty ovations, the hands of millions waving gaudy banners. He had invested all this amassed political capital in the two great chances—one in Paris, one in Tokyo. Now it was spent—all of it. There were not even any more gold medallions left.

There remained, therefore, in the summer of 1960, nothing for the President to do but to fix his gaze upon the political conflict in the domestic arena, as the national campaign boisterously proceeded toward the people's choice of a man to take his place —and a man to define, anew, his office.

5

While the voice of Dwight David Eisenhower, with its broad and warm Midwestern twang, was proclaiming the purposes of America—to European prime ministers, to Latin American congresses, and to millions of the people of Asia—there was heard in Washington, at precisely the same time, the voice of John Fitzgerald Kennedy. And in the cool and clipped accents of New England, he spoke of the office of the President itself . . .

In the challenging, revolutionary Sixties, the American Presidency will demand more than ringing manifestoes issued from the rear of the battle. It will demand that the President place himself in the very

thick of the fight, that he care passionately about the fate of the people he leads, that he be willing to serve them at the risk of incurring
their momentary displeasure. . . .

He must above all be the Chief Executive in every sense of the
word. He must be prepared to exercise the fullest powers of his office.
. . . He must master complex problems as well as receive one-page
memoranda. . . . He must re-open the channels of communication
between the world of thought and the seat of power. . . .

No President, it seems to me, can escape politics. He has not only
been chosen by the nation—he has been chosen by his Party. And if
he insists that he is "President of all the people" and should, therefore, offend none of them—if he blurs the issues and differences between the parties—if he neglects the party machinery and avoids his
party's leadership—then he has not only weakened the political party
. . . he had dealt a blow to the democratic process itself. . . .

Despite the increasing evidence of a lost national purpose and a
soft national will, F.D.R.'s words in his First Inaugural still ring true:
"In every dark hour of our national life, a leadership of frankness
and vigor has met with that understanding and support of the people
themselves which is essential to victory."*

The young Democratic senator, through the months of his
campaign for presidential nomination and election, probably delivered no more trenchant or persuasive speech—along with the
common quota of those of lesser merit. The nation, of course,
was not weighing a choice between academic definitions of the
office of the presidency. And the Democratic candidate—even
as he sketched a profile of the President not possible to confuse
with Dwight David Eisenhower—politically shunned nothing so
scrupulously as direct clash with the man whom he sought to
succeed. Yet the sense of politics and the sense of history of this
one speech reflected themselves in much of the candidate's bold,
brawling pursuit of his goal. John Fitzgerald Kennedy fought
his primary battles with the verve of a man deeply committed to
the political life and passionately eager for its prizes. Could one
conceive his ever raising—amid the heat and fury of a presidential
campaign—the self-protective shield of reserve of an Eisenhower:

* New York *Times,* January 15, 1960.

"If the people don't want me, that's all right: I've a lot of fishing to do."?

The young, articulate Massachusetts senator gave firm denial, too, to all the presidential assurances of progress in the nation and prestige in the world, and he proceeded to lament a national sense of drift, while crisply promising to "get America moving again." Thus a great part of the campaign of 1960 came to turn upon a curious anomaly. Both Eisenhower and Kennedy shied from personal conflict. The former did so from his distaste for such abrupt political attack, the latter from his respect for so difficult a political adversary. Both men agreed and insisted, therefore, that the contest and the choice lay between Kennedy and Nixon. Yet the differences in *substance* between these two young veterans of the Senate—whether measured by their views on national defense, their precepts of foreign policy, or their passion for civil liberties—were so small as almost to elude expression. And the real and profound contrast that gave some historic meaning to all the rallies, jousts, cheers, jeers, confetti, slogans, and banners—the contrast between the President and the President-to-be—was left in discreet silence.

The young senator could not, in the deepest sense, ever win the 1960 campaign: he could only hope and wait for his opponent to lose it. And the final result would newly prove that there is no such political event as a national campaign in which assets and liabilities are so rigidly and unequally distributed that the outcome is immutably assured. There were three great political burdens with which Kennedy began his battle: his youth, his religion, and his wealth. These were not only formidable in weight: they were also utterly impossible to change. Such political misfortunes of person were, moreover, matched by misfortunes of circumstance: his challenge had to be hurled at an Administration that, through most of its life, had benignly presided over a time of unprecedented national prosperity and apparent world peace. A more uninviting political prospect could not easily be designed.

But in the ruthlessly untidy ways of politics, the apparent design was to be undone. A superstitious Richard Nixon probably would have read the warning augury as early as the day in May when he learned of the fall of the U-2. Without that event to spoil the political drama of a Summit Conference and a presidential journey through the Soviet Union—even if both were largely innocuous and ceremonial—the Republican Administration could plausibly have stood before the nation as the gifted guardians of all hopes for world peace. They could have proclaimed themselves the wise men whose persistence had lifted the Iron Curtain—the leaders whose strength and dignity had brought even the masters of the Kremlin to give grudging respect, to enter rational dialogue with the West, and to practice civilized political table manners. The fantasy would have been irresistible. Alas, it fell in the Urals, punctured by the fire of antiaircraft guns—manned by unknown soldiers of the Soviet Union quite unaware that they were helping to elect the next President of the United States.

The uncomprehending Soviet soldiers needed assistance, however, from Richard Nixon. And this he contributed quite as abundantly, just as unintentionally.

It is not possible, of course, to single out definitively the lapse or blunder in an election so close that its final result could have been reversed by a strategic redistribution of less than twenty thousand votes in all the nation. Precisely this fact, indeed, set the price that Nixon would pay for so narrow a defeat: in all his host of mourners or detractors, each individual could—and would—claim to have possessed the small and priceless key to victory, foolishly ignored or disdained by the defeated candidate. A prompt and candid denunciation of the arrest in Georgia of a prominent Negro preacher; a more blunt disavowal of the anti-Catholic statement of a prominent Protestant preacher; a less spectral appearance, or a more confident argument, in the first critical television debate with his opponent—any one of these, or a score more of similar and equally plausible speculations, could be arbitrarily cited as the fatal fault. And yet . . . some more grave process of erosion had to have done its work—to leave a presidential candidate's political position so exposed, so vulnerable, to mere mischance of minor error.

The many flaws and lacks appeared, in fact, to have a single essential source: a want of resolution—a chronic personal incapacity for commitment—on the gravest political issues of the day. The pain of irresolution seemed to grow, moreover, with the size of the issue. The Vice President could be fiercely vehement and explicit on such immaterial or imaginary matters as the impropriety of blasphemy uttered by anyone in high office: He calculated correctly that very few citizens cast their ballots in favor of impure public speech. But he found it exceedingly hard to be explicit or compelling on questions of more great and urgent moment. He calculated correctly—again—that an unknowable number of voters might hoard their dissents until Election Day. This seemed an appalling risk.

Thus—in national affairs—the historic and divisive issue of civil rights left Richard Nixon, too, divided. The failure to intercede swiftly on behalf of the arrested Negro minister, the Reverend Dr. Martin Luther King, Jr., did not result from some mere administrative lapse. It followed logically from the exhausting and enervating uncertainty that he suffered in this sphere of crucial controversy and political peril. On the one side, there was the massive weight of the Negro vote in the great northern metropolitan centers. On the other side, there was the tantalizing lure of enough southern electoral votes to tip the balance in a close election. How—without feeling deep commitment in principle—*could* one choose?

Thus—in world affairs—there was no politically unhazardous choice to be made in appraising either the strength of national defenses or the height of national prestige. Nixon was not unaware, of course, that both were reasonably and anxiously questioned, at home and abroad. But to acknowledge this—and thereby to blunt the critical thrusts of his opponent—was to risk

315

the anger and the alienation of Dwight David Eisenhower, a formidable political asset to put in jeopardy. And so the Vice President turned to giving oddly mixed retorts. These were belligerently phrased but slackly reasoned. "I've been in the Soviet Union," he reminded his listeners, in Portland, Oregon, "and anybody who says that the Soviet Union is going to catch up with the United States economically just doesn't know what he is talking about." Or as he assured Peoria, Illinois: "If they do launch a man into space, we're not going to get downhearted, because our program is coming along splendidly." And the *reductio ad absurdum* was oddly reserved for the sophisticated audiences of New York: since the great city itself had given a conspicuously warmer welcome to President Eisenhower than to Premier Khrushchev, arriving to attend a session of the United Nations, did not this show of popular preference refute all ugly assertions discounting American prestige?

There was a tone to many of these arguments that strongly suggested the extravagance of a man angrily defying his own private doubts as much as those of the public. And the fact was that, for many months in Washington, there had been—not for the first time, his critics would have insisted—two Richard Nixons occupying the office of the vice presidency. The first, the public Nixon, acclaimed Eisenhower as a savior of world peace, a statesman of rare acumen, and a national hero whom a thankful electorate would not dare to slight by a vote for the Democratic party. The second, the private Nixon, patiently explained to visitors and journalists, in off-the-record conversations or over intimate dinners, his dismay with White House leadership, his dissent from decisions in the field of national defense and foreign policy, and his anxiety to offer the nation a more youthful, more vigorous, and more coherent presidency—in the person of himself.

But the "person" of Nixon was—*who?* Few men in the national politics of modern America had suffered such vehement attacks from their critics. Few had engaged in such vituperative attacks upon their opponents. And few finally emerged—after all the words, all the charges, all the venom—so gray a figure, pallid in philosophy and blurred in profile.

I had observed Nixon, closely and often, through all the earlier days of the Eisenhower Years: at regular Cabinet meetings and at special White House conferences, on formal political occasions and on relaxed social occasions. And the evidence mounted overwhelmingly that this man did not neatly fit the acid caricature of his enemies. To them, he appeared either a lion of Republicanism and reaction or a fox of ambition and guile. To closer witnesses, he seemed neither. His private discourse betrayed scarcely any of the partisan excess he reserved for public consumption. He brandished few of the clichés or prejudices of conventional Republican oratory. Indeed, the philosophy of any policy interested him, quite evidently, far less than its efficacy: he judged any declaration or speech not by its content but by its impact. At his intellectual best in offering tactical counsel, he came to appear more and more the kind of politician who, but for some accident of partisan affiliation, could have rendered such service just as heartily to the Democratic party. Significantly and logically, then, the most effective period of his vice presidency had come with the awkward political suspense following Eisenhower's heart attack in 1955. Then, poised and restrained, he had given an exemplary performance as a man close to great power *not* being presumptuously or prematurely assertive. This discreetly empty time was surely his finest official hour. As for the private citizen, most qualities displayed in public—the gregarious air and the simple manner, the assurance of voice and the banality of phrase—largely vanished along with the witnessing throngs. Alone, he appeared vastly different: laconic and clinical, reflective and withdrawn, not confident but—groping.

This unseen personality ruled much of the spirit and the conduct of the 1960 campaign. Throughout, he coldly, ever more

317

coldly, kept his own counsel. Virtually every close adviser, more than once in the course of the electoral struggle, resolved to resign in rage and leave him to the two things that alone he seemed to cherish: the privacy of his decisions and the advice of his wife. Most irate and abused of all, perhaps, was the man most tirelessly devoted to his cause, Leonard Hall. Rarely consulted, frequently insulted, and regularly overruled, Hall served the Nixon campaign perhaps most effectively by stifling mutinies that stirred at lower levels and that tempted his own sympathy. To wider audiences, such as the American press, Nixon addressed a suspicion and a hostility that his own subsequent account of the campaign made clear. Time and again, a close adviser would press him to attend a meeting with newspaper editors in centers as crucial as New York or Washington, and his stubborn retort would be: "What for? They're all against me, anyway."*

But nothing was so remarkable about the man, perhaps, as the passionate self-assurance that he seemed to reserve for one belief. This was the unshakable faith that he was, in an almost unique and surely superior sense, a "professional" politician, loftily surveying a scene cluttered with "amateurs." This particular form of self-esteem was curious for two reasons: it starkly contrasted with his lack of confidence in most other areas of thought, and it was singularly unwarranted. As one of his close counselors in the 1960 campaign subsequently remarked to me: "The crazy, almost incredible, fact about the man is that he's not a particularly good politician at all, on the simplest level. He does not even handle people intelligently—or carefully. He could —and did—manage even to insult and alienate a Herbert Hoover! No real 'professional' could be as willful and self-centered and withdrawn as he was." Indeed, Nixon's own political memoirs later revealed the remarkable naïveté of the man who avowed such scorn for "amateurs." Thus, in recalling the crisis of

* All commentary on Nixon's performance in the 1960 campaign is based upon post-election accounts directly gathered from men active on both the Nixon and Eisenhower staffs.

his personal political fund in the 1952 campaign, he could describe those days of distress—nine years later—and detailedly
report how he acquired "a lump in my throat" when he was
assured by two friends from his California home town that "all
the folks back in Whittier are behind you 100 per cent."* The
almost pathetic ingenuousness of a "professional" politician, so
solemnly recording so meaningless an accolade, is suggested by
the improbability of his opponent for the presidency ever reciting
such sentimentalized trivia for posterity.

To the many who tried to seek out the true identity of the
man, one conclusion finally seemed inescapable: this identity
remained elusive because *he* was deeply engaged in the same
quest as *they*. Here again his later memoirs would prove remarkably revealing. Thus he would recall the disaster of his first
televised debate with Kennedy and the agonizing self-reappraisal
following upon it. . . .

. . . in the final analysis, I knew that what was most important was
that I must be myself. I have seen so-called public relations experts
ruin many a candidate by trying to make him over into an "image"
. . . I went into the second debate *determined* to do my best to *convey . . . sincerity . . .* If I succeeded in this, I felt my "image" would
take care of itself. [italics mine]†

Only the most shallow exercise in self-scrutiny could conclude
with such a resolve to appear "sincere." Yet it was characteristic
of the candidate, the politician, and the man. For his mastery of
tactic or technique, at its best, never seemed quite to compensate
for his uncertainty in strategy or substance. He was always the
pupil who "heard the music but yet missed the tune." He was the
host obsessed with the setting of his table—but with no taste for
food. And for the President who was his most powerful sup-
porter he had to remain the candidate who was "just not presidential timber."

* Richard M. Nixon, *Six Crises,* p. 98.
† Ibid., p. 344.

Thus—again—the latest events of the Eisenhower Years carried echoes from its earliest moments. The silent sense of detachment, if not estrangement, between Eisenhower and Nixon had dated from 1952 and had been underscored in 1956 by the President's failure to rejoice at Nixon's companionship on the national ticket. Now in 1960 this heritage placed the White House at a peculiar distance from the man striving so actively to defend it and so ardently to inherit it. This man was not unaware of the potential political power that the President could wield in this election. Yet Nixon was no less aware that a large part of the electorate complained that he had never stood, alone and free, beyond the comforting shade of the taller figure of the President. A vigorous show of self-sufficiency, then, seemed the order of the day—along with a reserve of political aid, of course, to be summoned in emergency. And so the counsel of ambivalence prevailed once again.

In this climate, both personal and political relations between the Eisenhower staff and the Nixon staff grew chill as the political battle grew warm. Men around the President, anxious to lend assistance to guard Eisenhower's personal stake in the electoral verdict upon the past eight years, met repeated rebuff from men around the Vice President, anxious to be rid of the burden of past mistakes and to shape their own vision of the next four years. And this venturesome spirit prevailed—until little more than a fortnight before the day of decision. Then a candid survey of the political scene warned that the price of this spirited independence almost certainly would be the reduction of the life expectancy of the four-year vision to some fourteen days. And there seemed no escaping the conclusion: only Eisenhower might yet save the Nixon candidacy.

So, with sudden urgency, the presidential travels began again—for a last time—now on no grand global scale but in the narrower circuit of Pennsylvania and New York, New Jersey and Ohio. As the cheers rose and the confetti fell, Eisenhower glowingly looked back upon the eight years "since millions of us—Republicans, Democrats, independents—joined together to build a better America." It had been "a happy and fruitful partnership," as he told the throng in Philadelphia: "You have increased personal income . . . by 48 percent. . . . You have built nine million new homes, more than ever were built in the same length of time. . . . You have increased the Gross National Product by one hundred fifty-eight billion dollars—almost 45 percent. Our interstate highway system was talked about for years. . . . Now we are building forty-one thousand miles of these great new avenues of commerce. . . . The St. Lawrence Seaway, for decades a dream; finally it came true. . . . In the meantime, you have expanded Social Security, improved our national parks, forced passage of a good labor-reform bill, and took the only significant steps in civil right in eighty years. . . . My friends, never have Americans achieved so much in so short a time. . . ."*

As I listened to the familiar voice or read the familiar statistics —both sounding plausible and persuasive in their flat and undramatic way—I found myself again thinking that this election, too, could conceivably be ruled by a familiar irony. For the number of acceptable achievements of the Republican Administration in *domestic* life would have very little political impact upon an electorate basically distrustful of Republican economics. And the same electorate might view so differently—with grudging respect or open awe—such seemingly impressive credentials in *foreign* affairs as: Dwight David Eisenhower, a veteran of more than forty years in the nation's Armed Forces, proclaiming that "our military strength . . . is the most powerful on earth"; Henry Cabot Lodge, a veteran of years of forensic clashes with the Soviet Union at the United Nations; Richard Milhous Nixon, hailed by Eisenhower as a man of "character, ability, responsibility, experience," a man who had spent eight years as an intimate witness and student of the presidential office to prepare himself not merely to debate with Khrushchev but to contend

* New York *Times,* October 29, 1960.

with the whole aggressive thrust of Soviet Communism. . . . Were these not imposing political weapons? . . . Yet the President himself, when he spoke of foreign affairs, seemed reduced to submitting such measures of achievement as: "More than 120 heads of state and government have visited our nation's capital in the past eight years, an unprecedented occurrence."* . . . Or he could boast that the Latin American policies of his Administration had "forged new and strong ties with our neighbors to the south"—in a speech wholly free of any mention of the name of Fidel Castro. . . . Or he could make his climactic campaign appearance before a rally of enthused thousands in New York's Coliseum—already reassured by Ethel Merman's lusty rendition of "Everything's Coming Up Roses"—and could angrily cry that he could not "understand how, in the face of *such* a record, anyone can seriously argue that the world leadership of the United States has been impaired."* . . . And so I found myself listening and wondering: *was* it conceivable that—even as the mass of voters refused to give fair weight to Administration claims about the national economy—they would quixotically allow the scales of decision to be tipped by the weight of these brightly painted feathers?

It was, of course, not to be.

For Eisenhower, abetted by Nixon, had contrived to make the 1960 election, essentially, one more rendering of the tale, repeated so often through the years, of the fatally belated act. Through all the span of his presidency, no man, *either* in the United States *or* in any other free nation on earth, could match the resources of political power commanded by Eisenhower, *both* at home *and* abroad. Yet it had been the pattern of action, if not the purpose of the man, to husband and to guard these resources—like savings earned by the sweat of a lifetime—so that they not be spent in the rough and contaminating play of power and politics. The pattern had been almost faultlessly con-

* Ibid.
* Ibid., November 3, 1960.

sistent—whether the arena of world challenge was outer space or the nearby Caribbean, whether the issue was a menace to national sovereignty in the Middle East or a menace to civil rights in Little Rock. In the broad perspective of the world politics of all the 1950s, the President had waited too long for his encounter with Khrushchev. In the more narrow perspective of the national politics of 1960, he had waited too long, now, for his counterthrust to Kennedy.

Richard Nixon, at the same time, helped to forge his own defeat by decisions and actions just as authentically characteristic of his own political personality. In the most serious analysis, he did not lose the 1960 election merely because he failed, as Eisenhower later shrugged, to make "a couple of telephone calls" to impress the Negro urban vote. Nor did he lose because he displayed on the nation's television screens a face whose beard defied all disguise by lighting or cosmetic. If any one specific and deliberate decision contributed fatally to his defeat, this was his personal readiness ever to appear in televised debate with Kennedy. The mere fact of the closeness (and frequent diffuseness) of the debate between the two men sufficed, of course, to destroy any presumption of superior wisdom or greater maturity on the part of Nixon. For Kennedy, at the same time, the debates afforded more than occasions for display of his command of facts and of language: they were essential simply to make himself known and familiar to a national audience only casually acquainted with him. The challenge, however, had carried an irresistible temptation to a Nixon who, only the year before, had "won" his "debate" with Khrushchev in the Soviet Union. Such success encouraged him confidently to leave a large part of his political fate to a like encounter on the more familiar soil of the United States. And so a most incongruous fate was reserved for the man whose political fame rested upon his passionate combat with all whom he viewed as agents of Soviet Communism: to triumph in Moscow—and to blanch in Chicago.

The second term of the Eisenhower Years thus came to its end.

323

Each one of the latter years of the Eisenhower presidency had been marked, for him, by a personal and explicit kind of loss.

In 1957, he had lost his closest intellectual comrade in the government with the departure of George Humphrey—after the Secretary of the Treasury had inflicted upon the prestige of the President a damage as great as it was unintended.

In 1958, his closest political aide in the Administration, Sherman Adams, had been lost—a casualty, at least in part, of his own irresolution.

In 1959, he had lost to death his most trusted mentor in world affairs, John Foster Dulles—with whom were buried, too, the precepts and practices that had constricted American world policy for the better part of a decade. This latter interment, however, like the political damage endured in 1957, had gone unheralded and unacknowledged.

All this left him to spend 1960, politically, with Richard Nixon. And Nixon simply lost.

6

A few weeks later, the youngest man ever to be elected President of the United States stood on the Inaugural Stand on Capitol Hill and briefly shook hands in farewell to the oldest man ever to leave that office. Their murmured words were perfunctory and formal. Now linked in the sequence of history—even as they contrasted in its understanding—they could profess little else in common.

No President, upon retiring from his unique office, can seriously contemplate the possibility of his successor being more discerning and accomplished than himself. The official retreat must be covered, as it were, by a protective presumption that the affairs of the nation cannot be quite so well handled, at least for some considerable while. And, in this particular instance, the deeply felt differences in the two men's views of the very nature of *their* office set them at great distance from each other, even as they touched hands.

A few hours later, the path of retirement to private life meandered through the Maryland hills. It passed not far from Camp David, where Khrushchev had been entertained in a genial "spirit" only sixteen months earlier. And the snow-laden road, now traveled by the slenderest of motorcades, carried on toward the farm on the southern edge of Pennsylvania, not many miles from Philadelphia.

As I read of the little personal details of his itinerary, I found that my own thoughts went back to the political scene in Philadelphia, four years earlier. There and then, in stately Convention Hall, Dwight David Eisenhower had given the final speech of the 1956 campaign that was to bring him so resounding a mandate for his second term. Outside, the night had been bleak and damp under a dismal drizzle of rain. Inside, the hall had felt warm with the crowd's gift of cheers and the President's sense of confidence. He had delivered his speech with uncommon force, as his words touched on the fate of most nations and peoples on earth—the hostile, the friendly, the neutral. His most fervent words of hope had been reserved for the seven hundred million people in eighteen nations, new-born to independence since World War II. It was natural for an American President, standing there in Convention Hall, to think particularly of these nations. And such had been the spirit of his peroration, in this last of his campaign speeches . . .

. . . They summon to our minds another moment of greatness. It was here in Philadelphia, and it was in 1787. The Constitutional Convention had come to its end. . . . And . . . Benjamin Franklin pointed to the chair where Washington had been sitting. There—on the back —was painted, in brilliant gold, the half sun. And he said quietly: "Now, at length, I have the happiness to know that it is a rising, and not a setting, sun."

We today scan the wider horizon of all the world.

Proud of our principles, persistent in peace, we prayerfully may dare to say the same.

325

There was, that night, an ovation great enough to match the hope of these last words. . . .

Now—a few miles and four years away from that scene—the President neared Gettysburg and home. No rainy November night, it was now a gleaming January afternoon. The winter sky was clean and icy-bright, and the crooked thrusts of trees and shrubs whitely glinted in the sun.

But the hour in the day was late. And, this time, the sun was setting.

CHAPTER TEN

A Word of Conclusion

"The human story does not always unfold like a mathematical calculation on the principle that two and two make four. Sometimes in life they make five or minus three; and sometimes the blackboard topples down in the middle of the sum and leaves the class in disorder and the pedagogue with a black eye."

Winston Churchill

A free and prosperous people in the second half of the twentieth century, amply attended by all the time-saving marvels of modern technology and automation, enjoys far greater leisure than any generation of its ancestors. This historic dispensation extends to nearly all phases of a free nation's life. But there is one stunning exception. And this is the enterprise upon which the nation's survival may depend—the attainment of a wise and fair understanding of its own immediate past.

Here the very rhythm of revolutionary change, so generously favoring all other endeavors, harshly exacts its price. For it leaves to a free people—contemplating the sudden crisis or the instant challenge—less time, less chance for perception and reflection, than any other epoch of man. An age not long dead when the sound of musketry on Boston's Bunker Hill would take a fortnight to echo in London's House of Commons—and an age when the firing of an intercontinental missile from the far side of the globe might leave citizens of Detroit a quarter of an hour to prepare themselves for the blast—are two ages distant and distinct from each other by measure more profound than clock or calendar. For the newer of these ages does not challenge merely the speed of sound: it defies the speed of thought. It requires the processes of democratic decision to revolve and to react as fast as all the world in historic upheaval. And it prescribes a rate of obsolescence that dispenses as harshly with yesterday's ideas as with yesterday's weapons.

Thus all witnesses to such an age are denied the chance to wait for those comforting prerogatives of the historian—dispassion and detachment. The witnesses must speak, instead, from the swiftest of glances and the briefest of visits. For the long-deliberated and delicately balanced judgment, finally pronounced after exhaustive examination of amassed archives, can emerge to the light only to peer around for the once-living, once-urgent dilemma—and squint in vain. The dilemma will be dead, beneath the rubble of accomplished facts.

And so, falteringly and presumptuously, one can only try to catch some glimpses of the fleet shapes of the men or the events . . . to touch with the senses some part of their meaning, before they vanish over the rim of remembrance and understanding . . . someday to be recovered for the learning, but too late for the living.

This much one must try to do, as the Eisenhower Years slip fast into the past. . . .

2

What happened to all those fine young people with stars in their eyes who sailed balloons and rang doorbells for us in 1952?

Dwight D. Eisenhower (to Sherman Adams), July 1960*

Dwight David Eisenhower, the man of many paradoxes, left the office of the presidency as the most widely popular—and the most sharply criticized—citizen of his nation. By almost unanimous consensus of all political leaders of both parties, only the constitutional bar to a third term kept him from inflicting upon John Fitzgerald Kennedy an electoral rout as severe and complete as those twice suffered by Adlai Stevenson. By almost equally unanimous consensus of the national community of intellectuals and critics—journalists and academicians, pundits and prophets—his conduct of the presidency was unskillful and his definition of it inaccurate. And these fiercely contradictory judgments inspired two images: the profile acidly etched by his detractors, the portrait warmly painted by his idolators.

The caricature was—as always—easier to draw.

Here, in this vignette, was a weak and irresolute man, surrounded by vastly stronger men, their vision small but their will powerful. To them, this man delegated the powers of the presidency slackly and carelessly. To the role of national leader, he came unequipped by experience, by knowledge, by temperament, or even by taste for politics. To the role of military responsibility, he brought the prejudices of a professional life that had effectively ended before the advent of nuclear weapons. To the role of world statesman, he brought a genial and gregarious disposition, undisciplined and unsophisticated, never holding promise of a diplomacy more profound than a rather maudlin

* *First-hand Report*, p. 453.

kind of global sociability. On the world scene, he sought to check the power of Soviet Communism by complacent citation of the "spiritual" superiority of American life; and he thereby showed a blindness to national danger reminiscent of a Stanley Baldwin of the 1930s, assuring the people of Great Britain of their serene immunity to the menace of Nazi power. On the national scene, he persisted, too, in facile exhortations on "spiritual" and "moral" values—even while he practiced an aloof neutralism toward the struggle for civil rights that seemed, to many of his citizens, the most pure and urgent moral issue to confront his presidency. As a politician, he set forth to remake the blurred image of the Republican party, but he merely ended by suffering himself to be remade in *its* image. As an intellectual, he bestowed upon the games of golf and bridge all the enthusiasm and perseverance that he withheld from books and ideas. As a President, he sought to affirm the dignity of his high office by the simple device of reducing its complex functions to the circumspect discharge of its ceremonial obligations. As the leader of the world's greatest democracy—charting its flight through all the clouds and storms of the mid-twentieth century, on toward the mysteries and perils of the Age of Space—he elected to leave his nation to fly on automatic pilot.

The appreciative portrait was—as almost always—not so easy to draw.

Here, by this portrait, was a man of selfless and serious patriotism. Physically, he gave of himself unstintingly, in bearing the burden of the presidency, despite three illnesses that would have crippled weaker men. Morally, he gave uncompromising scorn to all temptations of expediency, despite knowing full well the easy accolades to be won at almost any instant—by publicly chastising a McCarthy, by blaming congressional leadership for failures, by wrathfully denouncing a Faubus, by combating recession with tax reduction or government deficit, by appeasing critics with the replacement of a Dulles or a Benson, or, most dramatically, by proclaiming himself the soldier-champion of gigantic military programs to assure American supremacy in the Age of Space. Whatever the crisis or the clamor, he stayed defiantly faithful to the policy—or to the man—as honest conviction decreed. As a national leader, he avoided, through the greater part of a perilous decade, his and his people's two greatest fears—war in the world and depression at home. As a partisan leader, he steered Republicanism toward new historic ground, far from its isolationist traditions; and, for all the conservatism of his economics, he left the policies of the New Deal and the Fair Deal intact and secure after eight years of a Republican Administration. Personally, he led his party to two successive and smashing national triumphs, after it had endured twenty years of failure and rebuff. He brought to the White House itself a personal sense of dignity and honor that could only elevate the office of the presidency in the eyes of his people. When he entered this office, the political air of the nation was sulphurous with bitterness, recrimination, and frustration. And when he left office, this air was clean of all such rancor, fresh with good will and good feeling.*

The two portraits of the man deny and taunt each other. It is easy and obvious to note—as I believe—that each contains some pieces and fractions of the whole truth. It is less easy—but more important—to discern that both suffer from the same flaws and tricks. Both confuse the plausible with the actual, the logic with the reality. Both ignore the capricious and the imponderable and the elusive in history. And so, by the neat fancy of fitting every event to some intent, they contrive the most seductive distortions: the happy occurrence confers credit, where none may be

* Nine months after leaving the presidency, Eisenhower cited this as the first item, when asked to enumerate "your greatest achievements." In his words: "When I came to the presidency the country was rather in an unhappy state. There was bitterness and there was quarreling . . . in Washington and around the country. I tried to create an atmosphere of greater serenity and mutual confidence, and I think that it . . . was noticeable over those eight years that that was brought about." ("Eisenhower on the Presidency," CBS telecast with Walter Cronkite, October 12, 1961.)

due, and the mourned occasion decrees guilt, where blame may be impossible.

A few instances may give warning. Thus, for example . . .

The hugeness of a President's popularity may be consoling or alarming, according to the viewer's prejudice, but it is of little relevance to a historian's judgment. Through the years, the upward graph of Eisenhower's popularity seemed a fact of formidable meaning. Yet almost immediately upon his departure from office, the significance of this fact seemed dramatically to depreciate, for his successor in the presidency—a man with a wholly different concept of the office and with a record of only mingled successes and reverses—scaled even higher peaks in the favor of opinion polls. The generosity of such popular tributes to both men suggests that these accolades may reveal not much about either of the men, but more about the temper of the nation. For the awareness of national peril seems inevitably to inspire an anxious sense of dependence upon the presidency, unbridled by the strict appraisal of logic or fact. And this sense—of both danger and dependence—may be greatly quickened, in fact, by a manifest lapse in presidential leadership. Thus the humiliation suffered by Eisenhower on his Far Eastern journey, in the summer of 1960, only brought forth new signs of popular acclaim. At such moments of national stress, partisans cannot rejoice and critics cannot gloat—and a Chief Executive's political error or diplomatic defeat can acquire a weirdly self-nullifying quality. In a democracy—whose very life may depend upon the clarity and courage of its faculties for self-criticism—this could be an alarming sign of intellectual slackness. It cannot be confused, in any event, with a true estimate of the merit or the vigor of a President's leadership.

And the national political scene, quite as much as the world scene, carries its own warnings against the too simple and sweeping judgment. An indictment of Eisenhower, for example, for allowing himself to be a meek creature of traditional Republican conservatism, rather than a bold creator of a new Republican liberalism, must start from the premise that Eisenhower was not, in fact, a conservative. The passage of years proved this premise largely false. Initially, the reality was obscured by Eisenhower's *foreign* policies, for his stands on mutual security or reciprocal trade invited the label of "liberal," even as they invited the hostility of most Republican traditionalists. But Eisenhower, after leaving the presidency, candidly compared himself and Robert Taft: "I found him to be more liberal in his support of some policies even than I was. . . . I laughed at him one day, and I said, 'How did you ever happen to be known as a conservative and me as a liberal?' "* The progress of his presidency brought a more and more heavily conservative accent to Eisenhower's policies and pronouncements. But this was not a matter of slow acquiescence to new political pressures: it meant a gradual reaffirmation of old political persuasions. And to appreciate this, one need only imagine the personal politics of a Dwight David Eisenhower from Abilene, Kansas, who never served in World War II; who passed no memorable years in Europe, there to become the comrade of a Churchill or a De Gaulle; and who became known to the political annals of the 1950s as the quite predictable congressman from the Fourth District of his native Kansas.

For like reasons, there is some unrealism in any tribute to Eisenhower for ratifying or consolidating the social gains of New Deal and Fair Deal. Eight years of a Republican Administration did leave intact all such laws and measures. Yet it is hardly accurate to ascribe this to presidential statesmanship, liberalism, or even choice. The Administration was not required to defend these measures against challenge, but merely to accept their immutability, as a matter of political necessity. And even with this tacit act of acceptance, the President himself held an antipathy toward TVA—and at least a tolerance toward right-to-work laws —scarcely reminiscent of the basic social attitudes of the New

* Ibid.

Deal. There was exceedingly little here, then, to suggest the
labor of a President who was *trying* to be a farsighted consolida-
tor of past social legislation. And it is not easy to assign historic
credit to a man for achievements he never attempted.

All these cautions and qualifications bring some light to the
question of the final fate of one of the supreme objectives of the
Eisenhower presidency.

This purpose was the invigoration and the rejuvenation of the
Republican party.

This purpose ended in defeat.

The size of the defeat was easy to measure. The loss of Executive power in the 1960 elections, despite all advantages enjoyed
by the incumbent Administration, could not be ascribed, harshly
or entirely, to popular distaste for the personality of Richard
Nixon. For the signs of Republican weakness and ineptitude
were visible almost everywhere across the political landscape.
The Republican party that in 1930 claimed governorships in
thirty states could boast of merely sixteen in 1960. Of the nation's forty-one major urban centers, the Democrats in 1960
swept a total of twenty-seven. Through all the Eisenhower Years,
in fact, the total polling strength of the GOP had steadily de-
clined despite the President's personal electoral triumphs—from
49 percent in 1950, to 47 percent in 1954, finally to 43 percent in
1958. In the Congress convening as Eisenhower left the presidency, the GOP was outnumbered three to two in the House
of Representatives and two to one in the Senate. Such a stark
reckoning more than sufficed, in short, to justify Eisenhower's
own unhappy query to Sherman Adams: "What happened . . . ?"

The answer clearly lay, in great part, with the man who asked
the question. The very definition he imposed upon his roles as
President and party leader approached a political philosophy of
self-denial. Months after leaving office, for example, he was asked
if he had "ever sort of turned the screw on Congress to get
something done . . . saying you'll withhold an appointment or
something like that." And with disarming accuracy, Eisenhower

answered: "No, never. I took very seriously the matter of appointments and [their] qualifications. . . . Possibly I was not as shrewd and as clever in this matter as some of the others, but I never thought that any of these appointments should be used for bringing pressure upon the Congress."* The President proudly forswearing the use of "pressure," of course, comes close to brusquely renouncing power itself. And such smothering of his own voice must have two inescapable consequences: the floundering of his legislative program in the halls of the Congress, and the blurring of his party's image in the eyes of the electorate.

As he treated the political present, so, too, Eisenhower faced the future: he served as a passive witness, rather than an aggressive judge, in the choice of leadership to follow him. It is reasonable to accept the sincerity of his belief—by 1960—that "experience" significantly qualified Richard Nixon for the presidency. It is no less certain, however, that—before 1960—Eisenhower constantly reviewed and privately discussed many alternatives to a successor whom he regarded as less than ideal. Along with such personal favorites as Robert Anderson or Alfred Gruenther, he faced—after the 1958 elections—the far more serious political possibility of a Nelson Rockefeller. Even if all calculations of simple political success were disregarded—including John Fitzgerald Kennedy's own calm judgment that his defeat could have been easy—the striking fact is that Eisenhower did nothing to encourage his party to weigh such alternatives, even while he pondered them within himself.

The conclusion must be that—for the Republican party under the leadership of Eisenhower—the 1950s essentially were a lost decade. Let the measure be the growth of the party in popular vote or popular confidence. Let it be the record of specific legislative achievements. Let it be the less specific but more meaningful matter of clear commitment to abiding prin-

* Ibid., Part II, November 23, 1961.

ciples or exhilarating purposes, relevant to an age of revolution. By all criteria, the judgment must be the same. And it darkly suggests no political truth more modern, perhaps, than the venerable warning of Edmund Burke: "The only thing necessary for the triumph of evil is for good men to do nothing."

And yet, there can be no just criticism of a political leader, obviously, without full reference to the political circumstances. And of the Republican party itself, the serious question must be asked: would some other kind of presidential leadership, more vigorous and more creative, have cleanly prevailed over this party's capacity to resist change? The chance of revitalizing a major political organization depends critically upon the nature of the material with which the work must begin. And, in this instance, the circumstances confronting Eisenhower might at least be called mitigating.

For the full half-century since the historic struggle of 1912 between Theodore Roosevelt and William Howard Taft, the Republican party has been known to the nation, of course, as the citadel of conservative orthodoxy. In this span of time, it summoned from its own ranks no President who could lay serious historic claim to greatness. It collectively offered no leadership that could be hailed, by a grateful nation, as imaginative, bold, or memorable. For thirty of those years, the party could not win a presidential election except under the leadership of a war hero. Over this same thirty-year period, it held control of the Congress for a meager total of four years. All this added up to a distinction of the most unwanted kind.

Yet, behind this near-barren half-century, there lies a Republican tradition of a vastly different fiber. This was, almost instantly upon birth, the party that abolished slavery. Throughout the decades of frenetically expanding capitalism—and the lawless acquisitiveness of "the robber barons"—this was the party that conceived and wrote the national laws most vital to the public good and welfare. These included: the first laws of civil service, the anti-trust legislation, the control of the railways, the first federal regulation of food and drugs, the first acts to conserve the nation's natural resources. And throughout this full and rich earlier life, the Republican party logically was both the home and the hope—rather than the enemy and the despair—of the American intellectual.

The third half-century of the story of the Republican party has now just begun. The party, quite obviously, still does not know which of its two selves to *be* in the years immediately ahead. And Dwight David Eisenhower—by his own austere and negative prescription for the role of party leader—could not help it to make up its deeply divided mind.

I have witnessed closely some of this party's recent inner travail. I confess to frequent and sharp dismay at the pettiness of its calculations and the narrowness of its vision. And yet, I presume to believe that the choice before it, as it faces its *third* half-century of life, is as clear as it is historic.

It must, if it is to be a live and generous force in American politics, stir with the energy of enduring convictions, rather than appeal for saving moments to the popularity of a new hero or the plausibility of an ancient shibboleth. It must comprehend and assimilate, in its own mind and spirit, some of the political and intellectual qualities that have enabled British Conservatism to hold power for a full decade and that have animated Christian Democratic parties on the European continent ever since World War II. It must honor, too, its own very origin as a party—by conscientious leadership in the struggle for civil rights. It must learn to use political power in some exercise other than the reflexes of opposition and denunciation. It must forswear the charades of hysterical duels with the imagined menaces of "socialism" and "totalitarianism." It must learn to assess its own political worth by some arithmetic more elevated than the facile addition of its own congressional votes to those of southern Democrats, to contrive the frustration of a fairly impressive number of Executive actions in any congressional session. It must attain a self-respecting sense of identity—and sense of purpose—that can turn

337

cold and confident scorn upon the tawdry political temptations proffered by a Senator Joseph McCarthy or a John Birch Society. And—with these and a host of kindred acts—it might begin to celebrate each political year, each session of the Congress in Washington, by offering the nation a modest minimum of one proud sign of imaginative political action, dedicated unabashedly to the common weal.

To inspire and to lead—indeed, to *re-create*—such a Republican party can only be, still, a patient and painful labor.

To this labor, there was, perhaps, not a great deal that such a President as Eisenhower could bring. This was not only because of the nature of the Republican party long before he encountered it. It was also because of the nature of the man long before the party encountered him. For he appeared upon the national scene as the political father of a phenomenon called "modern Republicanism." Yet his economic and social views could not convincingly be described as "modern." And his political behavior could not, with rare exception, be described as militantly and passionately "Republican." The fact is that the President who was supposed to lead the Republican party toward new, high ground—both "liberal" and "modern"—could not seriously be distinguished from a conservative Democrat.

If this suggests some kind of political paradox about the man, it suggests a more profound paradox about the system of political parties by which America governs itself in the middle of the twentieth century.

And it suggests the final reason why Dwight Eisenhower left the Republican party—politically and intellectually—where first he found it.

3

Things are in the saddle,
And ride mankind.

Ralph Waldo Emerson

The second and the grander of the two high purposes pursued by the Eisenhower presidency was the quest of "peace with justice."

This, too, ended in frustration.

The President's own appraisal of himself as a peace-maker, as fully and finally spoken, sounds rather like a judgment at odds with itself. Thus—on the one side—he publicly recited, within a year of leaving the presidency, what he called "my greatest disappointments," and concluded: "I suppose the most important . . . is a lack of definite proof that we had made real progress toward achieving peace with justice."* Yet—on the other side—he had proudly voiced, only a week before surrendering office, a quite different and less disparaging opinion in his final State of the Union message to the Congress. According to this review of the eight years of his presidency, he professed to see "Communist imperialism held in check." And he invited the Congress to share the Chief Executive's pleasure in his conclusion: "We have carried America to unprecedented heights."†

The two contrary appraisals were not as hard to reconcile as they might appear, even apart from the fact that one could not reasonably have expected Eisenhower's final address to the Congress to catalogue his personal disappointments. For the State of the Union message did not, in truth, presume even to suggest "definite proof" of "real progress." Instead, all the alleged achievements merely attested to the practice of a diplomacy of

* "Eisenhower on the Presidency," Part I, October 12, 1961.
† New York *Times*, January 13, 1961.

"containment," although its rewards were hailed—now—as "unprecedented heights."

The satisfying summits cited by the departing President were quite specific. They numbered seven in all. And they are worth quick scanning to appreciate the nature of the diplomatic terrain upon which he looked back. . . .

1. Whereas "when I took office, the United States was at war," the nation had "lived in peace" since the Korean Armistice of 1953. *But* . . . there seemed some irony in the fact that this list of eight years of diplomatic accomplishments should be headed by the prudent acceptance, seven years earlier, of a military status quo whose toleration, even at the time, had elicited only frowns and doubts from the Secretary of State.

2. The United States had "strongly supported" the United Nations in the 1956 Suez Crisis, thus achieving "the ending of the hostilities in Egypt." *But* . . . the prologue to this crisis had entailed the chronic deterioration of Anglo-American relations —and the epilogue had consisted of the alarming expansion of Soviet influence throughout the Middle East.

3. "Again in 1958, peace was preserved in the Middle East"— by prompt American military action in Lebanon. *But* . . . while this action had been vitally required and efficiently executed, its very necessity implied rather critical comment on the political heritage from American Middle Eastern diplomacy two years earlier.

4. "Our support of the Republic of China . . . restrained the Communist Chinese from attempting to invade the offshore islands." *But* . . . the honoring of this defensive action as the major triumph of eight years of diplomacy in the Far East seemed oddly to mock the "initiative" of 1953—supposedly freeing Nationalist China to assume a more menacing military posture toward the Communist mainland.

5. As for Latin America, there was not much that could be said beyond this: "Although, unhappily, Communist penetration of Cuba is real and poses a serious threat, Communist-dominated

regimes have been deposed in Guatemala and Iran." The fragile apologia could not even find sufficient supporting evidence in all the Western Hemisphere.

6. As for Europe—while the peripheral issues of an Austrian peace treaty and a Trieste settlement could be remembered from the first term with some justified satisfaction—there was no echo of the 1953 cries of "rollback" or "liberation," but the most modest of observations: "Despite constant threats to its integrity, West Berlin remained free."

7. Finally, there were alleged to be "important advances . . . in building mutual security arrangements." Thus: SEATO was established in Southeast Asia and the CENTO Pact in the Middle East, NATO was "militarily strengthened," and the Organization of American States was "further developed." *But* . . . a number of dispassionate critics would have felt compelled to note the following: (a) the political or military value of SEATO was highly questionable; (b) the birth of CENTO merely followed the death of the Baghdad Pact when Baghdad itself severed this tie to the West; (c) the political structure of NATO betrayed signs of growing division rather than greater unity; and (d) the OAS probably faced a graver crisis over Cuban Communism than it had ever known in all its political life.

The President's own chosen list of historic events thus strikingly revealed the limits and the lacks of eight years of American diplomacy, and the nation might well ask—as the President himself occasionally must have wondered—why his pursuit of peace, so ample in both motion and emotion, had yielded such meager reward. A part of the answer, it is true, might cite sheer bad luck. Only a glibly assured student of contemporary history could profess to know the course of East-West diplomacy in 1960, at least in its appearances and its amenities, if there had been no disaster with the U-2 flight. But one such mischance could not suffice to explain the sum of nearly a decade of national policy.

The climactic global effort of Eisenhower's peace-making suggested a peacetime variation on a familiar wartime lament. This was the case of—too much, too late. Through all the years ruled by the taut doctrines of John Foster Dulles, the national policy had decreed an almost religious kind of commitment to a moralistic definition of the relations between nations. By the terms of this orthodoxy, the promise of salvation lay in a kind of political excommunication of Soviet power. The means of grace, moreover, were assured: the political weakness of Soviet power was ultimately guaranteed by its moral wickedness. And the contaminating stigma of sin therefore attached to all acts or gestures of diplomacy that, by directly touching the unclean enemy, might give countenance to the damning offenses of his tyranny at home and his conquests abroad. It was as bad and unthinkable as selling indulgences.

Time and history, however, played a cruel trick. For the years when these strictures had been respected were precisely the years when the advantages of politics and power had rested with the United States. Militarily, American nuclear power then had stood beyond challenge. Politically, the Soviet Union had to suffer through all the complex conflicts wracking the Communist state after Stalin's death. But such factors were drastically changed by the time the clenched fist of Dulles came to be replaced, in the world of diplomacy, by the outstretched hand of Eisenhower. The Soviet power that Eisenhower now confronted was the new and ingenious pioneer of the Age of Space. The Soviet leadership that he faced, now no longer strife-torn, was personified by a Khrushchev politically more agile and skillful than a Stalin. Conversely, the American power that Eisenhower now commanded had passed under a cloud of world doubt. The American diplomacy that he directed was caught in a cross fire between colonialism and anti-colonialism, all through the very areas of Asia and Africa marked for political aggression by new Soviet leadership. And the American leadership that Eisenhower himself personified now could boast—by the constitutional law of his nation—only a few more months to live.

There was a moral as well as political edge, moreover, to the sad incongruity of all this. The Soviet leadership so righteously shunned by the diplomacy of Dulles stood indicted—a little belatedly—for political crimes essentially rooted in World War II. The Soviet leadership so hopefully encountered by the diplomacy of Eisenhower came—quite freshly—from the savage suppression of Hungarian freedom. And so American policy of the 1950s fashioned its supreme irony: a host of decent intents, generous gestures, and dramatic acts of peace were scrupulously hoarded—through years proclaiming the need for them—to be lavishly spent only when the moral occasion was least appropriate and their political value was least impressive.

The confused timing of such major diplomatic acts had to betray, too, some lack of substance, since the fully reasoned acts would have borne the much earlier dates. And this fact gave to the President's personal diplomacy its disconcerting overtones of impetuosity and improvisation. The reach of the leader was undeniably long, but his grasp did not seem firm; his manner was kind, but uncertain; his words were benign, but unclear. And all this explained why so many national capitals, warm as they felt in the presence of the man, also sensed a little shiver of unreality as they watched and listened. Even as he disarmed his critics, he disquieted his friends. For they could not suppress a fear that perhaps he had never understood the lesson recorded by one historian who had personally witnessed the travail of peace-making, as long ago as 1919: "It would be interesting to analyze how many false decisions, how may fatal misunderstandings, have arisen from such pleasant qualities as shyness, consideration, affability, or ordinary good manners."*

The strivings of Eisenhower to conciliate the world of nations thus markedly resembled his equally earnest attempts to conciliate the Congress of the United States. Over the years, the tortuous struggle to evolve Republican legislative programs with the help of political leaders as unreconciled as William Knowland

* Harold Nicolson, *Peacemaking: 1919*, p. 67.

was no more remarkable than the effort to evolve a foreign policy by mingling, in equal measures, Eisenhower's views of the world and those of John Foster Dulles. The truth was that all the public allusions to a "Dulles-Eisenhower" foreign policy were no more sensibly descriptive than some fantastic diplomacy proclaiming itself "radical-reactionary" or "bellicose-pacific." And in the councils closest to Eisenhower, the deep conflict of premises found a kind of analogy in a conflict of persons, also unadmitted by the President. For in Eisenhower's Cabinet, through all the years, no two men stood closer to him than Dulles and Humphrey. In the same Cabinet, no two men clashed more fundamentally on national policy. And the President warmly respected them both—equally.

A foreign policy beset by such inner contradictions inevitably could attain results of only one kind: the negative or the passive. Such results were not wholly to be scorned: they could include acts as important as countering the threatened chaos in Lebanon or the presidential veto upon military intervention in Indochina. But a national policy so nearly schizophrenic was powerless to create a positive political design.

In the deepest sense, it could neither conceive nor execute a truly *historic act*.

This was not because it lacked the courage to act.

This was because it could not decide upon a definition of history.

And so the years inscribed a record, not stained with the blots of many foolish or reckless acts, but all too immaculate. All the acts of omission signified a waste of something more than a briefly enjoyed military superiority. The great waste could be measured only by the vastness of the unused political resources at the command of the most powerful and popular leader of any free nation in the world. For Eisenhower had constantly enjoyed the freedom, so fantastically rare in a modern democracy, of the full and affectionate confidence of a people who would have followed him toward almost any conceivable military enterprise or diplomatic encounter.

The final reckoning upon such a period of singular opportunity truly revealed, in short, a "lack of definite proof" of the achievement of "real progress." At the end of his presidency and confronting his harshest critics, Eisenhower never had to suffer hearing criticism as biting as the accusation that Macaulay once hurled in the House of Commons at Sir Robert Peel: "There you sit, doing penance for the disingenuousness of years." But the chargeable offense might have been the exact opposite: the ingenuousness of years.

A last, small irony was reserved for his last months in office. The President then was fighting an increasingly bitter battle against critics who insistently warned of a faltering of American purpose and American power. While some of these critics focused their concern upon domestic issues—from the health of the aged to the education of the young—the majority saw the world scene as the sharpest cause for anxiety. Essentially, the sources of this anxiety were the multiplying signs of Soviet achievement, from progress of their missile power to education of *their* youth. The President found himself harassed by questions and laments upon a single theme: could not, should not, would not the federal government do more to spur comparable American achievement? Emphatically, then stubbornly, at last almost petulantly, Eisenhower insisted that such demands threatened an enlargement of federal authority that would "take our country and make it an armed camp and regiment it." And he went further—to contend angrily that such acknowledgment of Soviet power implied an almost unpatriotic disparagement of American life, as he gruffly admonished one press conference: "Our people ought to have greater faith in their own system."* Thus—strangely—did an intensely patriotic President come finally to argue that the nature of American freedom, and the resourcefulness of the American people, were so limited that they could give retort to the challenge of Soviet Communism only by fractional sacrifice and rationed effort.

* New York *Times*, February 4, 1960.

345

The distance in time and in spirit, from the First Inaugural, seemed—in these last days of the Eisenhower presidency—more than the meager sum of seven or eight years. . . . "We must be ready to dare all for our country. . . . The peace we seek . . . is nothing less than the practice and fulfillment of our whole faith. . . . It signifies much more than the stilling of guns, easing the sorrow, of war. More than an escape from death, it is a way of life. More than a haven for the weary, it is a hope for the brave."

The presidency that had followed upon these words had appeared only occasionally to be inspired by any such preachment about peace.

It had settled, instead, for the half-solace of a series of truces.

4

> O! it is excellent
> To have a giant's strength, but it is tyrannous
> To use it like a giant.

> *Measure for Measure*

The man who, for these several years, entered his office each morning to nod approvingly at the legend on his desk—"Gentle in manner, strong in deed"—would have commended Shakespeare's admonition on "a giant's strength" as an admirable definition of the proper use of power in the presidency of the United States. Because he so believed, he would be charged—quite justly—with refusal to give vigorous leadership even to cherished purposes. And he would also be condemned—not at all justly—for wholly lacking any concept of presidential leadership.

The Eisenhower who rose to fame in the 1940s, under the wartime presidency of Franklin Roosevelt, brought to the White House of the 1950s a view of the presidency so definite and so durable as to seem almost a studied retort and rebuke to a Roosevelt. Where Roosevelt had sought and coveted power, Eisenhower distrusted and discounted it: one man's appetite was the other man's distaste. Where Roosevelt had avidly grasped and adroitly manipulated the abundant authorities of the office, Eisenhower fingered them almost hesitantly and always respectfully—or generously dispersed them. Where Roosevelt had challenged Congress, Eisenhower courted it. Where Roosevelt had been an extravagant partisan, Eisenhower was a tepid partisan. Where Roosevelt had trusted no one and nothing so confidently as his own judgment and his own instinct, Eisenhower trusted and required a consensus of Cabinet or staff to shape the supreme judgments and determinations. Where Roosevelt had sought to goad and taunt and prod the processes of government toward the new and the untried, Eisenhower sought to be both guardian of old values and healer of old wounds.

The contrast was quite as blunt in the case of an earlier—and a Republican—Roosevelt. For the Eisenhower who so deeply disliked all struttings of power, all histrionics of politics, would have found the person and the presidency of Theodore Roosevelt almost intolerable. He would have applied to this Roosevelt, too, the homely phrase of derision that he reserved for politicians of such verve and vehemence: they were "the desk-pounders." Echoing back across the decades would have come the lusty answer of T.R.—exulting in the presidency as the "bully pulpit." And it is hard to imagine a concept of the presidency more alien to Eisenhower: to preach and to yell.

A yet more exact and intimate insight into the Eisenhower presidency was revealed by his particular tribute to the Abraham Lincoln of his admiration. He was asked, on one occasion, to describe this Lincoln. And he chose these adjectives: "dedicated, selfless, so modest and humble." He made no mention or suggestion of such possible attributes as: imagination, tenacity, single-mindedness, vision. Pressed gently by his interrogator as to whether Lincoln were not something of a "desk-pounder," Eisenhower denied such a notion and spontaneously related the one episode of Lincoln's life that surged to the surface of memory . . .

Oh no. Lincoln was noted both for his modesty and his humility. For example, one night he wanted to see General McClellan. He walked over to General McClellan's house . . . but General McClellan was out. He . . . waited way late in the evening. But when the general came in, he told an aide . . . he was tired and he was going to bed, and he would see the President the next day. And when criticized later . . . someone told Mr. Lincoln he ought to have been more arbitrary about this. He said: "I would hold General McClellan's horse if he would just win the Union a victory."*

The Eisenhower appreciation of Lincoln, in short, reflected one sovereign attitude: all esteemed qualities of the founder of Republicanism were personal and individual, and not one was political or historical. And if the logic of such an estimate were carried coldly to its extreme, it would end in the unspoken implication that the highest national office should be sought and occupied less as an exercise of political power than as a test of personal virtue. To excel in this test, the man would live not *with* the office but *within* it—intact and independent, proudly uncontaminated by power, essentially uninvolved with it. Rather than a political life, this would be a life in politics. Its supreme symbol would be not the sword of authority but the shield of rectitude.

While this self-conscious kind of idealism sprang from deep within the man who was Eisenhower, it found reinforcement—and rationalization—in his explicit theory of political leadership. This theory was profoundly felt and emphatically argued. It claimed even to bespeak a sense of responsibility more serious than the conventional shows of leadership. And no words of Eisenhower stated this theory more succinctly than these:

* "Eisenhower on the Presidency," October 12, 1961.

I am not a . . . leader. I don't want you to follow me or anything else. If you are looking for a Moses to lead you out of the . . . wilderness, you will stay right where you are. I would not lead you into this promised land if I could, because if I could lead you in, someone else could lead you out.

These words might have been spoken by Dwight David Eisenhower—at almost any moment in the years from 1952 to 1960—to the Republican party or, indeed, to the American people at large. They were actually spoken, however, by one of the great leaders of American labor, Eugene V. Debs, more than half a century earlier. And they are worthy of note here as simple evidence that, quite apart from all impulses of personal character, the political posture assumed by Eisenhower toward the challenge of national leadership could not, in fact, be curtly described as negligent, eccentric, or even entirely original.

This posture *was* Eisenhower—remarkably and unshakably —because it was prescribed for him by *both* the temper of the man and the tenets of his politics. In any President, or in any political leader, these two need not necessarily coincide: they may fiercely clash. A man of vigorous and aggressive spirit, restless with the urge for action and accomplishment, may fight frantically against the limits of a political role calling for calm, composure, and self-effacement. Or a man of easy and acquiescent temper, content to perform the minimal duties of his office, may strain pathetically and vainly to fill the vastness of a political role demanding force, boldness, and self-assurance. Eisenhower suffered neither kind of conflict. The definition of the office perfectly suited and matched the nature of the man. And neither critical argument nor anxious appeal could persuade him to question, much less to shed, an attire of leadership so appropriate, so form-fitting, so comfortable.

The want and the weakness in all this was not a mere matter of indecision. The man—and the President—was never more decisive than when he held to a steely resolve *not* to do something that he sincerely believed wrong in itself or alien to his office.

349

The essential flaw, rather, was one that had been suggested a full half-century ago—when the outrageously assertive Theodore Roosevelt had occupied the White House—and Woodrow Wilson had then prophesied that "more and more" the presidency would demand "*the sort of action that makes for enlightenment.*"* The requisite for such action, however, is not merely a stout sense of responsibility, but an acute sense of history—a discerning, even intuitive, appreciation of the elusive and cumulative force of every presidential word and act, shaped and aimed to reach final goals, unglimpsed by all but a few. And as no such vision ever deeply inspired the Eisenhower presidency, there could be no true "enlightenment" to shine forth from its somber acts of prudence or of pride.

This is not to say that the record of the Administration wholly lacked zeal—of a kind. It is doubtful if the leadership of any great nation can endure for nearly a decade without at least the flickering of some such flame of commitment. The man who came closest to a display of such fervor in these years, however, was not the President but his Secretary of State. This man possessed at least his own understanding of what Theodore Roosevelt meant when he spoke of a "pulpit." And yet, this particular ardor of John Foster Dulles could not be enough. For this kind of zeal was neither creative nor impassioned. It was austere, constrained, and cerebral. And in lieu of fire, it offered ice.

Ultimately, all that Eisenhower did, and refused to do, as a democratic leader was rigorously faithful to his understanding of democracy itself. When the record of his presidency was written and done, he could look back upon it and soberly reflect: "One definition of democracy that I like is merely the opportunity for self-discipline."† He lived by this definition. And by all acts of eight years of his presidency, he urged its acceptance by the people of his nation.

* Woodrow Wilson, *Constitutional Government in the United States*, p. 81.
† "Eisenhower on the Presidency," October 12, 1961.

The implications of this simple political credo could not instantly be dismissed as shallow. Forbearance and constraint, patience and discipline—those are not virtues for a democracy to deride. They can be fatefully relevant to the ways of free men.

And yet, by the year 1960, they did not seem to serve or to suffice, as full statement of either the nation's purpose or a President's policy.

What was so wrong or wanting in them?

Perhaps one might have caught some hint of the answer, if one were listening attentively, on Inauguration Day in 1961. The provocative moment came shortly before John Fitzgerald Kennedy took his oath of office. At this moment, there stood at the lectern of the Inaugural platform on Capitol Hill not a politician but a poet. His white hair was whipped by the chill January wind. His fingers fumbled clumsily with his text. He was eighty-six years of age—old enough to forget some of his own written lines. But the voice of Robert Frost was strong, and his meaning was clear . . .

> Something we were withholding left us weak
> Until we found it was ourselves
> We were withholding from our land of living
> And forthwith found salvation in surrender.

5

> "Beware the terrible simplifier!"
> Jacob Burckhardt

John Fitzgerald Kennedy—the student, the politician, the senator, and finally the President—had long been engrossed in the meaning and the power of the presidency. He talked of it often and openly, both throughout his audacious quest of it and during his first years in the White House. But he probably voiced no insight into the true nature of presidential leadership so luminous and so pertinent as his words upon one occasion when he was talking about something else.

The occasion, in the spring of 1962, was a formal dinner at the White House, and it was to pay honor to forty-nine Nobel Prize winners. Physicists, poets, peace-makers, dramatists, and mathematicians graced and distinguished the unusual gathering. And the President paid them tribute with these words: "I think this is the most extraordinary collection of human talent, of human knowledge, that has ever been gathered at the White House—with the possible exception of when Thomas Jefferson dined alone."*

The presidency of the United States—and all its subtle powers, challenges, and requisites—has been scanned and appraised by several generations of fascinated essayists, historians, lawyers, and statesmen. Thanks to them, we know rather well the myriad and rare gifts and faculties which the office summons and tests. But I doubt if any of these capacities is surpassed—and perhaps all are nearly encompassed—by the one particular and precious faculty suggested by the youthful President's bow to the memory of Jefferson. And this is the capacity to be—and to believe and to decide—*alone*.

Be this as it may, the American nation needed but a few weeks to sense the historic contrast, in act and in word, between the Eisenhower and the Kennedy views of the presidency. Before the public, the accent and speech of the two men seemed as different as their ages. Within the government, the Cabinet system so exalted by Eisenhower fell into almost instant disuse in the new Administration: there was to be far less reliance upon the broad consensus of many minds, far more upon the personal resolve of the President himself. The Executive would look upon the Congress, too, with a new and a colder eye: there would be no further self-denying solicitude for Legislative sensibilities, but rather the affirmative leadership of a White House strongly summoning the Legislature to act—and to follow. All

* New York *Times*, April 30, 1962.

the world of nations, indeed, would appear to be viewed differently—not as a surely hospitable place, respectful of the better instincts and nobler intents of the American people, but as
a revolutionary environment daring Americans to prove their will
and their power to prevail against the most menacing forces
ever to haunt their history. And back of all these contrasts in
politics—as seemingly vivid as if a Roosevelt had returned to
the White House—there had to be, of course, a matching contrast in persons. The new President did not frown upon politics:
he relished it. He did not shy from power: he wooed it. He did
not shun the world of books and ideas: he devoured them. He
did not view the centers of the American intellectual community
with suspicion: he appealed to them—and called men from them
to join in the aggressive enterprise of his leadership.

A President, like any man, may reveal himself most profoundly by the smallest of signs: an unintended inflection, an
unguarded gesture, a quick glance or grimace. And such signs
may tell more than the most thoughtfully pondered professions
of faith.

With Kennedy and Eisenhower, something like this happened
with each man's particular memory of the Lincoln whom both
admired. For Eisenhower, the memory had been of his "modesty
and his humility"—and the anecdote of McClellan's horse. For
Kennedy, the Civil War President excited a wholly different
image. Months earlier, even before his nomination, Kennedy
had spoken of this image—by recalling the occasion when Lincoln convened his wartime Cabinet to learn his decision to issue
the Emancipation Proclamation. And with warm admiration, the
young President-to-be had cited the words of Lincoln: "I have
gathered you together to hear what I have written down. I do
not wish your advice about the main matter—that I have determined for myself." Appealing to the same historic source, the
two men could hardly have discovered and treasured lessons of
more different force and meaning.

All these were some of the sharply suggestive signs that the

American presidency in the 1960s would not resemble the presidency of the 1950s. They seemed, too, hopeful and heartening signs of the only kind of leadership that could befit the most powerful democracy, in a world asunder.

And yet . . . It would have been all too easy to exaggerate the meaning of such signs to extremes of senseless credulity—or caricature. By so doing, the figure of one President could be made into a kind of superior and supercilious accuser of his predecessor. And there could seem to follow from this a host of deceiving simplifications—with their insinuated assurance that the sloth of age had been replaced by the vigor of youth, superficiality by profundity, shallowness by intellectuality, irresolution by certitude, timidity by boldness, sheer weakness by sheer strength.

A mature people, however, does not traffic in such crisp and foolish fancies. It does not populate its political world with demons and fairies, sinners and saviors. It shuns alike the hopes of the credulous and the cures of the huckster. And it presses the long and fatiguing quest for what is deeply true, rather than what is instantly consoling.

A people, mature in freedom, knows and accepts the obstinacy of all problems that can be called great or historic. It knows the fallibility of all men whom it calls to be its leaders. It expects of them no magic arts of exorcism, but the devoted exercise of their highest—and their limited—faculties. And it sees the fact that each such leader, and each President of the United States, will be a man surely suffering some lack of past experience, some want of present talent. Each, hopefully, will be the possessor of gifts, and the author of achievements, peculiarly his own. But each, certainly, will also be the unique designer of his own mistakes.

The Eisenhower presidency did not and could not suffer, therefore, any instant and peremptory judgment by the Kennedy presidency.

Both men—and both Presidents—in great part were, as they

354

had to be, not judges but witnesses to the politics of their age. And sometimes, too, they both were its creatures. . . .

It was thus even in the realm of personal political conduct.

The cautious and conservative Eisenhower, who so self-effacingly temporized with a McCarthy throughout the first year of his Administration, could not be mocked by the boldly liberal Kennedy for such temporizing. For in that same year of 1953, one could look in vain through the record of all deliberations of the Senate, including its final vote of censure upon McCarthy, for a single word or vote of criticism from the cautious young Massachusetts senator. In the year 1952, his relations with Senator McCarthy were so cordial and satisfactory as to dissuade McCarthy from entering Massachusetts, even to deliver a single speech in support of Kennedy's Republican opponent, Henry Cabot Lodge. Kennedy thereby narrowly averted defeat in that year of sweeping Eisenhower triumph. And the rude political reality had to be accepted: if the vigorous young President's view of Joseph McCarthy had been publicly and candidly more critical, at a time when such courage counted, he almost certainly would not have reached the White House in 1960.

It was thus, too, in terms of governmental practice.

Although the excessive deference of an Eisenhower toward the Congress undoubtedly had cost him many legislative battles, the first two sessions of the Kennedy administration did not yield notably richer reward to an Executive practicing far tougher tactical use of power and patronage. Whether the vital issue were federal aid to education, or medical care for the aged, or reorganization of Executive departments, or review of the federal tax structure, the first two Kennedy Years witnessed very little quickening of the pace of progress over the eight preceding Eisenhower Years. By the end of these first two years, in fact, a number of keen-eyed observers of the Washington scene detected and reported that the spirited Chief Executive showed signs, more and more, of the profoundly tempering influence of his own senatorial experience—in *his* caution and deference

355

toward former colleagues, as they threatened to defy the will of the White House. All this sufficiently indicated that (such is the nature of American politics and American government) the apparent errors and lapses in Eisenhower's congressional relations were not to be wholly redeemed by mere brisk show of Executive force. A stubbornly conservative Congress could prove quite as indifferent to one kind of presidential leadership as another.

It was thus—again—in the critical sphere of civil rights.

Among the many who deplored the passivity and neutralism of President Eisenhower in this area, few political leaders had been more explicit or eloquent than President Kennedy—before his election. As late as September of 1960, the Democratic candidate had assured the electorate that "a bill embodying all the pledges of the Democratic platform . . . will be among the first orders of business when a new Congress meets in January." A year and a half after President Kennedy's inauguration, however, the legislation to be "among the first orders of business" had yet to appear before the Congress.

And it appeared thus, too, in one tragic encounter in the world struggle against Communism.

It had been impossible for Eisenhower or Nixon to give effective retort to the Democratic candidate who charged, throughout the 1960 campaign, that Administrative laxness must partly account for the rise of Communism in Cuba, shattering Western Hemisphere unity and clouding the nation's prestige throughout the American republics. Yet it is hardly conceivable that an Eisenhower could have presided over so abortive a military action as the half-invasion of Cuba in April of 1961. The ill-designed venture reflected more than a failure of military judgment on the chances of success for such an amphibious operation without benefit of air cover. No military adviser, obviously, would argue *against* the usefulness of air cover. The tragedy rested, inevitably, upon a *political* judgment. This judgment had sought to reconcile and assimilate utterly contradictory appraisals of the wisdom of the venture, by reducing both the measure of overt American involvement and the margin of the operation's chances for success—to the same safe-dangerous minimum. Remarkably, the whole performance suggested just such a flawed and compromised judgment as might have emerged from the most hesitant councils attending Eisenhower, fumbling toward the broadest consensus with the least hazard.

The sum of all these matters, in the first months and years of the 1960s, meant no fatal marring. They did not proclaim any deep or lasting indictment of the Kennedy presidency. And they did not refute the essential rightness of the young President's definition of his office, its vast powers, and their proper and passionate use.

They served rather—again—as reminders to his people.

They served—particularly—as caution to the people, as they might look back upon the presidency and the politics of the 1950s.

They warned afresh that the governing of free men in any age, and especially American freedom in this age, does not impose such modest demands, or confront such puny perils, that all can be met and made safe by any swiftly saving dispensation of human personality.

There can be no such reprieve.

The powers of the presidency are great, but they can be no more great or more various, obviously, than those of the people. A Harry S. Truman wanted not at all for courage in the use of the powers of the office. And he concluded: "I sit here all day trying to persuade people to do the things they ought to have sense enough to do without my persuading them. . . . That's all the powers of the President amount to."*

Perhaps it is not quite all, but nearly so. For not even the presidency can grandly excel the range of wisdom, the strength of will, the clarity of purpose of the people it must serve by

---

* Cited by Richard E. Neustadt, *Presidential Power*, pp. 9–10.

leading. And this is true no matter *whose* presidency it be. For it remains, always and ultimately, *theirs.*

It surely was so with the most popular—and the most criticized —of modern Presidents.

6

I sense deeply, without pretending wholly to understand, a vital and subtle relation, in all politics, between the faculties of passion and compassion. The first belongs to the realm of ideas. And the second must be reserved for men.

Each of these faculties needs the other—in its rightful sphere. A free people, I seriously believe, have few graver obligations than to exercise these two faculties, courageously and honorably, without confusing them. For the life of freedom does require great passion—all the resources of *caring*—to fire both reason and conscience to judge, to acclaim, or to renounce. But this clean passion becomes twisted and ugly if it inspires only the inquiry that seeks not cause but blame, not reasons but victims, not discernment but punishment. This is why the rage or the revenge of super-patriots—the angry champions of any extreme, armored in hate—always threaten to prostitute the ways of freedom. For only the gross tyranny seeks its defense against falsehood, or its rescue from failure, by directing its passion at *men.* And such a tyranny then acts by its own pitiless logic: it exiles, it shoots, or it hangs.

The heart and mind of a free society respond, think, and do otherwise. This society honors the intent of men of good purpose—while it condemns the false idea, the unreasoned premise, or the tremulous policy. It distrusts passion that is not directed to ideas or to convictions, for such passion must inevitably be on the prowl for human sacrifice—to appease its own confusion. This free society knows that its most mortal enemy is the teaching or the living of an untruth. But it knows, no less well, that a deceptive premise cannot be lynched.

And free and thoughtful men keep remembering, too, that—as there is no art known to man so rare and so elusive as the art of governing other men—this has never been more sternly true than in the government of a great democracy caught in the historic upheavals of the twentieth century. This world of government is a world of spinning and jarring motion—violent and capricious—unbridled by ancient theory, unaided by modern machine. For the wider world with which it must contend respects no sovereignty of law or reason, measure or rhythm. And so the challenges of events—as they test or torment all men who govern—seem a little like missiles fired from hidden guns, swinging wildly in great darkness, at ruthless random. And the size and shape, the meaning and the direction, of the hurtling matters—from the stately councils of Western diplomacy to the savageries of African jungles—forever and fantastically vary. Some seem black and blunt and staggering, making men reel back and fight for balance. Some seem silvery and wispy and swift, and they dart maddeningly through and past the frantic clutch of outstretched hands. And yet others loom golden and great and awesome, leaving men to do little but turn and gasp as they soar overhead.

No leader and no President, in such a world, can be made to suffer the judgment of senseless—and heartless—simplification.

I knew this one President fairly well, and I have thought of him a very great deal.

I—and my own passions and preconceptions—grew to meet his only in deepening dissent.

I liked and respected him.

Whether or not these seeming contradictions blurred my own senses, and rendered obscure many things that appeared sure to the more distant viewer, I do not know.

He came, in his own way, to seem to me as toughly defiant of

359

"the terrible simplifier" as the world in which he lived—and with which he grappled with so odd a mixture of force and weakness. . . .

He was the man of strong will—who reserved his greatest force for keeping unwanted things from being done.

He was the man who gave of himself unstintingly in the public service—physically; and who restrained and withheld himself—politically.

He was the politically inexpert leader who made his unhappiest blunders when he deferred to the counsel of men of greater experience.

He was the veteran of military life who reserved his sharpest skepticism for the insistent "requirements" of career soldiers.

He was the man whose public speech seemed almost chronically careless of language and meaning—who made not one politically significant verbal blunder throughout eight years of press conferences and public addresses.

He was the soldier rather easily awed by great civilian names such as a Lodge or a Rockefeller—who ended by declaring a Nixon to be sole beneficiary of his political testament.

He was, in world affairs, the unabashed believer in conciliation and compromise—who conferred all his trust, and much of his power, upon a Secretary of State unique in modern American diplomacy for his distrust of compromise or conciliation.

He was, among all Presidents for at least a generation, the one least interested in historical theories or political abstractions—who elected to discipline almost all acts of his presidency by a purely theoretical view of the proprieties and the limits of Executive power.

I do not know the final and precise sum of all these equations.

This grand computation belongs, in any event, to the historian at safe and confident distance.

I am reminded only, again, that it is wise and necessary to separate—and to see apart—the man and the office, the person respected and the idea lamented.

I lately have found the reminder sharpened—by chance reading of a public speech. This is a relatively old and forgotten speech from a now remote scene. And it was delivered by Winston Churchill.

The scene was the House of Commons, and the date was November 12, 1940. Led and inspired by Churchill, Great Britain then was in its death duel with Nazi Germany, and much of London daily burned in flame. To this dread time, the long and dreary prologue had been the years of conciliation and appeasement. These had been the years patiently and vainly presided over by Neville Chamberlain. And through these years, Churchill had fought Chamberlain with a patriot's fear and fury.

This day, however, Chamberlain was dead. The House of Commons listened to the simple eulogy. And it was Churchill who slowly lisped the words . . .

The only guide to a man is his conscience: the only shield to his memory is the rectitude and sincerity of his actions. It is very imprudent to walk through life without this shield, because we are so mocked by the failure of our hopes; but with this shield, however the Fates may play, we march always in the ranks of honour.

I know that President Dwight David Eisenhower always believed this.

And I believe he will be so remembered.

Index

Emmet John Hughes

For all his active participation in government and politics, Emmet John Hughes finds his deepest interests in history, writing and journalism. A *summa cum laude* graduate of Princeton, he spent more than a decade as a foreign correspondent in Europe for Time, Inc. He has been an editor of *Life* and *Fortune* and a columnist for *Newsweek*. For three years (1960–1963) Emmet John Hughes was senior adviser on public affairs to the Rockefeller brothers. From 1968 to 1969 he was special assistant to Governor Rockefeller. Currently he is a professor of politics at Rutgers University.